HISTORY OF COMPUTING AND EDUCATION 3 (HCE3)

IFIP – The International Federation for Information Processing

IFIP was founded in 1960 under the auspices of UNESCO, following the First World Computer Congress held in Paris the previous year. An umbrella organization for societies working in information processing, IFIP's aim is two-fold: to support information processing within its member countries and to encourage technology transfer to developing nations. As its mission statement clearly states,

> *IFIP's mission is to be the leading, truly international, apolitical organization which encourages and assists in the development, exploitation and application of information technology for the benefit of all people.*

IFIP is a non-profitmaking organization, run almost solely by 2500 volunteers. It operates through a number of technical committees, which organize events and publications. IFIP's events range from an international congress to local seminars, but the most important are:

- The IFIP World Computer Congress, held every second year;
- Open conferences;
- Working conferences.

The flagship event is the IFIP World Computer Congress, at which both invited and contributed papers are presented. Contributed papers are rigorously refereed and the rejection rate is high.

As with the Congress, participation in the open conferences is open to all and papers may be invited or submitted. Again, submitted papers are stringently refereed.

The working conferences are structured differently. They are usually run by a working group and attendance is small and by invitation only. Their purpose is to create an atmosphere conducive to innovation and development. Refereeing is less rigorous and papers are subjected to extensive group discussion.

Publications arising from IFIP events vary. The papers presented at the IFIP World Computer Congress and at open conferences are published as conference proceedings, while the results of the working conferences are often published as collections of selected and edited papers.

Any national society whose primary activity is in information may apply to become a full member of IFIP, although full membership is restricted to one society per country. Full members are entitled to vote at the annual General Assembly, National societies preferring a less committed involvement may apply for associate or corresponding membership. Associate members enjoy the same benefits as full members, but without voting rights. Corresponding members are not represented in IFIP bodies. Affiliated membership is open to non-national societies, and individual and honorary membership schemes are also offered.

HISTORY OF COMPUTING AND EDUCATION 3 (HCE3)

IFIP 20th World Computer Congress, Proceedings of the Third IFIP Conference on the History of Computing and Education WG 9.7/TC9, History of Computing, September 7-10, 2008, Milano, Italy

Edited by

John Impagliazzo
Hofstra University
USA

Springer

Library of Congress Control Number: 2008928945

History of Computing and Education 3 (HCE3)

Edited by John Impagliazzo

p. cm. (IFIP International Federation for Information Processing, a Springer Series in Computer Science)

ISSN: 1571-5736 / 1861-2288 (Internet)

ISBN 978-1-4419-3503-8 ISBN 978-0-387-09657-5 (eBook)

DOI 10.1007/978-0-387-09657-5

Printed on acid-free paper

9 8 7 6 5 4 3 2 1

springer.com

IFIP 2008 World Computer Congress (WCC'08)

Message from the Chairs

Every two years, the International Federation for Information Processing hosts a major event which showcases the scientific endeavours of its over one hundred Technical Committees and Working Groups. 2008 sees the 20th World Computer Congress (WCC 2008) take place for the first time in Italy, in Milan from 7-10 September 2008, at the MIC - Milano Convention Centre. The Congress is hosted by the Italian Computer Society, AICA, under the chairmanship of Giulio Occhini.

The Congress runs as a federation of co-located conferences offered by the different IFIP bodies, under the chairmanship of the scientific chair, Judith Bishop. For this Congress, we have a larger than usual number of thirteen conferences, ranging from Theoretical Computer Science, to Open Source Systems, to Entertainment Computing. Some of these are established conferences that run each year and some represent new, breaking areas of computing. Each conference had a call for papers, an International Programme Committee of experts and a thorough peer reviewed process. The Congress received 661 papers for the thirteen conferences, and selected 375 from those representing an acceptance rate of 56% (averaged over all conferences).

An innovative feature of WCC 2008 is the setting aside of two hours each day for cross-sessions relating to the integration of business and research, featuring the use of IT in Italian industry, sport, fashion and so on. This part is organized by Ivo De Lotto. The Congress will be opened by representatives from government bodies and Societies associated with IT in Italy.

This volume is one of fourteen volumes associated with the scientific conferences and the industry sessions. Each covers a specific topic and separately or together they form a valuable record of the state of computing research in the world in 2008. Each volume was prepared for publication in the Springer IFIP Series by the conference's volume editors. The overall Chair for all the volumes published for the Congress is John Impagliazzo.

For full details on the Congress, refer to the webpage http://www.wcc2008.org.

Judith Bishop, South Africa, Co-Chair, International Program Committee
Ivo De Lotto, Italy, Co-Chair, International Program Committee
Giulio Occhini, Italy, Chair, Organizing Committee
John Impagliazzo, United States, Publications Chair

WCC 2008 Scientific Conferences

TC12	**AI**	Artificial Intelligence 2008
TC10	**BICC**	Biologically Inspired Cooperative Computing
WG 5.4	**CAI**	Computer-Aided Innovation (Topical Session)
WG 10.2	**DIPES**	Distributed and Parallel Embedded Systems
TC14	**ECS**	Entertainment Computing Symposium
TC3	**ED_L2L**	Learning to Live in the Knowledge Society
WG 9.7 **TC3**	**HCE3**	History of Computing and Education 3
TC13	**HCI**	Human Computer Interaction
TC8	**ISREP**	Information Systems Research, Education and Practice
WG 12.6	**KMIA**	Knowledge Management in Action
TC2 **WG 2.13**	**OSS**	Open Source Systems
TC11	**IFIP SEC**	Information Security Conference
TC1	**TCS**	Theoretical Computer Science

IFIP

- is the leading multinational, apolitical organization in Information and Communications Technologies and Sciences
- is recognized by United Nations and other world bodies
- represents IT Societies from 56 countries or regions, covering all 5 continents with a total membership of over half a million
- links more than 3500 scientists from Academia and Industry, organized in more than 101 Working Groups reporting to 13 Technical Committees
- sponsors 100 conferences yearly providing unparalleled coverage from theoretical informatics to the relationship between informatics and society including hardware and software technologies, and networked information systems

Details of the IFIP Technical Committees and Working Groups can be found on the website at http://www.ifip.org.

Dedication

We dedicate this book

to the men and women who seek to preserve the legacy of the computing profession, particularly those associated with the education of future professionals in the computing field.

Contents

WCC 2008 Congress v

Dedication vii

Contents ix

Preface xi

HCE3 Conference Organization xiii

HCE3 Program Committee xv

Refereed Full Papers

Computer Education Support Structures in Victorian Schools in the 1980s
ARTHUR TATNALL AND BILL DAVEY 1

A Case Study: History of Polish Computer Applications in Power System Control
JOZEF B. LEWOC, ANTONI IZWORSKI, SLAWOMIR SKOWRONSKI, AND ANTONINA KIELECZAWA 23

Olivetti Elea 9003: Between Scientific Research and Computer Business
Giuditta Parolini 37

Cuban Experiences on Computing and Education
Tomás López Jiménez, Melchor Félix Gil Morell and Adriana Estrada Negrin 55

Computer Education in Spain: From Early to Recent Times
Ramon Puigjaner 79

The Emergence of Educational Technology
Elizabeth Koh and John Lim 99

History of Computing Education Trends: The Emergence of Competitive Intelligence
Kevin R. Parker, Philip S. Nitse, and Bill Davey 113

An Open Adaptive Virtual Museum of Informatics History in Siberia
Victor N. Kasyanov 129

Refereed Short Papers

ICT for Success of Education from an Indian Perspective
Rakesh Mohan Bhatt 147

Sinhala Computing in Early Stage – Sri Lanka Experience
S.T. Nandasara and Yoshiki Mikami 157

Poster Summaries

A Brief History of Choosing First Programming Languages
Leila Goosen 167

Programming in Japanese for Literacy Education
Ken Okada, Manabu Sugiura, Yoshiaki Matsuzawa, Megumi Araki, and Hajime Ohiwa 171

Erratum E1

Preface

These proceedings derive from an international conference on the history of computing and education. This conference is the third of hopefully a series of conferences that will take place within the International Federation for Information Processing (IFIP) and hence, we describe it as the "Third IFIP Conference on the History of Computing and Education" or simply "History of Computing and Education 3" (HCE3). This volume consists of a collection of articles presented at the HCE3 conference held in association with the IFIP 2008 World Computer Congress in Milano, Italy. Articles range from a wide variety of computing perspectives and they represent activities from six continents.

The HCE3 conference is an event of the IFIP Working Group 9.7 on the History of Computing, a working group of IFIP's Technical Committee 9 (TC9) on the Relationship between Computers and Society. In addition, it is in cooperation with the IFIP Technical Committee 3 (TC3) on Education.

The HCE3 conference brings to light a broad spectrum of issues. It illustrates topics in computing as they occurred in the "early days" of computing whose ramifications or overtones remain with us today. Indeed, many of the early challenges remain part of our educational tapestry; most likely, many will evolve into future challenges. Therefore, these proceedings provide additional value to the reader as it will reflect in part the future development of computing and education to stimulate new ideas and models in educational development.

These proceedings provide a interesting articles spanning several topics of historical interest. The reader will find that these fascinating articles capture a historical perspective on the manner in which computing has affected formal and lifelong education in different parts of the world. They also preserve the computing legacies for future generations.

The HCE3 Program Committee expresses it gratitude to the organizers of the 2008 World Computer Congress for without their support, this conference would not be possible. We look forward to joining the presenters and attendees of the HCE3 conference and welcome all participants to this historic and interesting event.

John Impagliazzo, Ph.D.

New York, 2008 April

The original version of this book was revised.
An erratum to this book can be found at DOI 10.1007/978-0-387-09657-5_13

HCE3 Conference Organization

The Third IFIP Conference on the History of Computing and Education 3 (HCE3)

A co-located conference
in cooperation with TC3 and organized under the auspices of the
IFIP World Computer Congress (WCC) 2008
Milano, Italy

John Impagliazzo
HCE3 Program Committee Chair
John.Impagliazzo@Hofstra.edu

Judith Bishop
WCC International Program Committee Co-Chair
jbishop@cs.up.ac.za

Ivo De Lotto
WCC International Program Committee Co-Chair
delotto@unipv.it

Giulio Occhini
WCC 2008 Congress Chair
g.occhini@aicanet.it

HCE3 Program Committee

John Impagliazzo – Program Chair (United States)

Corrado Bonfanti (Italy)

Rosa Maria Bottino (Italy)

Giorgio Casadei (Italy)

Bill Davey (Australia)

Lars Heide (Denmark)

Lena Olsson (Sweden)

Ramon Puigjaner (Spain)

Arthur Tatnall (Australia)

Jan Wibe (Norway)

Computer Education Support Structures in Victorian Schools in the 1980s

Arthur Tatnall[1] **and Bill Davey**[2]

[1] Centre for International Corporate Governance Research, Victoria University, Melbourne,Australia; Arthur.Tatnall@vu.edu.au
[2] School of Business Information Technology, RMIT University, Melbourne, Australia; Bill.Davey@rmit.edu.au

Abstract: Prior to the 1970s, the idea of introducing school students to the use of computers, or of a school owing its own computer was difficult to imagine. This situation began to change during the 1970s and accelerated in the 1980s. While microcomputers were much cheaper and more easily handled than minis and mainframes, in the late 1970s they were still quite foreign to most school teachers. This paper tells the story of how a Travelling Computer Road Show, teachers seconded as Computer Education Consultants, a Computer Education Centre, Subject Teacher Associations and several other support structures were used in Victoria to facilitate the Microcomputers in Education revolution that changed the education landscape in the early to mid 1980s. The paper also reflects on how the adoption of computers in schools really affected school education.

Keywords: Computer education, Teacher/curriculum support structures, Curriculum consultant, Computer education centre, History

1 Background – Schools in Victoria

In Australia in the late 1970s and early 1980s the use of Computers in Education in Schools was becoming an important national consideration. The Commonwealth of Australia is a federation of six states and two territories each having a considerable degree of independence. Constitutionally, State Governments have responsibility for School Education, but in matters of perceived national importance, the Commonwealth Government adopts a policy position and supplies funding for specific education projects. Nevertheless, the State Government Education Ministries determine school curriculum, and how it is supported and delivered.

Whereas, previously the idea of a school owing its own computer seemed quite preposterous, the advent of the relatively inexpensive microcomputer in the

---

Please use the following format when citing this chapter:

Tatnall, A. and Davey, B., 2008, in IFIP International Federation for Information Processing, Volume 269; *History of Computing and Education 3*; John Impagliazzo; (Boston: Springer), pp. 1–22.

late 1970s meant that schools could now afford to purchase one or more computer. Consequently, the use of computers in schools began to expand at a rapid rate. The tremendous and growing interest in the use of computers in education led the Commonwealth Government, in April 1973, to set up the *Commonwealth Schools Commission National Advisory Committee on Computers in Schools (NACCS)*, whose purpose was to provide leadership and funding for Computer Education across all Australian states and territories. Another of its goals was co-ordination of Computer Education facilities and offerings in each of the States. NACCS published its first blueprint for Computer Education in Schools in October 1983 [1].

This paper will consider some of the education support structures introduced in the 1980s to facilitate the growing needs of schools for advice and assistance in developing and maintaining their programs for computers in education. Both of the paper's authors were Secondary School teachers in the 1970s and early 1980s, and between them were also involved in most of the support structures described. While also considering some Australia-wide issues, this paper will concentrate its perspective on the State of Victoria.

In the 1980s, the State of Victoria had several different types of schools. Firstly, there was the divide between Government and Non-Government Schools. As the name suggests, Government Schools were controlled directly by, and received their funding from the Victorian Ministry of Education. Their teachers were appointed, their conditions determined and their overall curriculum guidelines set by the Ministry. Non-Government schools were of two main types: Catholic Schools and Private Schools. In each case, these schools received no funding from the State, but did receive some funding and support from the Commonwealth Government. They employed their own teachers and determined their own curriculum within broad guidelines laid down by the Victorian Ministry of Education.

In the Government School sector, students up to the age of about twelve attended Primary Schools and then moved to either High (Secondary) Schools or Technical Schools. The idea of dividing students into two streams for their post-primary education was to allow that some students were more academically inclined, while others needed a more practical education. (In the late 1980s, these two Divisions were merged into what amounted to comprehensive post-primary schools.) Administratively, each of these school types was attached to a Division within the Ministry of Education.

2 The Beginnings of School Computing in Victoria

School computing began in Victorian schools when a small number of mini computers started to appear in the early 1970s [2, 3]. This typically resulted from the exposure of particular teachers to computing during their university studies. In 1972, for example, Burwood High School in Melbourne was loaned a PDP-8 computer by Digital Equipment [4]. In 1973 McKinnon High School received a Government Innovations Grant to enable the purchase of an 8k Wang computer costing over $10,000 (AUS) and requiring an annual maintenance contract of 15% of the purchase price. Because of this high maintenance cost Box Hill High School agreed to share the use (and costs) with McKinnon High School, each school having access to 4k memory. Box Hill used a Teletype terminal with a paper tape reader and accessed the computer via a dedicated telephone line, but this arrangement was soon seen to be unsatisfactory. These early computers were typically used by mathematics departments almost exclusively for the teaching of programming [4], so having very little overall impact on other aspects of education.

The biggest early impact on schools however, was introduction of the Monash Educational Computer System (MONECS). Before the advent of the PC, it was impossible for an average school to provide students with hands-on access to a computer. In 1974 a group at Monash University produced a system using mark-sense cards that allowed a class of 30 children to each get two runs in a one-hour period [5]. The MONECS system was used to teach programming in FORTRAN or BASIC. At this stage schools saw computing as a branch of mathematics concerned with algorithm design [2, 6].

Another development at this time was experimentation by the Victorian Technical Schools with use of Control Data's 'PLATO System' [7] of computer-assisted instruction for the training of apprentices and for other possible applications. The system was, however, very expensive and not very useful or satisfactory in fulfilling its hope for educational purpose. Its use did not proceed. The arrival of the Apple II in 1977 saw the end of this period and the beginning of real advances in the use of computers in schools. At around $2000 (AUS) for a 16k Apple II that used a tape drive (not supplied – you simply used your own cassette recorder) and a television (also not supplied) set as a monitor, the Apple II was affordable for schools.

It was not long before several different streams of computer education emerged in Victorian schools:

- Computers across the curriculum – computer use in different subject areas
- Computer Science
- Programming in mathematics
- Use of word processors by secretarial studies students

- Logo
- Computer industry/business training in Technical Schools [2].

One of the early curriculum directions was 'computers across the curriculum' and AppleII software such as Lemonade, Hammurabi, and the First Fleet (convict) database showed the possibilities here. Acorn BBC computer software included a word processor, database manager and a role play simulation program called Suburban Fox (where students took the role of a fox and learned to survive). Several Teacher Subject Associations showed an early interest, particularly the Mathematics, Science and Commercial Teachers' Associations, and a new subject association: the Computer Education Group of Victoria (CEGV) was set up.

This was before the days of the ascendancy of the IBM PC and MS-DOS and schools made use of a variety of computers. The main ones were the Apple II, BBC (Acorn), Tandy TRS-80, Commodore 64, Microbee, (an Australian designed and built computer capable of running the CP/M operating system), Micromation (also an Australian built CP/M machine), IBM PC, and Macintosh. Other computers in use in schools included the Cromence, Sega, BBC Electron, Atari, Amiga, Sinclair ZX80 and several others.

There was little or no software compatibility between these early types of microcomputers and so it made a big difference to a school's computer education curriculum which computer they used. Like several other countries Australia even commenced a project to design an Australian Educational Computer [8], which fortunately (in retrospect) did not proceed past the design stage. One of the functions of the Victorian State Computer Education Centre (which we will discuss later) was to control the proliferation of these brands by supporting only a limited number on a 'recommended list'. This reduced the problem somewhat.

3 Microcomputers in Schools – An Education Revolution?

With today's mobile telephones that can send e-mail and take movies it is easy to forget the nature of the microcomputer revolution. The first microcomputer to catch the imagination of teachers and to appear in significant numbers in Victorian schools was the Apple II. In 1978, the early versions of this computer had 16 Kb of RAM and used a cassette tape recorder for loading software and a television set as a monitor. It is illustrative to look closely at the instructions that came with the demonstration tape to see what a person taking delivery of their first computer might need to deal with. Figure 1 shows a page from the booklet that came with the Apple II.

```
The Usual Procedure for Loading Tapes

1.  Make sure your computer is in Applesoft BASIC
2.  Rewind the tape
3.  Start the tape playing
4.  Type  LOAD
    After you press  RETURN  the cursor will disappear.  Nothing
    happens for from five to twenty seconds, and then the Apple
    beeps.  This means that the tape's information has started
    to go into the computer.  After some more time (depending on
    how much information is on the tape, but usually less than a
    few minutes) the Apple beeps again and the prompt character
    and the cursor reappear.
4a. If you got an error message such as  ERR , the tape did not
    LOAD properly.  Turn your computer off (with the switch in
    the back), and begin the process again at step one.
    NOTE:  You cannot recover from a LOAD error by using RESET.
5.  Stop the tape recorder and rewind the tape.  The information
    has been transferred, and you are finished with the tape
    recorder for the time being.

Enjoy your new Apple!
```

Figure 1 Loading tapes [9]

Most of the personal computers of interest to schools (Apple II, Tandy TRS-80, Commodore 64, and Atari) loaded their software from cassette tape and most adopted the Texas Instruments standard of 300 baud. The Apple, however, used a faster 1200 baud when loading from cassette. The Computer Education Road Show (described later) and most Computer Education Consultants from 1978 to 1980 used tape loading to demonstrate software. The knowledgeable consultant would leave the tape sound output on so that they would be able to hear when it was loading properly and when a restart was needed.

In 1979 the first disk drives appeared and a Word Processor program could be obtained from Apple. The instruction booklet advised (Figure 2 below), all in friendly CAPS, as most printers did not have lower case:

```
                      RUNNING UP THE SYSTEM
     AFTER SWITCH ON AND AFTER INSERTING THE WORD PROCESSOR DISK IN
THE DISK DRIVE, TYPE '6'; THEN HOLD DOWN THE 'CTRL' KEY WHILE
PRESSING 'P'; THEN PRESS 'RETURN'.
     WHEN THE DISK HAS STOPPED RUNNING THE SCREEN WILL DISPLAY AN
INTRODUCTORY MESSAGE. TO CONTINUE WITH THE PROGRAM PRESS ANY KEY.
```

Figure 2 Word Processor disk instructions [10]

Once this 'simple' procedure was undertaken the instructions assure the user that almost nothing could go wrong with the program. That is, unless they had done something silly like pressing the Reset Key or typing in "too many lines" (see Figure 3).

```
    WHEN YOU HAVE FINISHED WHAT YOU WANT TO TYPE IN, YOU CAN TYPE
'END' AT THE BEGINNING OF A LINE. ON PRESSING 'RETURN' YOU WILL BE
PRESENTED WITH A 'TRAFFIC DIRECTORY' TO HELP YOU CHOOSE WHAT YOU WANT
THE PROGRAMME TO DO NEXT.
   PLEASE NOTE -
    IF SOMETHING GOES WRONG WITH THE SYSTEM DURING THE TIME YOU ARE
ENTERING TEXT, IN MOST CASES THE PROGRAMME WILL RESCUE YOU FROM
DISASTER. VERY RARELY, THE SYSTEM WILL GO HAYWIRE AND YOU WILL BE
PRESENTED WITH AN ASTERIX (*) AND A SERIES OF UNINTELLIGIBLE NUMBERS.
THIS IS DISASTER INDEED. YOU WILL HAVE TO START ALL OVER AGAIN.
FORTUNATELY THE OCCURRENCE IS RARE. THE MOST USUAL CAUSE IS THAT YOU
HAVE PRESSED THE 'RESET' BUTTON. USUALLY YOU WILL BE RESCUED. THE
CAUSES OF THE PROBLEM ARE THESE -
   1. YOU HAVE RUN OUT OF MEMORY,
   2. YOU HAVE TYPED IN TOO MANY LINES.
   IF YOU HAVE RUN OUT OF MEMORY OR HAVE TYPED TOO MANY LINES, SAVE
THE FILE AT ONCE. YOU CAN BREAK IT INTO PAGES AND JOIN IT UP WITH
OTHER FILES LATER. THE MAXIMUM NUMBER OF CHARACTERS IS ABOUT 12,000
AND THE MAXIMUM NUMBER OF LINES IS 200.
```

Figure 3 Word Processor instructions [10]

These examples show that the first microcomputers, while more simple to operate than their predecessor minis and mainframes, were certainly not consumer or teacher ready. The next factor in this scenario was staff training. It is difficult for universities to train teachers in technology that has not yet been invented. Many Mathematics and Science teachers under the age of about thirty at the time had been given some computer training in the university with punch card machines using COBOL or Fortran (normally in a situation of a one or two day turnaround for each program). However, a teacher older than this would probably have attended a University or Teachers College without available computing facilities. The situation in schools was one of enormous excitement created by the promise of the new computers that were almost affordable, could be used for programming and had amazing on-screen graphics that fired the imagination. At the same time these computers were very unstable, had been put together by people who saw CTRL 6P as a logical way of starting a disk drive and had miniscule memory size, capable only of simple things like storing and handling the number of characters that could be contained in five pages of a book. The Victorian Education Ministry could see the future for computers and the need to have students learning about them, but a lack of human resources familiar with computers must have looked like a giant hurdle. The education system had responded to the need for science equipment in the 1960s with large equipment grants, but then it had science-trained teachers to implement this program and to make good used of the new equipment. In computing, the equipment deficit was just as large, but supplying teachers able to use it would not be a simple task. Support was urgently needed.

4 Early Attempts to Offer Support to Schools

The introduction of the personal computer in the late 1970s produced unprecedented growth in the use of computers in schools in Victoria during the 1980s. This situation was also reflected in other Australian states as well as in many other countries. The growth of use of computers, however, existed in the absence of enough trained teachers and without national or international models of the educational use of computers in schools beyond simple programming. In Victoria, a number of different approaches were used in an attempt to provide support to schools. In the early 1980s, most innovative developments were from individual teachers or small groups of teachers, and a systematic approach was not put in place until the mid 1980s.

Document analysis and interviews of the main protagonists at the time has identified a number of different models used in Victoria to address the need for computer education support for schools. These models included:

- The spontaneous formation of self-help groups amongst teachers.
- Use of existing professional teacher associations (- Mathematics, Science and Commercial Teachers Associations).
- Formation of the Computer Education Group of Victoria (CEGV) to raise and discuss issues.
- Creation of a Higher School Certificate (Year 12) level Computer Science subject.
- Use of special purpose computer education conferences.
- A locally produced computer education journal.
- Vendor-directed support for schools using specific types of computer hardware.
- An Education Department sponsored ‘travelling computer education road show’.
- Regionally-based computer education consultants provided by the Education Department.
- Creation of the Victorian State Computer Education Centre (SCEC) – a centralised support unit.
- A seeding program centred on specific types of teachers.
- At later stages, equipment grants and government-funded computer education demonstration schools.

A good deal of documentary evidence is still available to study these models. This includes policy statements, copies of journals from the period, conference proceedings and minutes of meetings as indications of intention, with curriculum statements and enrolment numbers as measures of success. To supplement these findings we conducted interviews with instigators and directors of each model. Interviewees included senior officers of SCEC, a traditional teacher organization, the originator of one of the largest spontaneous teacher groups, a writer of one of the innovative programs used in the curriculum, a past president of the CEGV, a conference chair from the subject specific conferences, a member of the government policy group, an examination panel chair from the Higher School Certificate (HSC) subject and people involved in the various types of seeding programs.

The study of these models over the ten years from 1980 to 1990 has shown that each contributed to the advance of computer use in schools, but that none was entirely successful in achieving all its stated aims. Details of these support models, and reasons for their success or failure, are discussed in this paper. The history of computers in schools is not one of hardware and software alone. This study has shown that the efforts of a wide variety of champions were needed to reach into the education community. The lessons of this history are obviously applicable today.

4.1 The Computer Travelling Road Show

In 1978-1979, the Computer Policy Subcommittee of the Victorian Education Ministry Director Generals' Policy Committee produced a plan for the introduction of computers to schools. A key feature of the plan was that: "There is an immediate need for post-primary divisions to appoint full-time/part-time regional consultants for 1980 to establish clearing houses and assist in school program development and to co-ordinate the development of appropriate skills within each region" [11]. The plan arose from talks between Bainbridge (one of the Regional Directors of Education) and a group of Inspectors of schools. As a result the Secondary Mathematics Committee set up a 'Computer Education' Subcommittee [12] in recognition of the potential of computers in mathematics education (and possibly also in other aspects of education).

This subcommittee then set up a Computer Travelling Road Show that in 1979 commenced visits to schools around the State to promote the use of computers in mathematics education as well as in other subject areas. Members of the group would travel in twos or threes, normally bringing a 16k Apple II with tape drive (on loan from Computerland in Sydney) to demonstrate computer applications involving graphics, mathematics, commerce and word processing (rather than just programming) to teachers at curriculum days and staff meetings. This represented the Education Department's first official recognition of the importance of computers in education [4, 12].

Interestingly, although teachers of Mathematics were the prime movers in these early days, they did not remain a significant force in this area into the later 1980s. What appears to have happened is that mathematics teachers, many having had some experience with computers at university, were quick to use their computers (typically the Apple II) in teaching programming, but then had difficulty in identifying other suitable mathematical applications. In many cases these teachers then moved over to the teaching of computing: Computer Awareness and Computer Science, and gave up any attempt to use computers in mathematics. Today, mathematics would be one of the subject areas making least use of computers.

Growth of interest in using computers in schools exploded at this time and at a regional computer conference in June 1979, twenty-five schools were represented. Of these only two had school computers (an Apple and a Cromenco), three used computers owned by a teacher, four were making use of a computer at a local tertiary institution and the rest were "interested in learning what was possible".

4.2 The Director General's Computer Policy Sub-Committee

During the period 1978-1980, the discretionary fund of the Director of Secondary Education was used to support microcomputer purchase in a limited number of schools. The *Director General's Computer Policy Sub-Committee* also commissioned Anne McDougall, from Melbourne University Education Faculty, to undertake a study of the potential uses of computers in Victorian schools [2, 3]. The report's recommendations [13] included a major commitment to in-service education of teachers, and that adequate numbers of Computer Education Consultants should be made available. The main recommendations were:

- Schools should be encouraged and assisted to offer Computer Awareness education for all students.
- In schools where it was desired that computer programming be taught, the establishment of Computer Science courses was preferred to the inclusion of programming in Mathematics courses.
- A major commitment should be made to the in-service education of teachers for Computer Awareness and Computer Science.
- Adequate numbers of Computer Education Consultants should be made available.
- Secondment should be arranged for some skilled teachers to work in Central or Regional Centres on the preparation of courseware.
- Standardisation of equipment and computer programming languages was recommended, to facilitate the exchange of courseware, transferability of teacher skills and for equipment maintenance.
- A large pool of courseware programs should be developed for use in a wide variety of subject areas. Central or Regional Centres should be established

for the preparation, modification, documentation and cataloguing of educational programs. These should be staffed mainly by seconded teachers.

- It was also recommended that a resource library for computer education materials should be established [13: 31].

The Computer Policy Sub-Committee agreed in the need to separate Computer Education from mathematics, and influenced the formation of three (divisional) Computer Education Curriculum Committees [3]. It also approved the appointment of three Computer Education Consultants with state-wide responsibilities. These (one year tenure) secondments were to commence in February 1980.

The Victorian Education Department at this time had three very separate (and often non-cooperating) divisions (Primary, Secondary, and Technical Divisions), each of which pursued its own policies and directions. This was evidenced in the Computer Education area particularly in the friction, often apparent, between the Secondary and the Technical Divisions. These divisions had radically different ideas on policy; that of the Technical Schools Division being towards *industry standard equipment* and training for employment, while the main concern of the Secondary Schools Division was (after the recommendations of the McDougall report) for Computer Awareness. This important distinction in policy was partly due to the historical differences between the two divisions, the Secondary Division having (traditionally) considered its role as in both provision of a general education to all students, and in preparation of some students for tertiary studies; while the Technical Division had always been primarily concerned with preparation of students for apprenticeships, and training students for employment. It is thus not surprising that the Technical Division should have stressed *computer industry compatibility* as important in education. The problem remained until 1983 when the divisions were finally abolished.

4.3 The Secondary Computer Education Committee

In 1980 the Secondary Computer Education Committee was formed [14] with a membership made up from members of the Board of Inspectors of Secondary Schools, seconded computer education consultants and practicing Secondary School teachers, including some from the Secondary Mathematics committee [15]. The Committee's brief was the production of Computer Awareness course guidelines, investigation of Computer Science as a discipline, publication of computer education articles, collection and propagation of 'public domain' software and provision of in-service education [14]. In 1980 a 'Software Library' was set up using available public domain software suitable for Apple II and CP/M computers [14].

During 1981 the Secondary Computer Education Committee, the Technical Division Computer Education Committee and the newly formed Primary Committee for Computers in Education all functioned to produce curriculum guidelines and newsletters, and to conduct in-service education for teachers. The Secondary Division appointed several teachers as part-time Regional Computer Education Consultants. Also at this time, 'Ardoch Computer Centre' was set up in metropolitan Melbourne by the Computer Policy Sub-Committee as a state-wide resource, and in a rare example of co-operation, a *software library* was set up as a joint venture of the Secondary and Technical Divisions. The mission of the software library was to sift through the available public domain software for Apple and CP/M and to distribute to schools that which was found to be suitable.

An important evolution in thinking about computer education occurred at about this time, in the realisation that computer hardware was not *all important*. Before this, long periods were spent by teachers in discussing the relative merits of Apple versus Tandy, and Commodore versus CP/M computers. The focus now began to move away from the hardware to the importance of software, systems, and applications.

4.4 Computer Awareness Courses

In developed countries around the world today secondary school students are quite aware of the benefits of information technology and of the many and varied uses of computers. In Victoria, secondary school students now know a good deal about the Internet and broadband, play computer games, make extensive use of computer software and take photos using their mobile phones. This was, however, certainly not the case in the late 1970s and early 1980s when the first PCs began to make their appearance in Australian schools [16]. In 1983 Moursund [17] suggested that the idea that there was a need for the general student population to become computer literate began in the U.S. in the late 1960s, leading to the development of a number of courses and individual units in the early 1970s. Morsund described these early courses as being in Computer Awareness rather than Computer Literacy, in that they aimed only to give students a level of understanding that would enable them to talk sensibly about computers, and involved little or no experience of actually working *with* computers.

Computer Awareness courses in Australia, however, began to appear in the late 1970s and early 1980s when the first microcomputers started to be seen in schools. Unlike the situation described by Moursund, however, distinctions between Computer Awareness and Computer Literacy were not made in Australia, and Victorian Computer Awareness courses were always much more practical and involved a good deal of computer use rather than being almost wholly theoretical.

In Victoria, the Secondary Computer Education Committee put an early priority on the introduction of Computer Awareness in the middle secondary school years. In a 1980 curriculum document [15] the Committee noted that although computers had become indispensable in the operations of science, business and government, they did not currently play a significant role in Victorian secondary education [16]. To justify the introduction of computers and related technology into the secondary school curriculum the Committee argued that as computers were beginning to exercise an important and growing influence on society, that part of the school curriculum concerned with preparation for living in society should contain at least some elements of computer education [15]. The Committee's Year 10 curriculum guidelines noted that: "... we define Computer Education in terms of computer 'awareness' – the possession of skills and knowledge to enable informed judgments to be made on the basis of what is seen or heard about computers." [15 :1]. It added that "... the future citizen, ignorant of computers, will be functionally disadvantaged in a computer oriented society. In terms of 'social obligation' therefore, a strong case can be made for Computer Education. Since computers have significant social, political and economic consequences, an awareness of these consequences is essential to informed decision-making and to the democratic process." [15 :1].

The guidelines proposed for a Year 10 Computer Awareness subject strongly stressed the interdisciplinary nature of this subject matter and that Computer Awareness should not be equated with Computer Programming. The document specified the following content [15 :4-14]:

- What is a computer and how does it work?
- Computer use and programming
- Computer Applications and Implications

The introduction of courses like this, however, both created a need for teacher professional development and acted to make many teachers themselves aware of the possibilities of using a computer for other aspects of education. These courses were a phenomenon of the 1980s and vanished after this, their task having been fulfilled.

4.5 Subject Associations and User Groups

The Computer Education Group of Victoria (CEGV) was formed in the late 1970s as an association of academics, computer salespeople, teachers, and other interested in the use of computers in education. It came into prominence in 1979 when it launched the first Computer Education Conference in Australia. The CEGV, and its counterparts in other states, exerted a considerable influence on computer education through professional development activities, annual conferences, journals and the provision of other publications and resources.

In September 1982, the authors, along with a secondary school principal, formed the Apple users group: VACE (Victorian Apple Computers in Education). From small beginnings VACE grew to have a membership in excess of 200 schools [12]. Unlike the CEGV, VACE was very much a 'grass roots' organisation involving mainly practicing teachers. VACE conducted about two meetings per school term and fulfilled an in-service function. It had its own services section and software library and the VACE charter listed aims covering in-service education, helping with hardware problems and opportunities, software swapping, providing libraries of books and software and bulk buying schemes. The organisation was furiously busy for about 5 years then became irrelevant as the number of teachers with self-sufficient skills reached critical mass. Although the Apple II was by far the most common computer used in secondary schools, the TRS-80, Acorn BBC computer, locally made Microbe and various 'industrial' computers used by Technical Schools were common enough to also need their own user groups. Many of these groups then delivered hours of useful in-service training and technical support.

5 Regional Computer Education Consultants

An important school curriculum support mechanism used by the Victorian Ministry of Education in the late 1970s and 1980s was the Regional Subject Consultant. This was a time of decentralisation and the Ministry had set up twelve Regional Offices around the state, and in Melbourne, where many administrative matters were dealt with at a local level. The regions were not in any way really independent, but were used as a means of localising policies and decisions made by the Ministry of Education. An important function of the Regional Offices was to act as a base for the Regional Subject Consultants who spent much of their time serving the curriculum needs of local schools.

The Consultants were practicing schoolteachers who were seconded from their schools, usually on a part-time basis, to work from the Regional Education Office. They were chosen for their subject expertise, teaching ability, willingness to adapt to and lead educational change, and ability to get on with and work with other teachers. They were subject specialists (in the case of secondary schools) and were appointed only for a period of twelve months at a time. The idea was that although they could be re-appointed for following years, they should not become permanent advisors who might then lose contact with the school classroom. Having to spend half of their time doing their normal teaching job in a school meant that there was little chance that they could forget what it was like to be a classroom teacher. In the curriculum consultancy part of their job, however, they rarely had any interaction with school students, working instead with teachers and school principals.

As some Commonwealth Government money went into funding the Regional Subject Consultants, although they themselves were Government School teachers, their brief extended to servicing both Government and Non-Government schools. The first three statewide Computer Education Consultants were appointed in 1980, with additional appointments following in 1981. Unlike most other consultants, Computer Education Consultants were pioneering a new area of education and had little in the way of established precedent, techniques, or materials to assist them. A common starting point for teachers in thinking out how to best present subject matter to their students is to remember how they themselves were taught. As the use of computers in education was an entirely new area, few teachers had any experience with this, and so had little idea of where to begin. Their task was thus to introduce, and offer suggestions on the use of computers in schools. This work had various different forms including:

- Professional Development activities run at the Regional Office and open to teachers from any school – often based around use of a particular software product, an example being use of the 'First Fleet Database' in history classes.
- Professional Development activities within a given school. Although this could be similar to the activities described above, more typically they involved discussion of how some aspects of computing could be taught, or how computers could be usefully employed in various subject areas.
- Demonstration of educational computer software, and discussion of how it could be used in the classroom.
- Configuration and other work with computer hardware.
- Consultations with individual teachers on curriculum related matters.
- Individual consultations with school principals.

Computer software available at that time depended on which microcomputer was being used. In the early 1980s the Apple II was the most common computer in Primary and Secondary Schools. There were also significant numbers of Commodore 64, Tandy TRS-80, Cromenco (CP/M) and Atari computers in use. Typically, those teachers involved in the early days came with a science or mathematics background.

With its main goal being to prepare students for the workforce, the Technical Schools Division saw a need to use only 'industry standard' equipment in all its teaching. The main use seen for computers was in the commerce area and as the Apple II did not use the CP/M operating system or the S100 bus, and run WordStar and dBASE software (thought by the Technical Division to be the standard at this time) it was not considered to be an 'industry standard' computer. Hence, it was not considered suitable for use in Technical Schools. Recommended instead was a CP/M computer called the Micromation.

The promise of personal computers in the early 1980s was just that; a promise. It could take several tries for an experienced hobbyist to load software from a tape drive and the first PCs were far from consumer items with well-developed interfaces and manuals. Some of the most useful programs were those written by teachers. As mentioned earlier, the Apple II Word Processor manual was presented entirely in CAPS. This meant that the Regional Computer Consultant was part repairman, part programmer, part innovation champion, but mostly visionary with just enough knowledge to help the growing tide of interested teachers. The amazing thing about this system of consultants was the success rate. By 1985 the majority of secondary schools, and many primary schools, had embraced personal computers to the extent of having a class lab, often supplied by funds raised largely at the local level.

6 The State Computer Education Centre (SCEC)

In Victoria, the early development of Computer Education in schools was 'bottom up', beginning with the efforts of a small number of teachers. It took some time for the Education Department itself to become sufficiently interested to set up any form of central involvement. When the Computer Education 'explosion' began in 1983 and the Victorian Education Department saw the need for some form of 'top down' planning and control, it became clear that there was a need for some central focus for computer education in the state. Formation of the State Computer Education Centre (SCEC) was the eventual result.

In January 1984, the State Computer Education Centre (SCEC) was set up in temporary premises at the old Moorabbin High School with 10 seconded staff, along with twelve regional computer education centres staffed by seconded teachers. In 1985, all positions were advertised and staffing at SCEC was formalised with the centre headed by the Senior Computer Education Officer, with a Software Co-ordinator, Professional Development Co-ordinator, Curriculum Co-ordinator, Educational Computer Systems Analyst, and Equal Opportunity Officer (Non-Government) holding Deputy Principal Positions. Seventeen Senior Teacher positions (five at SCEC and twelve in the regions), and four Assistant Teacher positions made up a total staff of twenty-seven professional officers [3].

SCEC played a significant role in setting the direction of educational computing in Victoria for the next three years. It developed policy, produced curriculum documents, evaluated and distributed educational software, evaluated computer hardware and produced the 'recommended list' of computer systems for use in schools, facilitated interstate contacts and the sharing of resources, conducted professional development activities, and generally co-ordinated computer education in the state.

6.1 The Notion of Central Operations

Stated policies of devolution and school-based decision making not-withstanding, in the early 1980s the Education Department of Victoria still retained a strong central administration. There were several key aspects of the computer education situation in Victoria that distinguished it from other curriculum areas and that pointed towards the perceived need for a central operation. The first of these was the smallness of the number of people with expertise in the area; when a human resource is limited it is a common response of any controlling group to centralise it, and this is what happened in the case of computer education. Secondly, in every state it was policy to recommend specific computer hardware for use in schools. This was necessary in order to comply with Government tender, offset and preferred supplier requirements. Government offset policy was designed to encourage local manufacture of computing equipment by requiring that 'foreign' companies re-invest, in the state, 30% of the profits they made as the result of being nominated as a 'preferred supplier'. The process of evaluating computing systems and recommending that preferred supplier status be conferred on a particular company was a task that needed to be done centrally. It would not have been economically possible for such a function to be regionalised, let alone left to individual schools, and so it was a task performed by all State Computer Education Centres. This task alone could be used as a justification by Governments for setting up these Centres.

After the Computer Education money began to flow, all states also need to determine how Commonwealth and State grant money in computer education would be allocated to schools. Giving advice in this area was also a function made easier by the existence of some form of State Computer Education Centre or central committee. In this, computer education is not unique and a similar situation would have applied to any curriculum area having a large number of dollars to dispense. Not too many other curriculum areas have, however, recently been in this position. Co-ordination of in-service education and the professional development of teachers was another function that was perceived as sensibly done from the centre, as was the co-ordination of the production of curriculum materials. Dispensing of services could however easily have been decentralised more than it was. The reasons this did not happen have been largely historical and become apparent after studying the history of the SCEC [12].

In a quite short period of time in the early to mid 1980s every Australian state moved to set up (or extend) some form of State Centre for Computer Education, becoming the source of advice for central policies and the vehicle, at least to some degree, for central control. Thus, the notion of a State Computer Education Centre as a curriculum arm of the central administration became accepted across Australia.

6.2 State Centres for Computer Education in Other Australian States

The state centres for computer education in Australia were primarily a phenomenon of the 1980s with few established before, and few surviving long past that time. Most of the services provided by these centres, while important to the new area of Computer Education at the time were, in most cases, later able to be provided in different ways on a more decentralised basis. Judgements on the success, or otherwise, of the centres is difficult to make without much more data than was ever collected, but the little we have suggests that they filled an important role without which the adoption of computers by schools would have been much more haphazard. It is also an interesting reflection on these centres that few of the professional teachers who staffed them in the 1980s remained long in school education into the 1990s, but that is another story. This paper provides a brief overview of the formation and role of Computer Education Centres in the various states and territories of Australia during the 1980s.

South Australia, Tasmania and (to an extent) Western Australia) commenced programs of Computer Education (mainly of computer programming) earlier than the other states, and the role of the central operation in these states was partly determined by a need to maintain a central computer and to use it to provide a service to schools. This was not the case in the other states [14].

6.2.1 South Australia

South Australia first became involved in Computer Education with the setting up of the Angle Park Computing Centre in 1968 [14]. The South Australian Education Department had a long-standing policy on 'School Computing Activities', which in part stated that:

- Computing is an object of study in its own right
- Computing provides the means of enhancing and extending traditional components of the school curriculum.
- Computing and related technology have the potential to change the curriculum, the manner in which that curriculum is implemented and to improve the general organisational procedures used by schools [18 :46].

To implement its policies, the South Australian Education Department established the 'Schools Computing Section' which comprised professional staff, support staff and regional advisers, and maintained the Computing Centre.

6.2.2 Tasmania

Tasmania also had an early involvement with educational computing, beginning with the introduction of a year 12 Computer Studies course in 1972. Tasmania developed a statewide timesharing network for educational purposes (TASNET) and, in the mid-1970s, set up the Elizabeth Computer Centre (ECC). The role of the ECC involved: "... development of educational and administrative software for the network and for microcomputers; the provision of expert advice on computing to the Department, to schools and to colleges; the provision of advice and training to Tasmanian teachers and the production of the regular newsletters ..." [18 :49].

6.2.3 Western Australia

Western Australia also involved itself with computer education before microcomputers were common. Policy on the educational use of computers in Western Australia, developed by the Schools Computing Branch, was published in 1980/1981. "The Schools Computing Branch has six full-time professional staff and five technical staff. These officers provide schools with advice on hardware, software and pedagogic matters and carry out all the other functions associated with the activities supported by the Schools Computing Centre." [1 :11].

6.2.4 Tasawa

In 1981 the states of Tasmania, South Australia and Western Australia began to co-operate in computer education. This co-operation was enabled by their common use of Acorn BBC computers. In frustration at what they perceived as a lack on interest from the other states, they set up the TASAWA consortium to facilitate this co-operation by sharing development of software and curriculum materials for computer education.

6.2.5 Queensland

Moving in a quite different direction to the TASAWA states, Queensland schools showed a preference for the Apple II, and Queensland made no move to set up a Computer Education Centre or to produce curriculum software. Arguably, Queensland's most significant contribution to the field was the development, during the mid 1980s, of a Year 12 *Information Processing* syllabus using fourth-generation database-query languages and conceptual schema. Most other Computer Science courses were concerned with the study of computer architecture, algorithms, and programming in third-generation languages like Pascal and BASIC. Queensland's course started a trend in a quite new direction.

6.5.6 New South Wales

Along with Victoria, the Education Department of New South Wales was a little slow in formally sponsoring of use of computers in schools [14]. The creation of a

'Computer Education Unit' in 1983 was described as follows: "This will provide a critical mass of expertise, combining complementary skills, and a visible focus for computer education activities and innovation to support work in schools and regions. It will bring together work on curriculum development; the evaluation, development and distribution of software and other resource materials, consultancy support and in-service education of teachers; and advice on the selection of computer equipment for schools. This will help avoid unnecessary duplication of effort and provide a much more effective basis for support to schools throughout the State, both secondary and primary." [19 :115].

7 Computing as a Study in its Own Right – Higher School Certificate Computer Science

In 1981, mainly because of many years of effort by a group of academics, Computer Science was first offered as a Higher School Certificate (HSC) subject in Victoria. Personnel from the Education Department had little involvement in creating or in determining the nature and content of this subject.

The content of this subject included the following areas: computer structure and data representation, algorithms and modelling, programming languages, data structures, input/output devices, file structures, system software, and social implications [20]. In addition, students undertook one of the following two optional units: computers in science and engineering, or computers in business and government. Practical work was seen as an important part of the course.

Of relevance to this paper, however, is the affect that this subject had on computing support structures. While some would have argued at the time that the existence of this subject drew resources away from other aspects of computers in education, we hold the opposite view. The argument that this group of university education faculty academics and some teachers put forward against teaching about computers in this way was that teaching programming meant setting up computer laboratories in schools and so concentrating all the computers in one place. They argued that the computers would then not be accessible to teachers of history, geography, English, and other similar subjects. They also argued that teaching Computer Science would tend to attract the boys and not the girls. We, on the other hand along with a good number of others, would argue that teaching Computer Science generated a need in schools for the purchase of a large number of computers that would otherwise have been difficult to justify. No doubt there were some instances where the teacher of Computer Science managed to exclude others from the computer laboratory, but in our experience of schools at the time (both authors were Computer Science examiners), this was very unusual.

The introduction of Computer Science also meant that a number of teachers now had a good reason to learn much more about computers, and not just programming, so becoming a useful resource to other teachers in the school. It was all very well for the opponents of this view to stress the needs of other teachers as an argument against Computer Science, but it is not clear where they thought these other teachers would get the support they so much needed if it was not from other teachers within the school – there were not enough Computer Education Consultants to provide this support at the level required, and this was something that the Computer Science teachers could assist with. Fortunately the problem did not last long as larger numbers of teachers became sufficiently computer literate, and the number of computers in schools increased significantly.

8 Conclusion

The first microcomputer used in schools in Victoria was installed around 1978. By 1985 a Year 12 Computer Science subject was in place and almost every High school in the state had at least one computer laboratory. This change in less than ten years is amazing, and reflects a climate of intense enthusiasm and vision for the microcomputer, and of the success of attempts to support and train teachers in a completely new area. Factors in this success were the Travelling Computer Road Show, the State Computer Education Centre and in particular, the Computer Education Consultant. These Consultants were taken from the classroom because of their expertise and enthusiasm so they could help their colleagues in full knowledge of the working conditions in schools. The people they helped as they came from the same background also extended them trust. The measure of their success is the speed with which they did away with the need for their services.

In the mid 1980s, several Regional Offices experimented with the concept of a *General Curriculum Consultant*, rather than subject Consultants. These teachers were typically seconded full-time and were chosen for their broad view of the school curriculum. They would still do some *subject consultancy* work, but would also work on other more general curriculum tasks. The early 1990s saw the end of the seconded Regional Consultant, when the State Government changed its funding model to give money previously spent on consultants directly to schools to spend on professional development in any way they chose. This meant that most of this work fell to either educational consultants working independently on a commercial basis and Education Faculty academics, neither group having much contact or experience with the school classroom. The State Computer Education Centre and most of the Regional Computer Centres also closed at this time and development of educational computer software by the Ministry of Education ceased.

Those of us involved at the beginning of the Computer Education revolution in Australia had great hopes that the introduction of computers would make a profound difference and significantly improve the quality of school education. Now that over 25 years has passed, when one looks back and asks if this has happened, the answer would have to be equivocal. School students are now very well aware of the computer, how it is used and its place in business and society. They now take computers completely for granted, as they do with other items of technology. They have very little idea of computer history or realise that we did not always use computers. Most Secondary School students now complete their assignments in Microsoft Word, and students frequently send each other e-mails and look for information on Google or in Wikipedia. However, the question of whether education has undergone some sort of fundamental change due to the introduction of the computer is still debatable.

References

1. Commonwealth Schools Commission, *Teaching, Learning and Computers. Report of the National Advisory Committee on Computers in Schools*. 1983, Commonwealth Schools Commission: Canberra.
2. Tatnall, A. and B. Davey, *Streams in the History of Computer Education in Australia*, in *History of Computing in Education*, J. Impagliazzo and J.A.N. Lee, Editors. 2004, Kluwer Academic Publishers / IFIP: Assinippi Park, Massachusetts. p. 83-90.
3. Tatnall, A., *The Growth of Educational Computing in Australia*, in *History, Context, and Qualitative Methods in the Study of Education*, I. Goodson, F. and M.J. Mangan, Editors. 1992, University of Western Ontario, Canada.: London, Ontario. p. 207-248.
4. Salvas, A.D., *Personal communication*. 1985: Melbourne.
5. Monash Computing Museum. *MONECS Deamon Educational Computer system*. [Web] 2003 [cited 2004 Feb 2004]; Available from: http://www.csse.monash.edu.au/museum/.
6. Tatnall, A., *Curriculum Cycles in the History of Information Systems in Australia*. 2006, Melbourne: Heidelberg Press.
7. Plato Learning. *History of Plato Learning*. 2004 [cited 2004 Feb 2004]; Available from: http://www.plato.com/aboutus/company_history.asp.
8. Tatnall, A., *Designing the Australian Educational Computer*. Education, 1990. **110**(4): p. 453-456.
9. Apple Computer Inc., *The Apple Tapes Introductory Programs for the Apple II plus*. 1979, Cupertino, California: Apple Computer Inc.
10. Apple Computer Inc., *Instruction booklet to accompany word processing disk*. 1979, Cupertino, California: Apple Computer Inc.
11. Bainbridge, W.J., *Internal memo to all policy committees*. 1979, Ministry of Education, Victoria: Melbourne.
12. Tatnall, A., *The Role of the State Computer Education Centre of Victoria*, in *MA (preliminary) thesis*, Education, Editor. 1985, Deakin University: Geelong.
13. McDougall, A., *Computers and Post-Primary Education in Victoria: a Study of Needs*. 1980, Education Department of Victoria, Computer Policy Committee: Melbourne.
14. Tatnall, A. *The Formation and Role of State Centres of Computer Education in Australia in the 1980s*. in *8th IFIP World Conference on Computers in Education (WCCE-2005)*. 2005. Stellenbosch, South Africa: IFIP.

15. Secondary Computer Education Committee, *Year 10 Computer Education: Guidelines for Secondary Schools*. 1980, Education Department of Victoria: Melbourne.
16. Tatnall, A. and B. Davey, *Early Computer Awareness Courses in Australian Secondary Schools: Curricula from the late 1970s and early 1980s*, in *History of Computing and Education 2*, J. Impagliazzo, Editor. 2006, Springer: New York. p. 107-116.
17. Moursund, D., *Precollege Computer Literacy: a Personal Computing Approach*. 2nd edition. 1983, Eugene, Oregon: International Council for Computers in Education.
18. Shears, L.W. and E.C. Dale, *Computers in Education. A report to The Honourable Robert Fordham M.P. Minister of Education, Victoria*. 1983, Ministry of Education: Melbourne.
19. Smith, B.W. *Computer Education in New South Wales Government Schools*. in *Could you use a computer? The 1983 Australian Computer Education Conference*. 1983. Melbourne: CEGV.
20. Victorian Institute for Secondary Education, *Handbook for 1985 Year 12 Curriculum and Assessment*. 1984, Melbourne: Victorian Institute for Secondary Education.

A Case Study: History of Polish Computer Applications in Power System Control

Jozef B. Lewoc[1], **Antoni Izworski**[2], **Slawomir Skowronski** [3], **and Antonina Kieleczawa**[4]

[1] BPBiT Leader, Powst. Sl. 193/28, 53-138 Wroclaw, Poland; leader@provider.pl
[2] Wroclaw University of Technology, Wyb. Wyspianskiego 27, 50-370 Wroclaw, Poland; antoni.izworski@pwr.wroc.pl
[3] Wroclaw University of Technology, Wyb. Wyspianskiego 27, 50-370 Wroclaw, Poland; slawomir.skowronski@pwr.wroc.pl
[4] Institute of Power System Automation, ul. Wystawowa 1, 51-618 Wroclaw, Poland; tosia@iase.wroc.pl

Abstract: In spite of the difference in the country development level, especially in computer and automation technology, between Poland and well developed countries, the history of local computer control applications in the Polish power industry is rather interesting. The paper has been prepared by the IFAC Technical Committee SWISS due to significant social political and cultural aspects of power system control and describes the history of the power system projects implemented in the country by the leading power system automation centre.

Keywords: Electric power systems, Energy expenditure, Automation, Monitoring, Computer networks

1 Introduction

In the pioneering times of computer control applications in the power industry in Poland, i.e. in the seventies, there was a big difference between this case study country and typical well developed countries of the West. In the computer technology, the time lag between the computers available in the case study country and those available in the West was assessed at some 5 – 10 years, what can be compared to infinity for this fast growing technological domain. In addition, the case study country was governed by communist system severely impeding normal human life to say nothing of High-Tech activities.

However, Polish implementations of computer automation in the power industry are rather interesting. In particular, this refers to the Institute of Power

Please use the following format when citing this chapter:

Lewoc, J.B., Izworski, A., Skowronski, S. and Kieleczawa, A., 2008, in IFIP International Federation for Information Processing, Volume 269; *History of Computing and Education 3*; John Impagliazzo; (Boston: Springer), pp. 23–36.

System Automation (IASE) in Wroclaw, the definite Polish leader in power industry computer control applications during the pioneering times.

This paradoxical situation has induced often questions concerning how was it possible to develop useful computer systems with so big time delays in available computers and how was it done.

To answer the questions, a series of three papers have been prepared: two for the 17-th IFAC Congress '08 in Seoul and one for the IFIP Congress in Milano. The present paper describes the history of power industry computer control applications developed by IASE. Another paper [1] describes major technical and political problems that must have been solved by the design and implementation team to develop and implement successfully the computer control systems in the power industry. Still another paper [3] describes major technical solutions applied in the computer control systems.

The three papers have been prepared by the IFAC Technical Committee SWISS (Supplemental Ways for Increasing Social Stability) within the statute activity range of the Committee since the problems addressed therein are strongly connected with the social, political and cultural aspects of technology and the power system control domain is of major technological, scientific and social impacts.

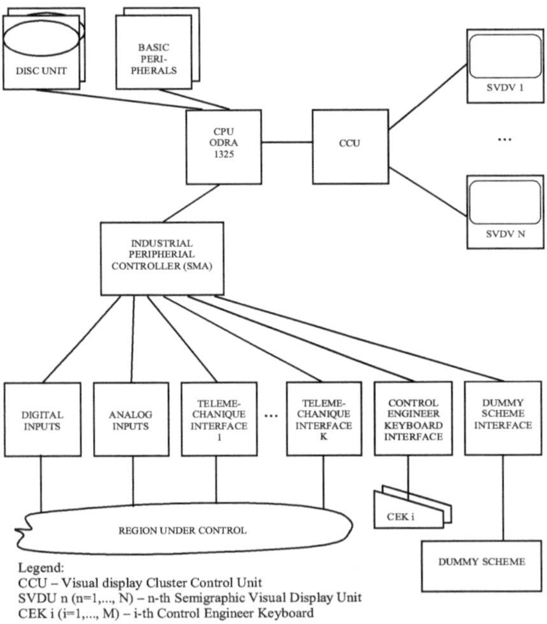

Figure 1 Hardware architecture of SAPI ODM

2 SAPI ODM

The first successful Polish large-scale computer automation system in the power industry and, at the same time, in any Polish industry was the regional power dispatching control system (SAPI ODM) (ref. Figure 1) [3]. The purpose of SOSAPI ODM was to collect information from the region under control, to enable effective monitoring of the information collected and to work out control decisions necessary to operate the power industry region in an adequate fashion, especially in emergency conditions. Some SAPI ODM functions (e.g. water power plant control) were to run in the automatic mode.

Some idea of the complexity of the problems to be solved may be given by the number of the inputs to be processed by SAPI ODM: several thousand analogue inputs and a similar number of digital inputs.

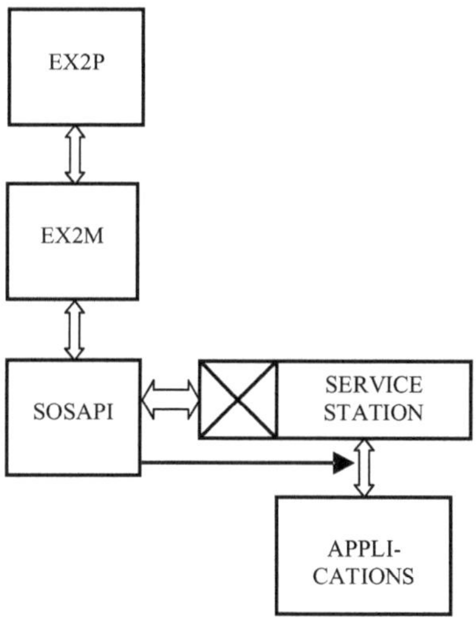

Figure 2a Software architecture of SAPI ODM

It was a prerequisite of the project that SAPI ODM was implemented on a Polish computer. The only available was Odra 1325 (ICL 1902a Compatible) [4]. The original computer (ICL 1902a) was oriented towards numerical data processing and not industrial control applications. Therefore, there was designed and implemented the industrial peripheral system (SMA) and specific peripherals needed for the power system monitoring purposes [4]. To run the hardware architecture of Figure 1, a software system was developed (ref. Figure 2a,), executing the functional diagram presented in Figure 2b. The SAPI ODM software consisted of the following basic components:

- EX2M executive, i.e. a general-purpose operating system for numerical data processing,
- EX2P industrial executive, i.e. EX2M + SMA industrial peripheral system drivers,
- SOSAPI, i.e. power system control oriented operating system (a trusted program running under EX2P and including the primary data processing routines,[5], of the most severe time constraints),
- APPLICATIONS, i.e. a set of data processing programs (PUCs (Programs Under Control)).

In spite of severe technical, social and political problems [1] and due to the solutions devised by the design and implementation team [2], the first successful version of SAPI ODM was implemented in the Central Power Industry Region in 1976. The two next versions were implemented in the Western and Eastern Regions; in addition, one big lower level power control centre was automated using the SAPI ODM solutions.

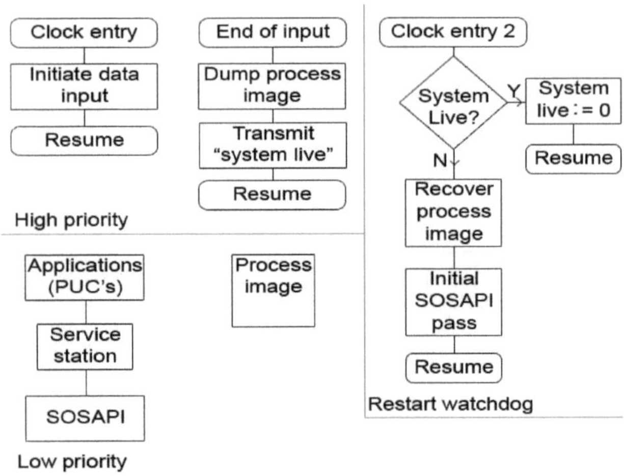

Figure 2b Functional architecture of SAPI ODM

SAPI ODMs controlled more than half energy flowing in the case study country grid for more than 15 years. Considering the problems that had to be solved by the design and implementation team, this was a remarkable technical success. But not only technical. Because of political reasons, nobody tried to evaluate the economic benefits generated by SAPI ODMs. However, it is not too difficult. In the case study country, it was accepted commonly to assess the economical benefits generated by a power control system at the level of a dozen or so percent of the price of the energy under monitoring. Assuming 10%, the benefits gained due to savings of more than 50% energy of the case study country during 15 years exceed $ 40 000 000 000. Even if the assumptions concerning the economic benefits are too optimistic, the figure is some measure of the economic success of the project SAPI ODM.

3 PGU Monitor

Since the results of SAPI ODM design and implementation teams were considered promising and there were major time delays in delivery of the industrial peripheral system SMA, the team was employed in development of a Power Generating Unit Monitor (PGU Monitor). This project was financed from the funds devoted to the nuclear power plant that was to be developed in the case study country (luckily enough, the decision was withdrew several years later). The simplified hardware architecture of PGU Monitor is shown in Figure 3.

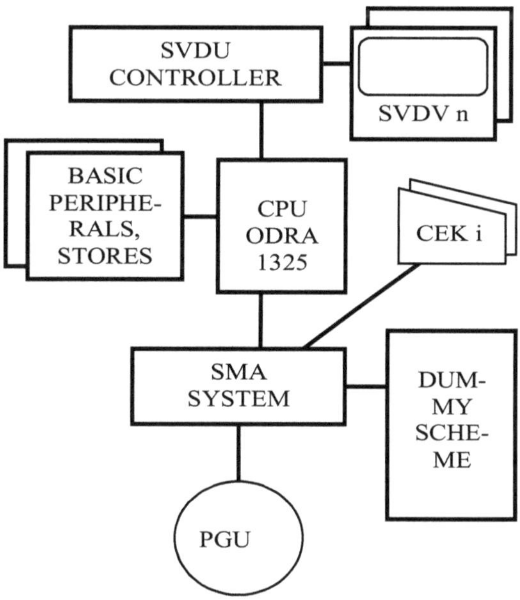

Figure 3 Simplified hardware architecture of PGU MONITOR

In the PGU Monitor, the software of SAPI ODM was used, except of the Application software that was to be written based on that employed in SAPI ODMs, [5]. PGU Monitor was commissioned successfully on a 200 MW power generating unit and during almost a yearly test operation period it enabled to acquire a lot of useful information concerning actual power generating unit monitoring problems.

4 Intelligent Cluster Control Unit

However, when developing SAPI ODM, a very good solution (at least, as for that time) was designed and implemented [1], the importation barriers in the case study country were a severe limitation for the cluster control unit. Therefore, it was decided to develop a home solution for the power industry visualisation systems. The design team decided to make use of a small home minicomputer and home scheme visual display units and to develop the first intelligent peripheral in the case study country.

The hardware structure of the intelligent peripheral (CCU emulator) [6] is shown in Figure 4 a while the functional architecture of the intelligent cluster control unit – in Figure 4b.

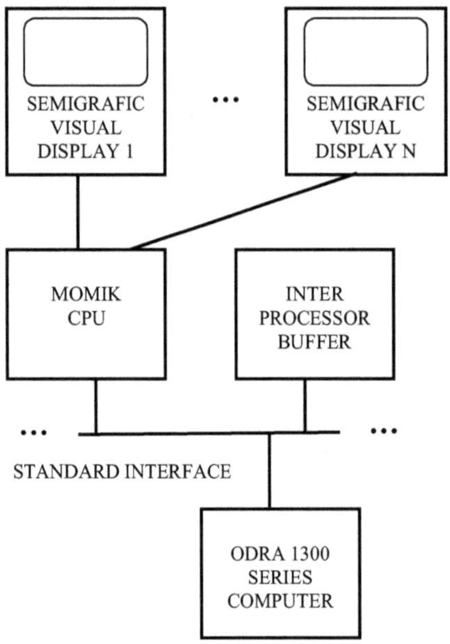

Figure 4a Hardware structure of CCU emulator

The CCU emulator software (Figure 4b) written in the Momik minicomputer assembler language made use of the Momik capabilities at their maximum: For the maximum configuration of 16 VDUs, there were only about 20 spare memory bytes left. This is an evidence for the team's approach consisting in taking the maximum possible use of available hardware.

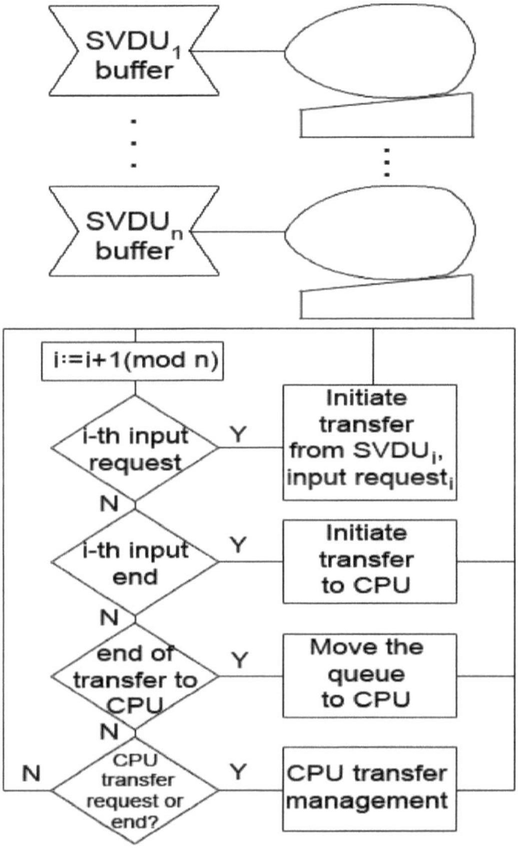

Figure 4b Functional architecture of intelligent power system visual display unit cluster software

The project was successful: the Polish SVDU configurations were successfully applied in several power industrial computer control systems, including the PGU Monitor (Figure Section 3) and the power system simulators (ref. Section 5).

5 Power Grid Training Simulator

Because of SAPI ODM, a power grid training simulator was developed intended for training power network control engineers (Simulator). The hardware structure of the simulator is that of a typical SAPI ODM (ref. Figure 1) plus a trainee console and a trainer console. However, the software architecture of SOSAPI had to be upgraded to enable running two types of PUCs: power grid models (at a lower priority level) and simulation co-ordinators of a higher pre-emptive priority (ref. Figure 5) [7], [8].

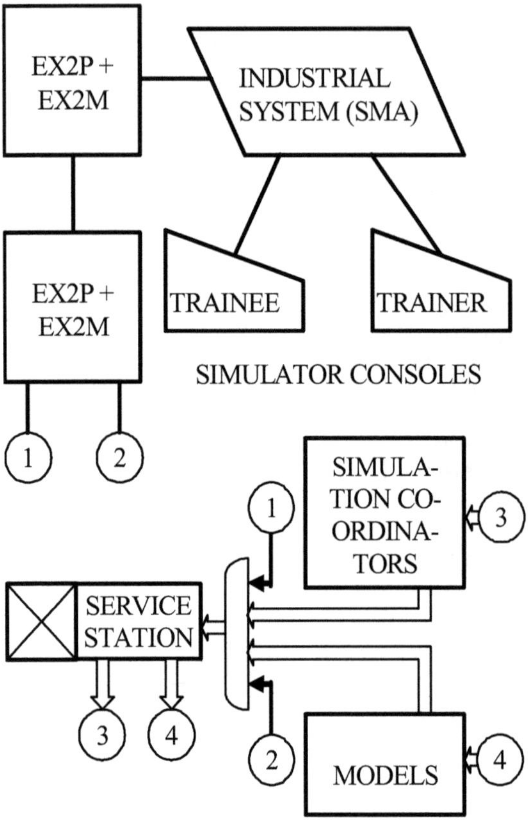

Figure 5 Software architecture of the simulator

6 Further Versions of SAPI ODM

6.1 Microprocessor Based Version

The success of various SAPI ODM applications and the new technologies being available in the case study country made the design and implementation team to think about other versions of the system.

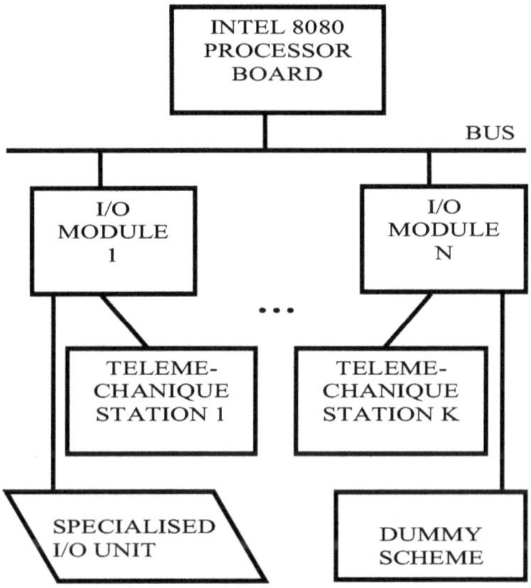

Figure 6 Hardware structure of KWP

For area power system control centres, a microprocessor version was developed reflecting, though in a much smaller scale, the computer system. This version, implemented on the Intel 8080 technology, was called a commutated measurement display KWP and had the hardware structure shown schematically in Figure 6.

KWP was successfully implemented in several lower level power control centres. Though its capabilities were lower than those of computer based SAPI ODMs, it was rather a handy tool requiring no too much room and no special environment [6], [10].

6.2 IBM PC Version

In early nineties, the basis SOSAPI version and APPLICATION PUCs were transferred on the IBM PC computer. Due to the complete documentation of software (complete detailed flowcharts were available), this task could be done rather easily and effectively.

There were two successful implementations of the IBM PC version of SAPI ODM, one in a big town electric power utility and the other in a big 400/110 kV switching station [11].

7 Computer Integrated Manufacturing and Management System for Power Plants

Already in late eighties, series work was undertaken to develop a combined integrated power manufacturing and management system for a big power plant under construction. Similar Computer Integrated Management systems (CIMMs) are severely needed by the users of various industries but, most regretfully, they are not available in the Information and Communication Technology (ICT) market so some work has been done in the domain ([12], [13], [14], [15], [16], being in a large part a continuation of the work mentioned in the present Section of this paper.

When commencing the planning work for this project, it was decided that it would be cheaper to develop a program generator and generate rather then program software for the six power generating units of the power plant under development and to develop the management and manufacturing solution by a single team under one order; therefore, hardware and software facilities should be provided for the CIMMs approach from the very beginning.

The hardware architecture designed for Badel (from Polish (rozproszona) Baza danych dla elektrowni = (distributed) database for power plants) is presented in Figure 7.

The hardware architecture includes N (N = 6 for the pilot power plant under construction) power generating unit (PGU) computing facilities $\{SC_{n,k(n)}\}_{n=1,k(n)=1}^{N,K(n)}$, that are the sequential control systems for the n-th PGU, and $\{DAQ_{n,k(n)}\}_{n=1,l(n)}^{N,L(n)}$, i.e. the data acquisition computers for the n-th PGU.

In addition, for each power generating unit $\{PGU_n\}_{n=1}^{N}$, there should be developed the control processor $\{CP_n\}_{n=1}^{N}$, the presentation processor $\{PP_n\}_{n=1}^{N}$ and the operator's visualisation system console $\{Console_n\}_{n=1}^{N}$

The single power generating unit outfit system was known as KSWDB (from Polish Komputerowy System Wspomagania Dyspozytora Bloku = computer power generating unit control engineer's supporting system).

The first phase of Badel (consisting of KSWDB passed successfully laboratory tests in the Institute in the early nineties. Unfortunately, this was a very low economy period in the case country, the demand for power was low and construction of the power plant was intentionally delayed of several years. Due to that, Badel could not be developed further and the design and implementation team had to be disassembled. Nevertheless, the work done by the team (some ready-made programs, flow diagrams and ideas devised when designing and testing KSWDB) has been used in further successful applications of ICT in the power industry control (some of this is mentioned hereinafter). Therefore, the authors considered it purposeful and worthwhile to mention Badel when describing the history of the most important ICT applications in the power industry of the case study country.

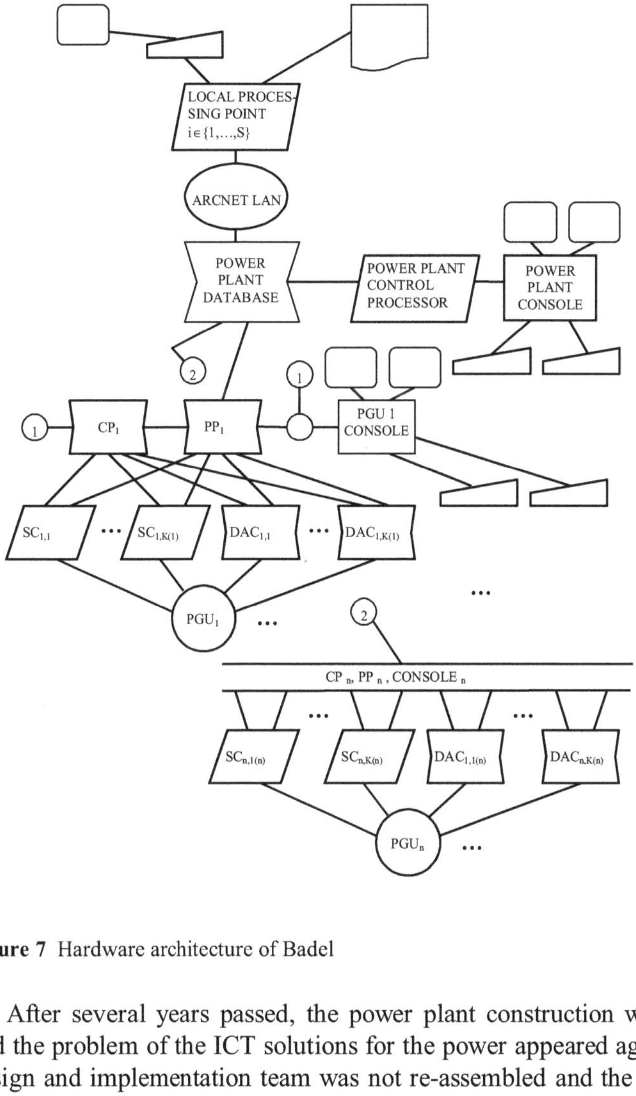

Figure 7 Hardware architecture of Badel

After several years passed, the power plant construction work was resumed and the problem of the ICT solutions for the power appeared again. However, the design and implementation team was not re-assembled and the job was entrusted to a big international corporation, a world leader, at least in theory, in the technology transfer in the domain of ICT for automation. The corporation had not offered the complex CIMM solutions but they also were not apt to re-assemble the Badel design and implementation team or to continue its work. Consequently, the system comparable with KSWDB was, for years, the only outcome of their actions. Thus, the work organisation decisions of the corporation resulted in a lose-and-lose solution: the design and implementation team members did not get the job they liked and the corporation did not get satisfactory results of their work. Unfortunately, the "technology transfer" process in the case study country was full of similar paradoxical events ([16], [17], [18]).

8 Computer System Powerster Supporting Power Generation and Distribution Facility Control

The history of computer power system monitoring and control in the case study country finishes, in practice, at the Powerster Dispatching System, being a successor of KSWDB (ref. Section 7 Hereinabove) implemented on IBP PC compatibles in early nineties and having been developed and upgraded till now, and implemented successfully in more than a hundred heat and power distribution and generation applications. See Figure 8.

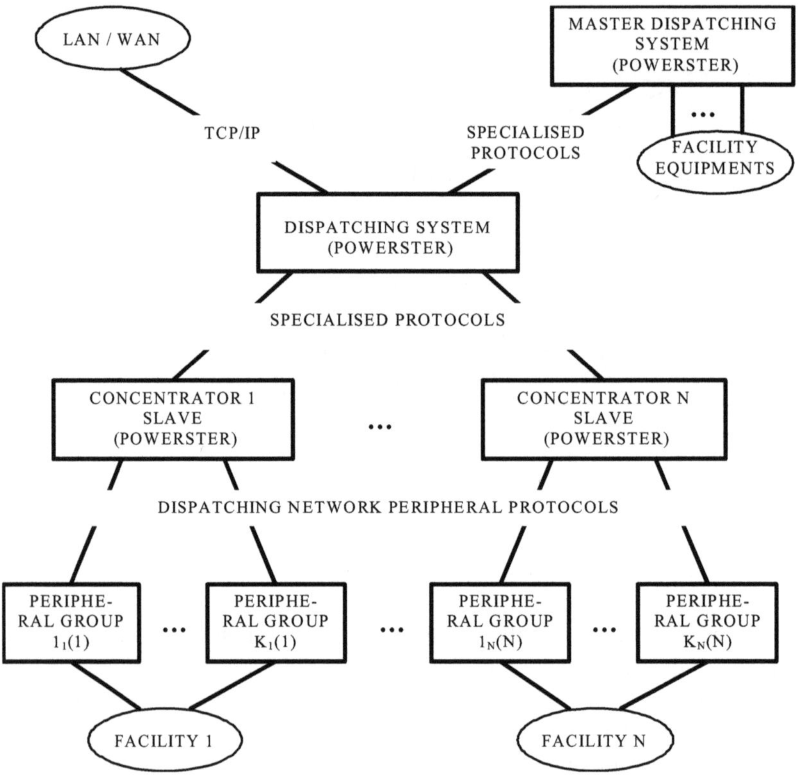

Figure 8 Typical Powerster-based dispatching system network

9 Performance Evaluation Work

Considering the fact that hardware and software tools available to the Team were always obsolete of some 5 to 10 years with respect to those used by designers in well-developed countries, serious approach to the performance problems was a must. The team started from event-driven simulators and, at the end, developed their own approximate throughput evaluation tool depicted in Figure 9 ([21]) with an exemplary closed loop investigated with the tool depicted in Figure 10.

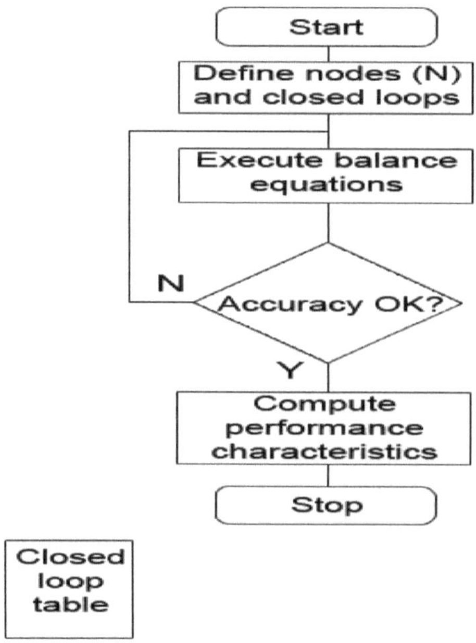

Figure 9 Functional architecture of approximate analytical performance evaluation tool

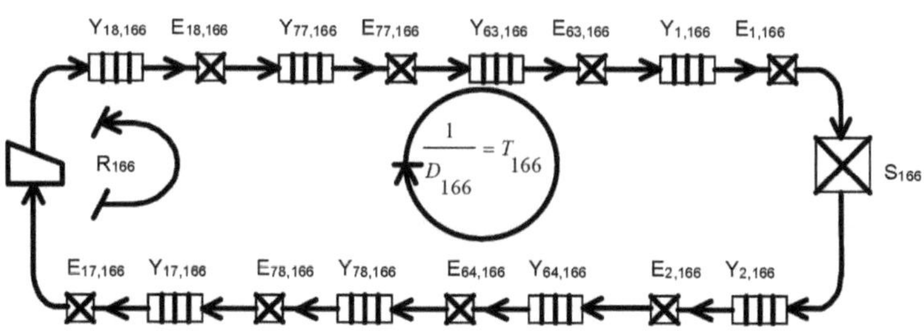

Figure 10 Exemplary closed loop investigated by the approximate throughput evaluation tool

References

1. Han M.W., Lewoc J.B., Izworski A., Skowronski S. and Kieleczawa A., Power Industry Computer Control System Design and Implementation Problems: A Case Study of Poland, In the 17-th IFAC Congress, Seoul 2008. .
2. Lewoc J.B., Kieleczawa A., Tomczyk A., Ziaja E. Izworski A. and Skowronski S., The Role of IASE In Design and Development of Pioneering ICT Systems for Power Industry In Poland, The 14-th International WOSK Congress, Wroclaw, 2008.
3. Sawicki J., Kowalski A.J. and Lewoc J., Implementation of the Automatic Data – Processing for the Power System Control in Poland, Data – Processing Conference, Nr 5.1.11, Madrid, 1974.
4. Elwro, Electronic Computer Odra 1325, Operating and Maintenance Manual (in Polish), Wroclaw, 1976.
5. Lewoc J. et al., Primary Data Processing Methods Applied in Power Generating Unit Computer Monitoring System, Power System Conference, Prague 1978.
6. Lewoc J.B., A Microcomputer Data Acquisition and Retrieval System for Power Distribution Boards, Microelectronics 1984, Prague 1984.
7. Lewoc J. and Rozent M., An Operating System for Digital Simulator of Power Generating Unit, In: Future Progress of Electrical Engineering, Prague 1975.
8. Lewoc J., Nawojski J. and Worsztynowicz E., Two-program operating system for digital simulators of complex power systems, Prace IASE, vol. 35, 1980 (in Polish).
9. Lewoc J.B., Rozent M. and Weksej E., A Power System Simulator: Participation of People Involved. In: ASBoHS (IFAC), Madison 1992.
10. Lewoc J.B. and Lanowska B., Microcomputer Data Display System for Power Industry Applications. In: MicroP '83, Budapest 1983.
11. Bujko J. and Lysiak E., IASE History. Prace IASE, Vol. 45, Wroclaw 1999 (In Polish).
12. Franasik L. et al, System Media – a Step toward Computer Integrated Manufacturing and Management Systems, Modelling, Measurement and Control (AMSE Press), vol. 22 No. 3, pp. 37-46, 2001.
13. Izworski A. and Lewoc J.B., Robustness Comparison of Enterprise Energy Distribution Systems of Various Topologies. In: Robust System Design (IFAC), Milan, 2003.
14. Izworski A., Lewoc J.B. and Skowronski S., Development of Computer Integrated Manufacturing and Management Systems. In: Information Control Problems in Manufacturing (IFAC), Saint Etienne, 2006.
15. Lewoc J.B., Izworski A. and Skowronski S., Alsis Case Study Computer Integrated Manufacturing and Management Systems. In.: Applications of Large Scale Industrial Systems (IFAC), Helsinki-Stockholm, 2006.
16. Lewoc J.B., Izworski A., Skowronski S. and Kieleczawa A., Some Problems with Technology Transfer in Lower Silesia. In: DECOM 2007 (IFAC), Cesme, 2007.
17. Izworski A., Lewoc J.B. and Piwowar B., Some Aspects of Technology Transfer – A Case Study, In: SWISS '01, Vienna, 2001.
18. Lewoc J.B., A Case Study: Practical Ethical Aspects for Technology Transfer and Change in Computer Control System Development. In; IFAC Congress, Prague, 2005.
19. Lewoc J.B., Izworski A. and Skowronski S., Economic, Ethical and Cultural Aspects of ICT Change in Power System Automation: a Case Study of Poland. In: ISA (IFAC), Prishtina, 2006b.
20. Wikipedia, QNX. Available at http://en.wikipedia.org/wiki/QNX, 2007.
21. J.B. Lewoc, Izworski A. and Skowronski S.. Performance Modelling of a Computer Integrated Manufacturing and Management System. Eurosim Congress, Ljubljana, 2007.

Olivetti Elea 9003: Between Scientific Research and Computer Business

Giuditta Parolini

Innovations in the Communication of Science (ICS–SISSA),
giudittaparolini@gmail.com

Abstract: About fifty years ago, Elea 9003, the first Italian mainframe fully transistorized, was built in the Olivetti Electronic Research Laboratory. The mainframe was realized with a drain of international expertise and training on-the-job of scientific staff. The head of the Laboratory, Mario Tchou, had a valuable experience in electronics in the U.S. and his collaborators, at first mainly Italian, were chosen for previous experience in pulse modulation methods. Elea 9003 was built with germanium diodes and transistors. They successfully sold the mainframe on the national market, but Olivetti electronic enterprise did not last. After the unexpected deaths of Adriano Olivetti (1960) and Mario Tchou (1961) there were inner contrasts in the management. Moreover, the national market was very limited and the Italian government did not help in any way the company. Therefore, in 1964 due to financial problems and shortsighted business strategies, Olivetti dismissed its main electronic assets and sold the Electronic Department to General Electric. However, the seeds of the work done by Olivetti Laboratory sprouted later on in computer science thanks to Programma 101, the first desktop computer.

Keywords: Second generation mainframe, Research & development (R&D), Technology transfer, Olivetti

1 Olivetti Electronic Research Laboratory

1.1 The Birth of Italian Computer Science

In 1959, the Italian company Olivetti, worldwide known for mechanical typewriters and calculators, officially announced a business mainframe, called Elea 9003, fully transistorized. The first computer designed and manufactured in

Please use the following format when citing this chapter:

Parolini, G., 2008, in IFIP International Federation for Information Processing, Volume 269; *History of Computing and Education 3*; John Impagliazzo; (Boston: Springer), pp. 37–53.

Italy was the outcome of the industrial research done since 1955 by Olivetti Electronic Research Laboratory.

The jump into business computer manufacturing was quite abrupt for Olivetti, but not unsuccessful in the Italian market were Olivetti computers competed with IBM mainframes. During the early 1960s, the Italian company manufactured about a quarter of the large and middle mainframes operating in the country. Olivetti built forty Elea 9003 in only four years and rented them out to important Italian companies – the first customer was in 1960 the textile industry Marzotto – and institutions (such as the Energy Corporation ENI and the Italian Insurance Agency Inps).

However, in 1964 due to financial problems and shortsighted business strategies, Olivetti dismissed the main electronic activities. The Italian expertise was taken over by General Electric, which purchased Olivetti Electronic Department.

However, Elea 9003 is a remarkable result because Italian computer science was at its very beginning. Besides Olivetti industrial research, there were only three more projects started in 1954.

Pisa University, in partnership again with Olivetti, began to develop a scientific calculator called CEP (Calcolatrice Elettronica Pisana) and two mainframes built abroad were installed in the country, a computer by National Cash Register at Milan Polytechnic and a Ferranti Mark I at INAC (Italian Institute for Applicative Calculations) in Rome. Both these computers belonged to first generation. In addition, CEP, officially presented in 1961, was only partially transistorized.

1.2 Olivetti Scientific Enterprise

The interest of Olivetti for research in computer science began in the early Fifties. Electronic systems were increasing more and more their power in US and Great Britain and Adriano Olivetti, the head of the Italian company, forecast an electronic development for mechanical products.

Olivetti should be prepared for this new business challenge, so, in 1952 the company founded a laboratory in New Canaan, Connecticut, in order to drain knowledge from the US expertise in the field. However, the aim of Olivetti was to create a laboratory in Italy. In 1955, the Olivetti Electronic Research Laboratory was founded in Pisa and hosted for a few months in the Physics Department of the University; the official headquarter instead was in Barbaricina, near Pisa, in a nineteenth century villa.

Olivetti chose Mario Tchou, the son of a Chinese diplomat in Italy, for leading the laboratory. Despite his young age – he was born in 1924 in Rome – he had a valuable experience in electronics. In 1945 Tchou moved from Italy to the US where he took a B.E.E. at the Catholic University of America in 1947 and a M.S. at the Polytechnic Institute of Brooklyn in 1949.

Since 1952 Tchou was working as Associate in Electrical Engineering at Columbia University. In those years the Department was chaired by Prof. John R. Ragazzini, whose team gave valuable contributions to classical theory of sampled-data control systems. Tchou himself added between his professional skills to be expert of «digital control system including electronic and electro-mechanical computers». (Rao 2003)

1.3 Tchou, Mario- Appointment Card at Columbia University[1]

B.E.E., Catholic University of America, 1947; M.S. Polytechnic Institute of Brooklyn, 1949

1952 (9/10) Appointment – Associate in Electrical Engineering 1952-53
1953 (5/4) School of General Studies 1953-54 – Engineering
1953 (6/24) Reappointment - Associate in Electrical Engineering 1953-54
1954 (6/11) Reappointment – Associate in Electrical Engineering 1954-55
1954 (5/3) School of General Studies 1954-55 – Engineering
1954 (10/5) Leave of Absence 10/15/54 – 6/30/55 without salary
1955 (5/2) School of General Studies 1955-56

1.4 International Experience for Olivetti Laboratory

Mario Tchou and Adriano Olivetti met for the first time in New York in 1954, while Mario Tchou was working at Columbia University. Adriano Olivetti was strongly impressed by Tchou who was very well educated and communicative. The young engineer had both scientific competence and managerial attitudes, which suited well with Olivetti's philosophy of a 'responsible' industry[2].

Thanks to his attitudes, Mario Tchou could promote electronic research between the company management, who did not support the new technology apart from the president Adriano, his son Roberto, and a few other people.

In September 1954 Mario Tchou required a *Leave of Absence without pay* from Columbia for the period October 15, 1954 to June 30, 1955 and he came back to Italy in December 1954 (Figure1 and Figure2 in Appendix A and B are the original documents from the Columbia Archives).

[1] By courtesy of Columbia University Archives.

[2] «Seriously interested in people, in social experiments, in the relationship among management, executive and workers», *The Asia Magazine* (22 October 1961).

The Olivetti Laboratory should be a national value, so Tchou's collaborators (some of them are shown in Figure 3) were mainly Italians at first and they were chosen for previous experience in pulse modulation methods. Only Giorgio Sacerdoti knew already mainframes because he had taken part in the set up of Ferranti Mark computer at Inac.
In the beginning, the only stranger was Martin Friedmann, a Canadian engineer who had developed the magnetic memories for the Ferranti Mark in Manchester. A drain of national and international experiences was necessary to set up the industrial laboratory and develop the ambitious project of a computer *made in Italy* (Filippazzi and Sacerdoti 1992).

Figure 3 A photograph taken at Barbaricina. We can see the staff of the Olivetti Electronic Research Laboratory (not all the members are present). Mario Tchou is the third on the left in the second row.

Mario Tchou assigned a different task to every member of the staff. In 1957 at Olivetti Laboratory, five different groups were at work for developing respectively a) the machine instructions, b) the government system for magnetic tapes, c) the central government unit, d) the mainframe memory, e) the arithmetic unit. In the Laboratory, besides the main electronic activities for Elea 9003, there were also minor works in electronic devices for Olivetti mechanical calculators. One example is a device necessary for using punched tapes, called *cbs*, built by Pier Giorgio Perotto who next developed also Programma 101.

The supervisor of the Laboratory activities was Roberto Olivetti, while the head of the company, Adriano, visited Barbaricina only from time to time.

1.5 From Scientific Research to Industrial Development

The manufacturing of the Elea computer developed into three main steps. In 1957, the first prototype was finished. It was mainly built with vacuum tubes and only the register for magnetic tapes was transistorized. This computer – known as *Macchina zero* (zero machine) and then called Elea 9001 – was not competitive in Mario Tchou's opinion. In fact, in those years the most important companies involved in computer manufacturing were developing transistorized mainframes. So, with the aid of his collaborators, Tchou restarted the project for a fully transistorized architecture and in 1958 the prototype of the business machine (Elea 9003) was almost finished. Between Elea 9001 and Elea 9003 another Elea machine (Elea 9002) – with standard vacuum tubes – was built.

In August 1958 Olivetti laboratory moved from Pisa to Borgolombardo, near Milan, where began the manufacturing of the transistorized computer. The laboratory building in Borgolombardo was on two-floor. On the ground floor the Elea central unit and the memory were produced – the I/O devices were built in Ivrea – while on the first floor there was the Elea 9003 computer at work. The prototype mainframe often required repairs and the servicing staff was set next to it.

Employees at Borgolombardo increased from some decades to some hundreds and then more than a thousand taking into consideration both the research staff and the manufacturing workers. Hierarchies substituted the flexible organization experienced in Barbaricina. Mario Tchou, now, was the head of the research activities but in Borgolombardo research and development had to coexist with the commercial goals.

In 1963, there was another move to Pregnana Milanese, in a strategic area along the Turin-Milan highway. The change of location happened after the official set up in 1962 of the Olivetti Electronic Department, which should coordinate all the factory activities in electronics.

Nevertheless, Olivetti electronic enterprise did not last. In 1960, Adriano Olivetti abruptly died and in 1961, Mario Tchou was also killed in a car accident. Two years later, in 1963, Olivetti suffered financial problems and the management decided to reduce loss selling to General Electric the Electronic Department, which required many investments. Due to unfortunate events and structural fragilities, the Olivetti engagement in computer science stopped in about a decade and the company went out of the mainframe market.

Although in 1965, the Italian company tried a new adventure in computer science with a desktop computer, Programma 101, which gained great business results. It was a forerunner of personal computer and its project had already started in the company Electronic Department.

1.6 The Architecture of Elea Computer

The Olivetti Laboratory developed the central unit of Elea 9003 by an original project, although I/O devices (tape punch and reader, cardpunch and reader, printer and teletypewriter) were commercial products built by Olivetti and Olivetti-Bull. The main components of the computer were the memory, the logical-arithmetic unit, the central government unit, the tape government unit, and the on-line unit synchronizer.

The mainframe had a clock time of 10 μs, 8 characters instructions (2 characters for function/command, 4 characters for the address, 2 characters for the length), variable word size, magnetic cores for the main memory and magnetic tapes[3] as secondary memory devices. It could perform about 5,000 additions per second and the capacity of the main memory was extensible from 20,000 words to 160.000. It was built with germanium diodes and transistors and its power consumption was 4.5 kW.

The most original features of the Olivetti mainframe were multiprogramming, the capability of handling an interruption, and optimize computer work (De Marco et al. 1999).

> Multiprogramming was based on a completely automatic priority system that depended on the availability of hardware resources and requests. The maximum "multiprogramming level" available on Elea 9003 [...] was three. [...] The main architectural components that made multiprogramming feasible were the Internal and External Transfer Channels. [...] With this architecture Elea 9003 was able to multiprogram operations on tapes, operations on online I/O Units [...] and logical-arithmetic operations.

1.7 The Problems of Technological Transfer

In the development of Elea 9003, technological transfer from research to industrial manufacturing highlighted some structural problem of the Italian system. The financial effort needed by electronics was very heavy for Olivetti, which was still a 'multinational shop', mainly governed by members of only one family. Moreover, the Elea computers were not sold to customers, but rented to them, as in IBM practice. In that way, initial investments were recovered in a longer time. Financial resources were also necessary for the development of new Elea machines as the smaller Elea 6001 devoted to scientific research.

The software development required also new efforts because Elea business mainframes could not be programmed easily. The Olivetti software team, born in the last days in Barbaricina, experienced all the difficulties of computer programming at its very beginning.

[3] The Elea 9003 brochure also referred to magnetic drums as secondary memory devices, but they were never added to the mainframe (Bonfanti 2007).

Mauro Pacelli, the mathematician who led the team, created PAlgol, a personal dialect of Algol, but an effective solution to software problems required the cooperation between Olivetti and its customers. For example, the Elea 9003 sold to Marzotto needed a long training period before it was fully operative.

The Italian situation was also peculiar because the national government did not help Olivetti in any way: it did not commission any computer – instead the national Treasury received free an Elea mainframe by Olivetti – nor it helped the company during the financial crisis occurred in 1963. When the Olivetti Electronic Department was sold to General Electric, the Italian government did not recognize as a national value the development of a home industry for computer research and manufacturing.

Mario Tchou, the leader of Olivetti Laboratory, had been aware of this criticality and he had already stated it in 1959 during an interview (published by the Italian newspaper *Paese Sera*) (Rao 2003)

> Nowadays we have gained the same qualitative development of our competitors, but they receive consistent financial aids by their national governments. Electronic research, mainly for military applications, is generously funded by the US. Also Great Britain invests millions of pounds in the field. Olivetti effort is great, but other companies could hope in a better future than us because they receive public funding.[4]

2 The International Framework of Computer Science

2.1 A Survey in Computer Science at the Beginning of the 1960s

During the age of transition between vacuum tubes mainframes and transistorized computers, engineers and public officers interested in the field wrote detailed reports about the worldwide development of computer science. Throughout the Fifties new technologies of information processing were growing in United States, Europe and Japan. At the beginning of the Sixties in the United States there were «over ten times the number of medium and large-scale data processing equipment installations [...] than in the rest of the world» (Auerbach 1961).

The US leadership was due to earlier start in the field and was maintained by the Government support in research and development. The main computer manufacturers – such as IBM, RCA, Remington Rand, Sperry, DEC – invested in new solid state technologies and exported their mainframes in many foreign countries. In 1958 Sperry Rand started the development of a full solid state mainframe and in the same year IBM announced the 7070 all transistorized computer series, which was put on the market in 1960. In 1960, too, DEC commercialized the Programmed Data Processor (PDP 1) computer, full

[4] *Paese Sera* (November 18, 1959). The translation is mine.

transistorized and very compact. In addition, in Europe and Japan the Fifties were a profitable age for development of information systems and at the beginning of the next decade digital computers were working throughout the area. In large part of Europe, computers were manufactured and seven countries were involved also in the commercial market. «[…] Great Britain clearly comes first (after the U.S.). She is followed by (West) Germany, the U.S.S.R., France and Japan» (Blachman 1961).

2.2 The Situation in Great Britain, France, and Germany

In Cambridge, Great Britain, was realized in June 1949 the Edsac, the first stored-program electronic digital computer. In Manchester, both University and Ferranti Ltd. did relevant efforts in scientific and industrial computer development. In particular, Ferranti manufactured Atlas, a fully transistorized computer capable of operating on several programs simultaneously. Besides Ferranti, there were seven more computer manufacturers in Great Britain and they delivered about two hundreds computers in about a decade.

In the Western European continent, Germany and France had a leading role in computer science. Germany was involved in computer science and making since the late Thirties, when Konrad Zuse realized the first relay computer. A decade after the II World War in the Western side of the country there were national computers manufacturers (as Zuse, Siemens, Telefunken, Standard Elektrik) and two factories of foreign builders as IBM and Remington Rand. Telefunken, in particular, was making the most advanced machine, Telefunken TR 4, fully transistorized. Many German universities were also involved in computer development and scientific training.

In France Compagnies des Machines Bull, Société d'Electronique et d'Automatisme and Société Nouvelle d'Electronique were the national computer developers. In particular, Bull was the most important punched-card machine manufacturer all over Europe, North Africa, and South America and since 1950, it had a business agreement with Olivetti for the sale of punched-card systems in the Italian market. Bull Gamma 60 mainframes had multi-threading capabilities through asyncronism of processing units and input/output channels. They were realized by a combination of germanium transistors, magnetic core memory and still a few vacuum tubes.

2.3 Computers in USSR and Japan

Moving toward the East, in USSR the development of computer science was mainly due to the Ukrainian engineer Sergey A. Lebedev. At Lebedev's Institute in Moscow there were laboratories working on transistors, core materials, thin magnetic films, and magnetic circuits.

In the Far East, instead, Fujitsu produced the first Japanese computers during the Fifties. In 1954 the company built Facom 100 with relay technology but in less than a decade it moved from old technologies (vacuum tubes and parametron, a kind of oscillating circuit with the same functions of transistors) to solid-state electronics. In 1956, Fuji Photo Film Company built with vacuum tubes the Fujic, the first Japanese computer with a memorized program, and between 1956 and 1957 a transistorized computer were built at the Electrotecnic Laboratory of Japan. The Japanese universities of Tokio, Keio and Osaka were also involved in computer science research.

3 Solid-state Electronics in Italy

3.1 The First Root of ST Microelectronics

In 1956, the Nobel Prize for Physics was awarded to William Shockley, John Bardeen, and Walter Brattain «for their researches on semiconductors and their discovery of the transistor effect» done ten years before at Bell Laboratories in US. Also in the field of solid-state devices, the US strongly kept a leading role. In Europe the main producers were Siemens and Philips. Solid-state components were not manufactured in Italy, another obstacle for the development of transistors computers.

Olivetti in joint venture with Telettra, an Italian telecommunication company that shared the same problem, founded in 1957 the SGS (Società Generale Semiconduttori). In fact, Roberto Olivetti, the manager of Olivetti electronic assets, and Mario Tchou, the head of the Olivetti Laboratory, thought that a computer factory should take part in the basic industry of electronic devices.

From 1960 also the US company Fairchild was involved in the society, which next developed into the multinational STMicroelectronics. At the beginning of the Sixties in the SGS laboratories near Milan worked also another key-figure of computer science, Federico Faggin who developed there a method of manufacturing MOS (Metal Oxide Semiconductors) integrated circuits and designed also the first two commercial ones.

3.2 International Cooperation

The first Italian staff in Olivetti Electronic Research Laboratory knew only a little about computers and physicists, engineers and technicians strengthened their competences by self-training and international experiences. This requirement was precisely stated in the company job advertisement appeared in 1955 on the main Italian newspapers for recruiting the laboratory staff.

Franco Filippazzi, who developed the Elea 9003 main memory, for example, visited more than once Philips Laboratories in Eindhoven, where he could see the most advanced European solid-state devices. Besides the drain of international knowledge, Olivetti management tried also to promote a grid of European electronic manufacturers.

There were meetings with the British company ICT (International Computers and Tabulators), the French company Bull, the German Siemens, but the effort was unsuccessful. European manufacturers could not find an agreement about common technological standard and scientific knowledge sharing.

4 Advertising and Science Communication

4.1 Olivetti Advertising Office

At the middle of the twentieth century, 'Olivetti style' was a recognized feature of the Italian company all over the world. In 1952 the Metropolitan Museum of Modern Art in New York exhibited some of the more successful Olivetti products as the mechanical calculator *Divisumma 14* and the typewriter *Lettera 22*.

The elegant design was a main component of the Olivetti brand and since 1931, the company founded an Advertising Office, whose consultants were architects, painters, writers and poets. The duties of the office were the design planning and the promotion of advertising campaigns. The office staff worked in strong collaboration with both the management and the project engineers.

Electronics, as a new and promising company assets, should be respectful of Olivetti style, so in 1958 Adriano Olivetti entrusted the architect Ettore Sottsass of the mainframe design. Elea 9003 cabinets created by Sottsass were about a meter high, far less than the big ones generally used for mainframes. The result was an open space where technicians and engineers could see all the system with only a look.

Moreover, every cabinet was connected to others by aerial conducts (shown in Figure 4) and so it was unnecessary to build a new pavement under which store cables and ventilation pipes. Elea cabinets could also be separated from one another (they had a "wing" structure) for easier transport and installation of the computer. Ettore Sottsass also designed the Elea console, very functional and user-friendly before this expression was born (an overview of the mainframe is in Figure 5).

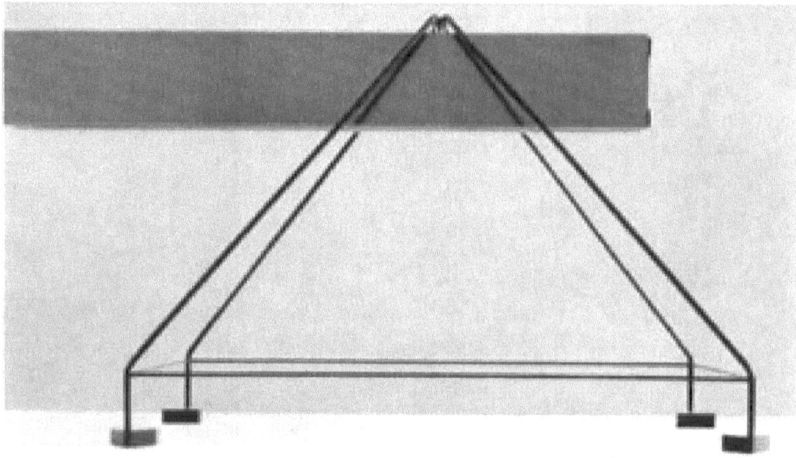

Figure 4 The aerial conducts between Elea 9003 cabinets. By courtesy of Associazione Archivio Storico Olivetti, Ivrea (Italy).

The aesthetic of Elea 9003 was strongly influenced by the sovereign Olivetti philosophy, in which machines should fulfil the greatest usefulness for people. This feature was highlighted also in the advertising campaign for Olivetti mainframe and the commercial name Elea is again a smart communication trick. On one side Elea is the abbreviation of the Italian words for Electronic Automatic Computer, but on the other it recalls the town of Elea where flourished in the Antiquity a famous philosophical school. It is claimed that the commercial name Elea was chosen by Franco Fortini, a famous Italian writer and translator who worked for Olivetti Advertising Office in those years.

4.2 The Future is Now

In 1959 and 1960, when Elea was officially announced, Olivetti promoted the new electronics activities with brochures, advertising, on the press and in broadcasting.

In October 1959 a popular Italian magazine of the time, *Epoca*, published a 'servizio industriale' (an article realized by the Advertising Office) about the Olivetti mainframe and the Electronic Research Laboratory. The article is a masterpiece of photojournalism. The first part of the article summarizes Olivetti approach to electronics as a key way for industrial development and shows photographs taken at Olivetti headquarters in Ivrea and in the Research Factory at Borgolombardo, where Elea 9003 was working.

Figure 5 Olivetti Elea 9003. In the foreground the console of the mainframe. By courtesy of Associazione Archivio Storico Olivetti, Ivrea (Italy).

The written text remarks the switching of lights in the console of the mainframe and the high potential of the computer («more than 100,000 characters could be written and are available for reading every minute»). In the second part of the article, a photographic gallery displays the main features of Elea 9003. Ten images with a legend explain the information process from data entry to output results, giving some remarks about the function of the main memory and the role of government units.

Elea 9003 and the Research Laboratory in Borgolombardo are also shown in the documentary *Elea classe 9000* produced in 1960 by Olivetti Film Office. In about half an hour there is a summary of calculating machines history and a perspective look of the Elea development and functions. Graphic animations, beautiful photography, and the original soundtrack make the film a masterpiece. The documentary explains both the research goals – there is also the head of the laboratory, Mario Tchou, who describes the work done by his team – and the business value of the machine. Graphic animations show how Elea is helpful in the management of car industry and a voice over suggests also that the mainframe could be useful in financial business, archives administration, registry office and much more.

Basic mainframe features and functions are explained to the documentary audience by metaphors, smart graphic solutions, and analogies. In fact at the beginning of the Sixties computer science was quite unknown in Italy and its popularization should be developed from nothing. Olivetti approached the challenge with a mix of advertising techniques (first of all, brand reliability) and science communication attitudes, explaining the great potential of Elea machine.

In 1960 also the annual diary[5] created by Olivetti was devoted to the evolution of writing machines from mechanical typewriters to the Elea mainframe, which was described as 'the electronic thinking machine'. The Italian painter Bruno Caruso, who realized the drawings for the diary, represented Elea mainframe thanks to the metaphor of the electronic brain. Logic circuits and the memory of the computer are related to human anatomy. Caruso plays with the identity of functions and at the same time, he underlines the substantial differences between the levers and the mechanisms in traditional typewriters and the greater potentialities of the Elea computer.

5 Conclusion

The development of the Italian mainframe Elea 9003 is an interesting case of industrial research because the architecture of the mainframe, which was original and competitive in the national market, started from scratch by a drain of international experiences and on-the-job training of the scientific staff.

Although, the challenge of technological transfer could not be properly overcome due to several factors: Olivetti experienced financial fragilities and there were inner contrasts in the management after the unexpected deaths of Adriano Olivetti and Mario Tchou. Moreover, the national market was very limited and the Italian government did not help in any way the company. Between scientific research and computer business there was – and in Italy often there is again – a tangled bond, which could choke even a promising project.

[5] It was a prestigious gift for customers created by Olivetti during the Sixties and devoted, year after year, to different topics. The 1960 diary was entitled *Dalla calligrafia alla memoria* (i.e. From calligraphy to memory).

Figure 6 A drawing of the Elea 9003 computer done by Bruno Caruso and published in Olivetti journal during 1960. The caption is a poetic description of how Elea 9003 works. "A question impressed on a magnetic tape pass through a logic circuit which decides the operation, perform it, decides, proposes, answers, searches for the truth and rejects the error. The result is imprisoned in the memory where it is stored, localized and, under request, proposed another time in the consciousness of the machine. The past survives in the machine, invisible and unchanging, because this memory has no mood. Elea, electronic brain, is at work for mankind". By courtesy of Associazione Archivio Storico Olivetti, Ivrea (Italy).

However, the manufacturing of Elea 9003 was one of the first computer science initiatives in Italy and, though not at all successful, it spread many seeds.

The first root of Programma 101, the scientific training of Italian computer experts and a few attempts in science communications are all outcomes of the activity done in a decade by Olivetti Research Laboratory.

Acknowledgments: I would like to thank all who have supported me in collecting information about Mario Tchou's international experience and Olivetti Electronic Research Laboratory. I am grateful to Jocelyn K. Wilk of the Columbia University Archives and to Giuseppe Rao who has done an extensive research about Mario Tchou and Olivetti Laboratory. Thanks to Franco Filippazzi for our conversation in Milan and to Corrado Bonfanti for documents and suggestions.

References

1. Auerbach IL (1961) The international impact of computers. Commun. ACM 4,10: 466
2. Blachman NM (1961) The state of digital computer technology in Europe. Commun. ACM 4,6:256-265
3. Bonfanti C (2007) L'industria del computer in Italia. In: L'informatica - Lo sviluppo economico, tecnologico e scientifico in Italia, Edifir, Firenze (in Italian)
4. De Marco G, Mainetto G et al (1999) The Early Computers of Italy. IEEE Ann. Hist. Comput. 21, 4:28-36
5. Filippazzi F (2005) Elea: storia di una sfida industriale. PRISTEM 12-13:43-57 (in Italian)
6. Filippazzi F. and Sacerdoti G. (1992) Progetto Elea: il primo computer made in Italy. Atti del Convegno Internazionale sulla Storia e Preistoria del Calcolo Automatico e dell'Informatica (Siena, September 10-12, 1991), 3rd edn, AICA, Milano (in Italian)
7. Gallino L (2003) «Un neo da estirpare»: l'informatica. In: La scomparsa dell'Italia industriale, Einaudi, Torino (in Italian)
8. Morelli M (2001) Dalle calcolatrici ai computer degli anni Cinquanta. FrancoAngeli, Milano (in Italian)
9. Rao G (2003) La sfida al futuro di Adriano e Roberto Olivetti. MEFRIM 115,2:643-678 (in Italian)
10. Rao G (2005) Mario Tchou e l'Olivetti Elea 9003. PRISTEM 12-13:85-119 (in Italian)
11. Soria L (1979) Informatica: un'occasione perduta. Einaudi, Torino (in Italian)
12. Ware W.H. et al (1960) Soviet Computer Technology – 1959. Commun. ACM 3,3:131-166

Appendix A

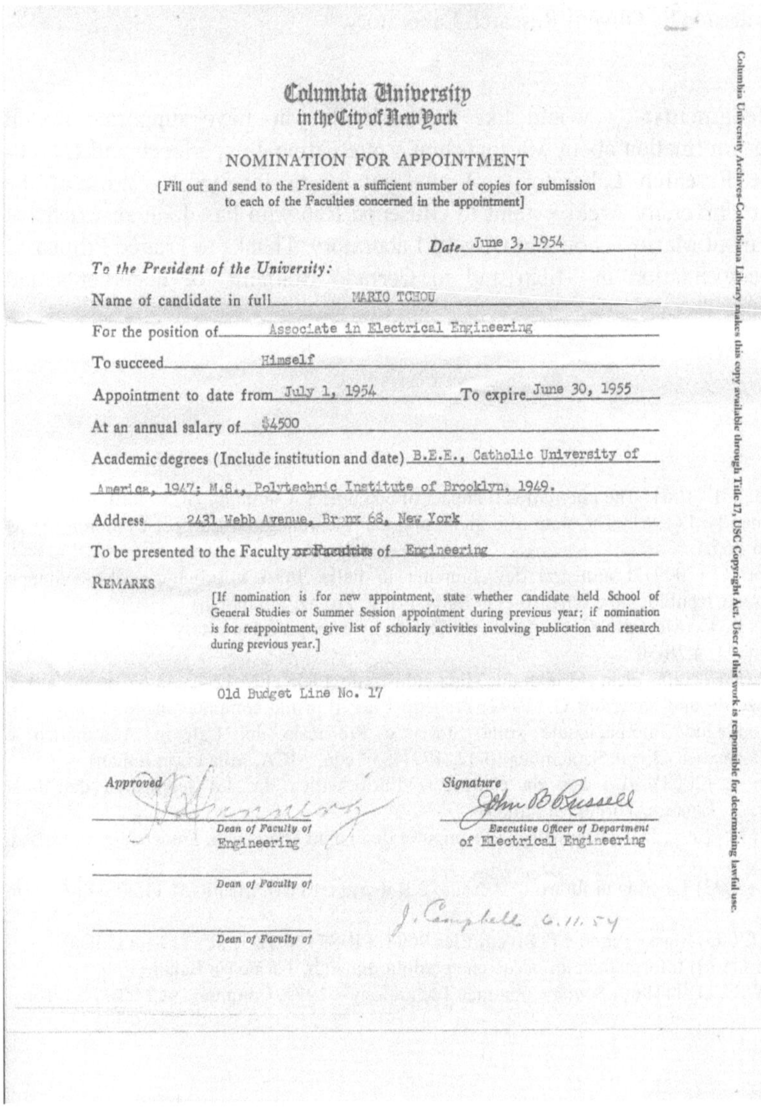

Columbia University
in the City of New York

NOMINATION FOR APPOINTMENT

[Fill out and send to the President a sufficient number of copies for submission to each of the Faculties concerned in the appointment]

Date June 3, 1954

To the President of the University:

Name of candidate in full MARIO TCHOU

For the position of Associate in Electrical Engineering

To succeed Himself

Appointment to date from July 1, 1954 To expire June 30, 1955

At an annual salary of $4500

Academic degrees (Include institution and date) B.E.E., Catholic University of America, 1947; M.S., Polytechnic Institute of Brooklyn, 1949.

Address 2431 Webb Avenue, Bronx 68, New York

To be presented to the Faculty ~~or Faculties~~ of Engineering

REMARKS

[If nomination is for new appointment, state whether candidate held School of General Studies or Summer Session appointment during previous year; if nomination is for reappointment, give list of scholarly activities involving publication and research during previous year.]

Old Budget Line No. 17

Approved

Dean of Faculty of Engineering

Signature John B. Russell

Executive Officer of Department of Electrical Engineering

Dean of Faculty of

Dean of Faculty of

J. Campbell 6.11.54

Figure 1 Mario Tchou's Nomination for Appointment from July 1954 to June 1955 at Columbia University. By courtesy of Columbia University Archives.

Appendix B

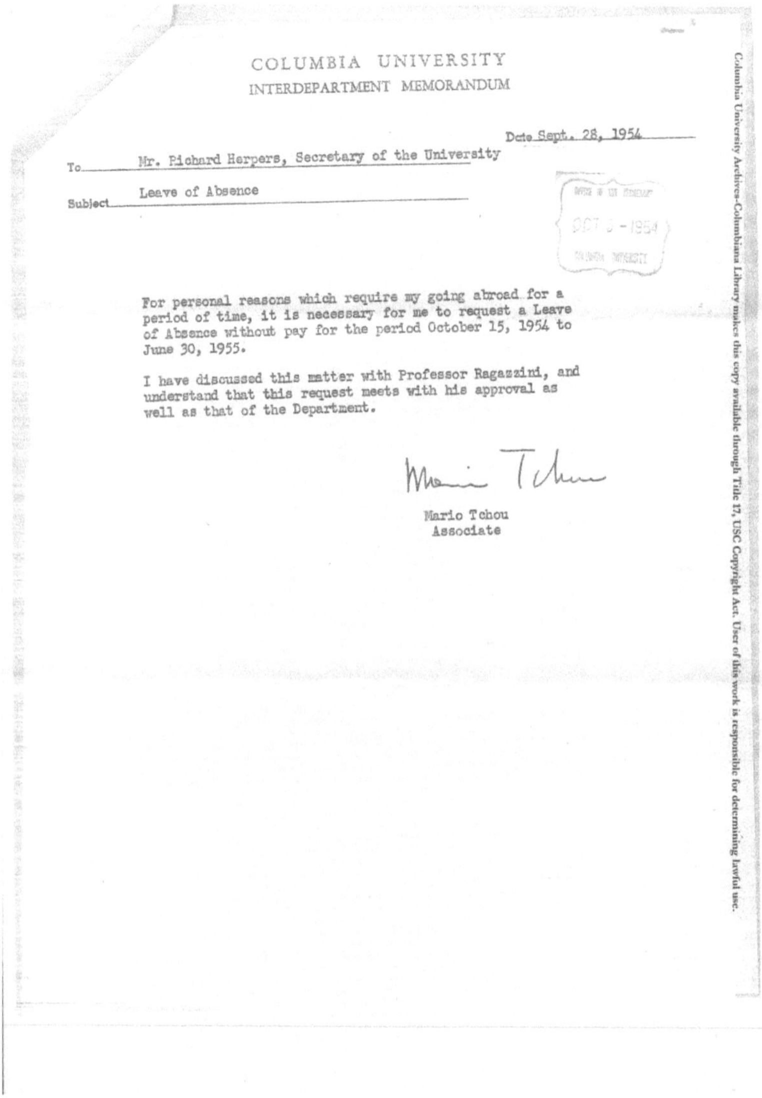

COLUMBIA UNIVERSITY
INTERDEPARTMENT MEMORANDUM

Date Sept. 28, 1954

To Mr. Richard Herpers, Secretary of the University

Subject Leave of Absence

OCT 5 - 1954

For personal reasons which require my going abroad for a period of time, it is necessary for me to request a Leave of Absence without pay for the period October 15, 1954 to June 30, 1955.

I have discussed this matter with Professor Ragazzini, and understand that this request meets with his approval as well as that of the Department.

Mario Tchou
Associate

Figure 2 Memorandum for Mario Tchou's Leave of Absence (Sept. 28, 1954). By courtesy of Columbia University Archives.

Cuban Experiences on Computing and Education

Tomás López Jiménez[1], Melchor Félix Gil Morell[2], and Adriana Estrada Negrin[3]

[1] *Universidad de las Ciencias Informáticas, Habana - Cuba, tlopezj@uci.cu*
[2] *Universidad de las Ciencias Informáticas, Habana - Cuba, rector@uci.cu*
[3] *Universidad de las Ciencias Informáticas, Habana - Cuba, adriana@uci.cu*

Abstract: In 1959 in Cuba, there was little knowledge regarding modern computing; the educational offerings at the university level were not enough and the diversity was low. Currently, this environment has changed completely obtaining levels over world average standards. Apart from the collaboration from abroad that the country has received, the domestic development has played a vital role since the 1960s. The main events on industrial and scientific development on computing in Cuba and its teaching at all educational levels in this country appear in this work. We show the issues that reflect how the early and systematic guidance and attention from the country's administration, together with the active and certain academic and scientific policy of the University of Havana were highly decisive. Although the main research covers through the mid 1990s, we also demonstrate the early events that would be of interest.

Keywords: Cuba, Computing, Informatics, Education, Science, Technology, History

1 Introduction

The history of computing still offers a passionate, important, and greatly needed research field for society, in which many events and approaches remain almost unknown or completely non-investigated. A large number of authors have given significant and valuable results on this field, with papers scoping different approaches of the development of science, technology, economics, and society itself. Generally, their foundations rest upon well-intentioned and recognized interests; however, they do not always focused on finding answers that can be of great use and impact to improve the needed knowledge for a better human development.

Please use the following format when citing this chapter:

Jiménez, T.L., Morell, M.F.G., and Negrin, A.E., 2008, in IFIP International Federation for Information Processing, Volume 269; *History of Computing and Education 3*; John Impagliazzo; (Boston: Springer), pp. 55–77.

From the historiography point of a view, there are many publications, most of them of great value, which report related events from the United States, Great Britain, Germany, Spain, some information from the former Soviet Union, Japan, and some other countries. In most of them, they use history to identify and reward pioneer personalities for their scientific and technological contributions; a similar situation results when they refer to countries, historical events, universities, research institutions, enterprises, or other entities. Some accounts even focus on technological generations, platforms, crises, and the software industry. It is quite common to find the presentation and defense of preconceptions and points of views somewhat unethical or even wrong, whether unconscious or on purpose.

Yet, it is quite difficult to locate a set of approaches that provides a platform of knowledge that facilitates the needed establishment of professional culture. Similarly, it is not easy to find the horizontal and vertical integration of learning within the undergraduate, post graduate specialized studies of computing and informatics, and at the same time, support the didactics and other pedagogical needs. This situation is even more critical when it refers to establishing a general and basic culture in this history for professionals from other working fields, which is without any doubt well needed.

This void is even more important when its intention is to address the measurement and understanding of economical and social impacts of computing and informatics. The relationship between both origins, human beings and informatics, should take into account the cognitive informatics approach [1]. That is, we should consider its role through the creation of a knowledge society and the thesis that it could generate a scientific revolution that could be the basis for a new social mode of knowledge production.

Nevertheless, this paper does not give solutions to problems mentioned above. It does compile some preliminary and partial results from the research on the history of informatics in Cuba. It offers some elements that address and contribute to the veracity of the events and the motivation and importance of the investigation itself. We pay special attention to the period from 1959 until now. We also show the basic elements from previous years with an emphasis to the ending of the past millennium.

Taking into account the scope of the HCE3 as part of the IFIP WCC 2008, the second section of this paper limits its contents to the period from 1959 to 1990. It depicts the implementation of domestic hardware and software capacities, while highlighting the main elements of computing education and training development between 1959 and today and we show its close relationship with the mentioned capacities. It is important to highlight how the Cuban government and specifically the further vision and systematic attention of its main leaders, have guided this process to foster a national development of its educational system in particular.

On the other hand and as a necessary terminology explanation, the nouns *computing*, *informatics*, and *information technology* appear in this paper in an indistinctive way, as synonyms of the name of the discipline of computing, having an analysis of the backward scope and a look to the present use since its origin as automatic electronics computing back in the 1940s. We give greater preference to the term *informatics* as the discipline whose working field is defined by *cognitive informatics* [1], considering it a more comprehensive phrase and having possibilities of a longer use. In addition, it offers a more practical and widespread reference for the research of this history in order to fulfill the objectives and reach the approaches stated in this paper.

2 Establishing Computer Capability in Cuba

2.1 Antecedents and Situation of Computing in Cuba during 1959

On January 1st of 1959 in Cuba, there were three public universities: the University of Havana (UH), the Eastern University (EU) and the Central University (CU). There were three other private universities, out of which the Catholic University of Villanueva (CUV) was the most outstanding. Before 1959 there were less than seven million inhabitants in the island; nowadays this population has stabilized having around 11.3 million inhabitants. The illiteracy rate at that time represented more than the 14% of the population. However, two years later, it reduced to a 3.9% because of a special literacy campaign carried out during 1961.

There are documental records regarding conventional data processing in Cuba from as far back as 1927; yet, in 1959, there was no established knowledge about modern computing. In 1927, IBM opened a field office in Cuba, the 27th outside the USA. One of its main recorded external business milestones was the installment of their tabulating and accounting machines in Havana. It is recorded as the 16th and the confiscation of their offices in Cuba in 1961 as the 52nd.[1] Actually, there was no confiscation; the manager paid employees, closed all operations, and abandoned the country. Later on, the Cuban authorities reopened the place and managed to maintain its services, even though it was impossible to acquire spare parts or new equipment and systems [2].

At the end of 1958, the first electronic computer arrived in the country; it was a RAMAC 305 with 350C magnetic disks – at the time still considered a world

[1] See frequent asked question about IBM in at http://www-03.ibm.com/ibm/history/documents/pdf/faq.pdf

novelty.[2] This was installed in 1962 after a proposal made by the Minister of Industry, Commander Ernesto Che Guevara. Initially, the government used it for processing social security information, for the development of applications as payroll calculations, and for other enterprise interests. It was also devoted to the training and development of programmers and system designers. With the breaking-up of diplomatic relations with the USA administration along with the harsh blockade imposed by them since February, 1962, access to North American science and technology was cut off, making it also harder to establish relationship with other countries. This and other related damages have brought about accumulated losses to Cuba for over 89,000 millions dollars throughout its fifty years of existence [2].

Before 1959 there existed a baccalaureate degree in Physics and Mathematical Sciences with subjects as mathematics and statistics at the UH and the CU; electrical engineering was also taught at the University of Havana since 1900. Linear algebra and notions of operations research were part of the curriculum at the CUV while the CU started electric engineering in 1960. The EU added mathematical studies in 1968 and electrical engineering in 1969.

2.2 Creating Basic Conditions. Period from 1959 to 1967

In 1959, wide-ranging transformations occurred in the country. They established a National Education system with universal and free access to all citizens. At the same time, the government implemented a program on Integral Teaching Reform. The universities were the main scenarios of the process. By June of 1961, the government proclaimed a law for the General Nationalization of Education. This law established the responsibility of the state for offering free educational services. On January 15 of 1960, Commander in Chief Fidel Castro stated, "*The future of our Nation has to be, necessarily, a future of men of sciences, of men of thinking...*" From the very beginning the mission and commitment of science and education within the Cuban society was clearly stated.

In March of 1962, Commander Ernesto Che Guevara, with an acute vision, pointed out electronics as one of the four fundamental lines for the future industrial development of the country. They created the Department of Automation and Electronics of the Cuban Industry Ministry right away; its mission was to train leaders and professionals who would establish working and research models on the fields of electronics, cybernetics, automation, and computing [3]. In 1963, making emphasis on his idea, he stated "*...in the future,*

[2] See IEEE Santa Clara Valley Section, Dedication: May 26, 2005 at www.ieee.org/organizations/history_center reporting that the IBM 305 RAMAC was commercially delivered from September 4, 1956.

no country can move forward if it does not develop the Electronics and Computing fields; this is the strategy and we have to work towards it" [4].

Preceded by the use of the RAMAC 305 since 1962, in 1965 the English second-generation computer Elliott 803B was installed at the National Calculus Center (NCC) of the UH. They purchased this computer as part of the scientific equipment for the National Scientific Research Center of Cuba, also inaugurated in 1965. Working jointly with national institutions, applications were developed to enhance projects such as the transportation systems, input/output models, mix balancing and optimizing, management of bird keeping farms, numeric forecasting of time, and geological research. The NCC trained its own programmers and system analysts, and from their clients or customers. In 1967, the School of Mathematics from UH founded the Institute of Applied Mathematics and Computing to increase the academic activities and services from the out-coming scientific discipline [5].

Although before 1959 one of the Cuban universities trained electrical engineers, two of them trained Licentiates in Physics and Mathematics. Furthermore, another one taught linear algebra and notions of operation research. We can undoubtedly stated that up to that moment there were neither academic nor research activities in the country that would develop capacities for the use and development of electronics in computing.

Because of the educational reform, the scientific policy and the industrial development started in 1968 was already in existence. It had gathered the basic and indispensable knowledge necessary to undertake a more advanced development and use of computing, as well as the training of specialists and scientists in this field with higher goals set for it.

2.3 Explicit Takeoff Strategy: Period from 1968 to 1976

Taking as the starting point the advances reached in the knowledge of the use of computers during the eight years gone by, coupled with the objective of strengthening its development for the interest of the economy and the Cuban society, in the period between 1968 and 1976, this led to the following parallel and complementary lines.

1. In charge of the Central Planning Board became the present Ministry of Economy and Planning. Originally, its mission was to carry out the 1970 population and housing census, and also to do the centralized statistical planning and control of all the national activities. With this purpose in mind since 1968, the Board organized the National Calculus Plan (NCP) and later on the National Direction of Electronic Calculus. The country imported both the technology and the technical assistance.
2. The second line for the creation of computing capacities in Cuba stimulated and empowered domestic scientific and technological development.

Conceived and aroused by President Fidel Castro, by the end of 1968 he entrusted the task to the University of Havana, with the immediate goal of developing a Cuban computer; this constituted a great challenge for the young scientific and technological policy of the university [6].

3. The bodies of defense and national security led the third line. Besides its own strategy and guidelines, it supported itself on the previous lines and on the collaboration of the European socialist countries, mainly that of the Soviet Union.

2.3.1 Brief Summary of the Main Activities Developed by the NCP

The NCP reached certain agreements in 1968 with the French government for the supply of two SEA 4000 second generation computers, followed in 1972 by two IRIS50 mainframes and little more than a dozen third generation IRIS10 minicomputers. Part of the IRIS10 were remote satellite terminals: three destined to the universities and the others to other organizations, most of which were already using the Cuban CID 201 minicomputer A and B, among which we can mention the University of Havana and the headquarters office of the sugar industry.

The two SEA 4000 were destined mainly to the processing of the 1970 population and housing census. Later on, they placed it into the service of the army with the incorporation of the IRIS computers since 1972. The introduction of French technology ended around 1975 with two additional IRIS50. The project and development of a tele-transmission system and a teleprocessing of data with these systems took place in the years between 1973 and 1976. The French alternative had begun between 1973 and 1974 to replace them gradually by a more viable and secure option with the European socialist countries. The use of mainframes continued spreading through the importation of various models of the unified series ES[3] from the member countries of the Council for Mutual Economic Assistance (CMEA or COMECOM as also was known) mainly the Soviet Union, the Democratic Republic of Germany, and Bulgaria, adding up to more than a hundred systems by the end of the 1980s.

A training process of some dozens of programmers and analysts preceded the introduction of the French technology. This initiated in 1969 by recruiting first year university students who were previously studying different undergraduate

[3] The ES systems were developed starting in 1969 under the agreement of the European countries members of the Council for Mutual Economic Assistance (CMEA). At the beginning only to mainframe computer were orientated. The Standard for functional analogies was established for IBM 360 and 370 Systems. The main models for this serial used in Cuba were 1020, 1022, 1035, 1040 and 1055. In 1973, the agreement was expanded with the introduction of the SM system for the unification of the minicomputer development. Cuba enters to this last amendment in 1974.

disciplines. In the beginning, they studied and were trained for programming and setting programs in machine code and assembly language for the Elliott 803B and the SEA 4000, respectively, for the AutoCode Elliott 803 Mark 3, and ALGOL 60 for the Elliott 803B. This personnel training was kept according to the needs to assimilate the IRIS computers, firstly for a pioneer small group in France and then in Cuba. Some specialized schools from the University of Havana and the Central University, trained their students and teachers for a while in the use of the IRIS 10, though the training was limited due to the fact of having only a few of those minicomputers.

Aiming to increase the range of organization in the country and its economic and social development, they proclaimed a new law for the organization of the central administration of the Cuban state in November of 1976. Because of it, the government created new ministries and organizations; priority for the development of computing increased significantly by creating the National Institute of Automated Systems and Computing Techniques (INSAC) that represented a special body of the Council of Ministries. Its main objective consisted of paying special attention to the development and generalization of computing in Cuba in all their lines – hardware and software industries, applications, technical services, imports, exports, and others. From that moment on, the NCP and the rest of the specialized computer institutions became part of INSAC, thus integrating themselves into new conceptions and programs. Education was empowered with the creation of the Ministry of Higher Education, expanded from the Ministry of Education from that moment onward in charge of the other subsystems of education.

2.3.2 National Trend of Scientific and Industrial Development of Computing

In April of 1969, the UH created the Digital Research Center (CID – acronyms in Spanish), having as an immediate assigned mission for the development of a Cuban computer. Led by the magnificence of Ph.D. Eng. Orlando Ramos Fernández (1938-1990), on April 18, 1978, the CID 201 was running, the first third generation Cuban minicomputer, with integrated DTL circuits and 4K words of a 12-bit ferrite core memory unit. For its architecture, it used the PDP-8 as a reference. In October 1970, five years before they reported the KCS[4], a compact audiocassette recorder was coupled to it as a more powerful I/O device, at a transfer ratio of 300 bauds; it was ten times faster than the original paper tape and had an auxiliary 64K words memory –equivalent to 96K bytes [7].

[4] See the KCS (Kansas City Standard), reported in BYTE February 1976. Afterwards the Processor Technology Corporation published the popular CUTS– Computer Users' Tape Standard, with option of 300 or 1200 bauds.

The production of the CID 201 started by the end of that year under the name of CID 201A. What made it different was the technological solution offered to its cabinet and wiring for a more efficient reproduction, enhancing its coordination and facilitating a man-machine communication as shown in Figure 1. We can see how it integrated the operator control console to the main body. Replicated through small neon lamps, in the console there are the binary contents of the arithmetic unit accumulator and its a bit link, the memory/address contents and the program counter registers, as well as six keys to interact with them in the setting up, debugging and running of the programs and the technical service. On the right frontal block, they installed an original I/O system as an alternative solution to the difficulties faced to obtain peripheral equipment due to the North American blockade against the country. The I/O system also maintained the monetary waste within the limited disposition of the project and of the country. Its output unit consisted of a decimal numerical display initially with tubes of seven segments. A luminous 4x4 dot matrix made it possible to correlate the numerical result of 16 tags or names of different variables – alphabetical or personalized – according to the case. The input unit was an integrated device with a conventional decimal numerical keyboard and three hot keys for the automatic launching of three different programs. This device, together with the corresponding programs, favored an economical and flexible I/O interactive system in octal, decimal, and symbolic characters for multiple purposes, including the setting up and debugging of programs.

The right side of Figure 1 shows the compact cassette audio recorder /reproducer for which the necessary communication protocol was developed in a binary format. In its configuration, there was also included a tele-printer with a five-channel paper tape reader and punch in the Murray code, produced by the RFT Complex of the former Democratic Republic of Germany.

Figure 1 First Cuban minicomputer. Left hand: Prototype CID 201. Right hand: Serial model CID 201A.

Having no access to US systems and facing program incompatibilities became a challenge for the fathers of the CID. Late in 1970, it released the domestic software for bootstrapping, input/output, and integer and floating-point arithmetic package. Early in 1971, it received the LEAL 201 (which in Spanish stands for algorithmic language, an auto-code language of high level, domestically designed; for whose development it was followed some concepts from Auto-Code Elliott 803- Mark III). In 1972, it had incorporated a compiler and an interpreter from a simplified FORTRAN and other library programs.

The next code is a sample of a LEAL 201A program implementing Euclid's algorithm to obtain the GCD of two integer variables. Note the use of Polish notation. The comment facility was not implemented; here it is used for clarity purposes and appears at right side of the code, beginning with the slash character.

```
LEAL
TO FIND THE GCD OF A AND B, THE RESULT IN A
ENT A B M       /Integer variable declaration;
FLO             /Its use was mandatory;
REF (2)         /Reference numbers declaration;
LEC A B         /Read A and B;
A-B? SSP (1)    /Go to (1) if A>B;
A=M             /A<B, interchanges the A and B contents;
B=A
M=B
(1)A=M          /The function MOD was not available;
(2)M-B=M        /implemented by successive subtracting;
M? SNN (2)      /Repeat (2) while M<0;
B=A
M=B
B? SNC (1)      /Repeat (1) while B≠0;
PER A           /Print A; in this moment A=GCD;
FIN             /Stops translating and halt execution.
```

Following research goals, in 1972 the experimental minicomputer CID 202 was finished. Its novel architecture allowed running two programs in parallel, using a common 16K central ferrite core memory unit with 16 bits words, having the possibility of giving control and resources to one of them. Its operator control console allowed two programmers or operators working simultaneously, interacting each with their respective programs.

By the end of 1972, CID 201B was completed; it had twice the speed of the 201A, with up to 32K by 4K modules, eight auto-indexing registers per module, having an interruption system and a direct access bus. Its development extended until 1976 under a particular concept of family of systems, reaching configurations of even four units of minidisks and magnetic tape mini-units, operating systems with a DOS version included, and a system of files management on magnetic tape with an original algorithm of direct access from the FORTRAN IV. In Figure 2 the central processing unit of the CID 201B is shown with possibilities of maximum configuration. In the left cabinet we see the central processor and the central memory, allocated up to 32K words of 12 bits. They placed the multiplexed channel bus and the disk unit controllers, magnetic tape units and other optional expansions in the right cabinet.

Its software included a powerful FORTRAN IV compiler. They also developed ALGOL 60, FOCAL, BASIC, SNOBOL compilers, and a COBOL compiler that was more powerful than the DIBOL of DEC.

Figure 2 Cuban minicomputer system CID 201B.

They used a self-developed LALR1 analyzer. Specialized languages included LEE for the electrical industry and LINCO for the teaching of computing at the intermediate level, with a multi-terminal configuration in shared time.

The FORTRAN IV compiler was entirely compatible with the ISO standard for FORTRAN IV full version. It generated an object program for an original virtual machine designed with the purpose of raising efficiency in the use of the hardware system resources. In a benchmark test to measure and compare the speed in the execution of programs, those written in this FORTRAN IV surpassed by more than 2.5 times the equivalent solution in the other languages and compilers implemented. A fast algorithm for binary-decimal conversion of variable speed for all the representation formats was also developed, reaching a minimum of 220 characters per second and a maximum higher than 1800. The virtual machine also made it possible to implement recursive subroutines and other novel characteristics for the time.

Following the most innovating trends, in 1973 they defined the CID 300 family of minicomputers under the basis of reaching total compatibility of programs with the PDP-11 family. Production started in 1976, gradually substituting the production of the 201B. This system fulfilled the SM standards of the CMEA (COMECON). As part of the system, they developed a wide range of video terminals. These emulated efficiently several of the VT DEC models, including the VT-220. The line of video terminals and keyboards became a Cuban specialization within CMEA, exporting thousands of units to the European socialist countries, mainly to the Soviet Union.

The system software CID 300/10 fulfilled the SM standards, equipped with operating systems of real and timesharing. Among the languages, C and Pascal were included besides those traditional ones. The Cubans were in charge of the development of an original COBOL, complying satisfactorily with the international tests of the CIC's CCP/SM. From that moment on, it was included in the software distributions carried out by the European countries of SM.

Among other developments more oriented towards applications the GES 300 system; the multi-terminal SMT 300 and the system of data base management dBASE 300 were included.

Figure 3 shows a calculus center with a CID 300/10 system in a basic configuration with a unit of minidisks with a fixed disk and an interchangeable cartridge. We can appreciate some other equipment such as a video terminal as an interactive console, 180 characters per second mosaic printer, and others. The tallest cabinet in the middle lodges the central processor, the memory unit, the main minidisk units, and other interfaces. The configuration of the system augments adding similar cabinets for lodging up to four units of minidisk, four units of magnetic bands, and other optional equipments.

The hardware development and production was not limited to the system of minicomputers. From 1974, work started on microprocessors for multiple purposes, including diverse microcomputers. Among them was the CID-1417, compatible with the IBM PC/XT. They also developed different systems for the industrial automation and other processes such as for medical computerized equipment in conjunction with other research centers and medical assistance institutions. Research on advanced medical equipment and applications began since the early 1970s. An important stage was marked when they delivered in 1982 the MEDICID 03. It was a computerized system for advanced brain research. The development of complex medical equipment and automated systems turned into the current specialization of the ICID (originally CID). With its serial productions, it supplies the national health system and increasingly exports to various countries. This alternative became a specialization reached within the CMEA and maintained until 1991, the year in which Cuba supplied some medical computerized equipment to the former Soviet Union.

Since 1970, CID produced its own minicomputer systems in laboratories and workshops of its principal site. Until 1973, through the development of their own technology, they built a first factory and started producing in the industrial area of the vocational school "V.I. Lenin" High school. Students participated in the production lines as part of their education. This experience provided them with excellent results in their future studies as professionals with a deep and advanced theoretical and practical knowledge early in their lives.

Figure 3 Cuban minicomputer system CID 300/10.

2.3.3 Development of Computing by the Defense and National Security Bodies

The Cuban defense and security bodies had developed their own computing strategy since 1959. Though facing hazardous situations and many disadvantages, they have been able to keep themselves updated in the computing science and technology fields as an important part for ensuring the freedom and sovereignty of the Cuban nation. Their conceptions, plans, and performance had equaled to what more developed countries have done. They encouraged, supported, and cooperated with the civilian institutions in charge of science, technology, and industry by responding with necessary and convenient services.

They created and developed their own systems and schools for teaching and training their human resources. They were the pioneers in the country creating the undergraduate studies on computing, founding in 1969 computing engineering at the higher Technical Military Institute – the first Cuban military university. Some years later, this discipline converted to one called Automated System Engineering. In addition, they were the pioneers in cooperating and introducing in Cuba the Soviet computing science and technology, effectively contributing to ensure their strategic activities.

2.4 Collaboration on Computing with the CMEA countries

In the early 1960s, the collaboration with the former Soviet Union was established. It became a very important and vital alliance for the development of the country during a long period. Nevertheless, CMEA did not accept Cuba as a full member until 1972, the moment in which they classified it as one of the three countries less developed of the agreement, jointly with Viet Nam and Mongolia. Opposite to what happened with the collaboration with many other economic and social sectors, it was not until this moment that gradually opened doors to the computing one.

In those times, a parallel committee to CMEA, the Intergovernmental Computing Committee (ICC), established in 1969, carried out the international socialistic collaboration for the computing development. Cuba was included in the ICC after the CMEA admission as full member, first as a future client of EC (US – Unified Systems), whose first deliveries started at slow rates since 1974. In 1973 the ICC extended the scope of its program, organizing the Main Constructors Council (CCP-SM as in Russian language), for joint development of the unified minicomputer systems, with the SM as general mark; the strategy of this Council was to achieve the full functional analogies with the Digital Equipment Corporation's PDP 11 minicomputers family. Once Cuba became part of this Council in 1974, it already had its own development in this field, as discussed in subsection 2.3.2 above.

In general, the autochthonous Cuban minicomputer software development and knowledge, in conjunction with their application in several social and economic sectors including education, were relatively more advanced than in the rest of the socialist countries of the Eastern Europe. They found a very similar behavior with hardware lines starting in 1969 in Cuba, especially in comparison with the knowledge about some of the leading DEC standards. This position happened in a very poor and more difficult condition that was different from that of those countries. The same occurred regarding the relative incipient microprocessors knowledge.

We now summarize briefly some examples to support the above affirmations.

- In March of 1973, when in Bulgaria they were starting up its IZOT 310 minicomputer – similar to the PDP 8 – the Cuban CID 201B was already running with the full memory unit working and the original basic software delivered.
- The same situation occurred in the Soviet Institute INEUM in Moscow, headquarters of the CCP-SM, when they were starting up the initial series of the SM-3 central processor – similar to the PDP 11/05 central processor. The Cuban engineers demonstrated that they were much more skilled than their Soviet partner was in solving complex problems, based on the knowledge of architecture they had from their studies that started since 1972.
- The software platforms for the European SM systems were mainly directly assimilated from the DEC development. However, Cuba developed the COBOL compiler and other original software products and, consequently, Cuba supplied them to the member countries of the SM agreement.

Nevertheless, some authors claim that Cuba developed its computing industry thanks to the European socialist help with the projects and the technological supplies. They also strongly state that the Cuban computing professionals were, in a massive way, educated and trained in the former Soviet Union and some other European socialist countries [15]. In this paper, we offer some details on how the history occurred. Apart from the negative factors that could have been present, the cooperation Cuba received from those countries represented a big importance and good contribution to the Cuban science, technology, and economics. Concerning the human resources education and training of the computing professionals and technicians in Europe, it was in a low percentage with respect to rate of people educated and trained in the country, even when its quantity in total terms was something greater since the second half of the 1970s.

3 Spreading Computing Teaching in Cuba since 1970

In 1970, the UH created the Computing Committee (CCUH) to widen research activities on this field, such as industrial development, applications and their teaching all over the country. During the academic period from 1970 to 1971, the UH set up programs for computing science (CS) and computing engineering (CE) undergraduate studies; this occurred only five years after the funding of first computing science department of the world at Stanford University. Students, who had an engineering specialty and who had finished their 4th grade in telecommunications or automatic control studies, had credentials for the CE; this last program became a full-time study by 1972. In 1970, the UH included the CS in mathematics bachelor degree studies. That same year, it introduced Analysis and Programming in FORTRAN IV as a subject taught at several universities and the CID opened a master degree program in digital systems in joint collaboration with Canadian universities.

The Professor PhD. José Antonio Presno Albarrán represented the School of Medical Sciences in the CCUH from its very beginning. Immediately, he organized the Computing Department at his school and increasingly added this subject into the curriculum. In 1974, he published "*Cybernetics: Computers at Health Systems*". In the 1970s, the Cuban Association of Medical Informatics was founded [10].

Since 1970, the CID started to deliver courses on operating systems, programming, applications, and technical services to their clients' staff. Since February of 1971, the first CID 201A was used on sugar cane train timetable planning and control systems and on the balancing and accounting of row material in process at "Camilo Cienfuegos" Sugar Cane Factory.

Since its very beginning, computing teaching on high education in Cuba followed approaches corresponding to those from international practices. The UH played a transcendent role since the 1960s. Nowadays, the universities have multiplied themselves by more than 20. Creating municipal universities to generalize high education system meant a growth in the enrollment to 700,000 during 2007 to 2008 in a country having only 11.3 millions inhabitants.

Informatics teaching in the other educational subsystems was also a national strategy since the first half of the 1970s. In 1972, in a visit to CID, Castro expressed, "... *Comrades, I have come after seeing that computer* (he meant the French IRIS 50) *where you could hardly have access, where the people have no access, to ask you to make many computers for the people, so that the students have access to them, study them, learn computing. We are a country without natural resources, but we have a very important resource, the intelligence of the Cuban people, which we have to develop and computing accomplishes that, and I'm convinced that Cubans have a special intelligence to master Computing*" [6].

From then on, attention focused on the evolution of this teaching in Cuba through the mid-1990s, and some transcendental events from the current century are also shown. We make the analysis based on the development and improvement of:

- Higher education in Informatics since 1970
- High school teaching since the first half of the 1970s
- General education since kindergarten
- Education and continuous training for all

3.1 High Education in Informatics since 1970

The first stage occurred through the consolidation of the computing bachelor degree studies and engineering took place between 1970 and 1976. Topics concerning solid state and microelectronics were included in the specialties of electrical engineering and physics, supported by researches and postgraduate studies from CID, the Solid State Research Laboratory (SSRL), and the Microelectronics Research Centre (MRC), together with all laboratories from the UH.

In April of 1970, the School of Technology of the UH created the Engineering Systems Study Centre (ESSC) to guarantee the inclusion and development of computing teaching to the different undergraduate disciplines, postgraduate courses, and to the professional practice as well [8].

In order to face the increasing number of 12th grade graduates, the government created new universities with more capacities within them. In June of 1976, the School of Technology of the UH became the Higher Polytechnic Institute "José Antonio Echeverría", (ISPJAE in Spanish); in 1977 studies of Automatic Systems Management Engineering began (SAD as in Spanish) with freshman and sophomore students reaching its first graduation in 1981. Their final profile turned out to be very similar to the American recommendations for information systems engineering.[5] Since 1990, such studies were renamed informatics engineering [9].

In 1982, higher pedagogical institutes included the bachelor in mathematics and computing as undergraduate studies for high school teachers. In 2000, a bachelor on informatics became an option to more than 10,000 computing teachers of that level. We must also mention the special program carried out to train the emerging informatics teachers at the beginning of the present century to guarantee the opening of municipal schools or the Cuban universities and for the spreading and introduction of the computing teaching in the national K-12 system.

The Informatics contents within the curricula of the medical sciences studies evolved systematically, incorporating subjects such as biostatistics and computing, network use, and other related topics. That situation remained the same until the discipline of medical informatics was created and consolidated in 1998; this discipline was later included within the nursery bachelor degree studies and its director plan was established for all medical sciences [10].

The outstanding development of the Cuban national health care system implemented the use of a growing and extended assortment of medical devices, imported or developed and manufactured by the country's institutions; by this means, it generated an important demand of a specialized professional. In 1989, the High Institute of Medical Sciences of Havana, experimentally started the

[5] See "Computing Curricula 2005. The Overview Report covering under graduate programs. The Joint Task Force for Computing Curricula 2005. A cooperative project of ACM, AIS, and IEEE-CS.

health technological bachelor course; since 2002, this successful program had spread to various similar institutes, expanding to twenty-one different profiles from its initial six. In most of them, computing and informatics contents played an important role, some of them are fully specialized in these disciplines [16]. Similar motivation led ISPJAE to establish the biomedical engineering studies in the School of Electrical Engineering in 2005 [17]; simultaneously, they implemented it also at the CU and at the EU [19].

The curricular programs for the Cuban higher education had the names A, B, C… according to their generation. In 1985, the enhancement of A and B plans began, in order to achieve higher integration and a better relationship to practice, pursuing, among other objectives, to produce graduates that are more suitable. From 1990, they introduced C programs, cutting the unnecessary disciplines, achieving a greater coherence and systemic scope [9].

Thus with the economic changes, with the new informatics Cuban software industry strategy, the computer machines and equipment and the electronic components engineering studies disappeared; the necessary contents were included into the studies of automatic engineering and electronics and of the telecommunications engineering studies as well. The computing bachelor studies began in 1970, which they later named cybernetics, finally changed its name to the computer sciences bachelor from C plans since 1990. Indeed, they also intended such changes for curricular updating and adjustment. Following similar criteria, the informatics engineering model and curricula were updated to a C program in 1990. These studies started at 1977; they gradually spread to the Cuban provincial universities, reaching the whole country by 2005. Since 2003, the ISPJAE opened these studies at all municipalities in the capital under a blended learning system. Today, there are numerous master and doctorate degree courses in many Cuban universities, some of them in jointly modules with other countries' academic institutions.

The University of Informatics Sciences (UCI in Spanish) was founded in September of 2002, starting its first year with 2000 students. On July 19 of 2007, 1334 students graduated as informatics sciences engineers. Its present recruitment consists of eleven thousand students spread within thirteen schools, ten of them on its main campus and three in different territorial allocation all along the country. The schools' main differences occur by their second profile of specialization. Other distinctive elements are for example: the discipline of professional practice with subjects all along the five years syllabus; the learning model comes from production and research activities and organizing students' work in teams playing different roles. An optional subjects program exists including level assessment, a kind of certification exams. Continuous curricular improvement has become important. Its own name encourages people to think differently.

The main speech delivered during the first graduation ceremony of this young university literally stated, "*The UCI has been born for socializing and multiplying as never before the higher informatics studies in Cuba. In five years, the country grew from 2483 to 16395 undergraduate students in computing, multiplying the recruitment in these disciplines almost seven times. Together with the young students from junior high studies on informatics, it represents a force of more than 50000 young people committed to the main idea of transforming the informatics field in the most productive and resource supplier sector for the nation, using the intelligence deeply*" [18].

3.2 Junior High Education from the First Half of 1970s

In 1970, the Ministry of Education organized a group for the development of computing in interaction with the CCUH; its mission was to prepare and develop the initial strategy for the use of computers in education and their introduction into experimental teaching in three of the six sub-systems that integrated general education K-12 system.

In 1971, the CID concluded the FOCAL CID 201A compiler oriented to education, performing experimental experiences in selected schools. In 1973, it developed the Language Introduction to Computing - LINCO CID 201B, in a multi-terminal environment with time-sharing; implementation started in the vocational senior high school "Vladimir I. Lenin". There, on January 1974, during its official inauguration, in the presence of L. I. Brezhnev - First Secretary of the CPSU, Fidel Castro explained some of its achievements. He noted that the school had a calculus centre for the teaching of computing, an industrial area for electronics, with a line for assembling Cuban minicomputers and other perspectives, stressing that no country of Latin America, including the United States, had a similar school. That experience gradually extended to schools of its kind in other provinces [11].

The introduction of personal computers in this educational level began in 1983, two years after launching the PC platform by IBM. It started at the vocational senior high school "Humboldt 7", which used a CID 201B since 1979. It became the first pre-university Professional Institute of Exact Sciences (IPVCE in Spanish) in the year 1983. In a visit to its laboratories, accompanied by the President of Angola, Fidel Castro said, "*Not far is the day when all our schools have the latest machines and that our compatriots use properly computers*". In 1989, the conversion of all vocational schools into IPVCEs was finished and by then they obtained enough PCs.

The U.S. blockade of Cuba hampered the early spreading of these experiences due also to the lack of financial resources for the broad socio-economic Cuban programs. The arrival of home computers offered a better alternative for their introduction into schools. Domestic industry developed models themselves, starting a serial production by the end of the 1980s, a process interrupted by the collapse of socialism in Europe and the deep crisis the Cuban economy had to face.

The development of specialized technological institutes continue today under the name of Polytechnic Institute on Informatics (IPI in Spanish); it constitutes a special program consisting of twenty-seven institutes, with a staffing of 27,000 students, graduated as high school technical sciences students specialized in computing.

3.3 General Education from Kindergarten

The Cuban children from kindergarten to the ninth grade are members of the José Marti Students' Movement and they participate in extracurricular activities as additional technical training, cultural, patriotic and sports actions. They freely offered this complement in the House of Students, those with classrooms, laboratories, or knowledge clubs (KC) for career guidance. In December 1984, they founded the KC of computing and electronics from the Central House of Students "Ernesto Che Guevara". This place was equipped with a minicomputer CID 300/10, home computers with BASIC, IBM compatible PC, calculators, and other electronic devices needed for children practice.

The deep economic depression in the early nineties affected the progress of this and other programs of these teachings. However, on March 29, 2002 the President of Cuba opened the "*Educational Informatics Program*". One of the fundamental objectives of this strategy was the computerization of the Cuban society. Currently it includes more than 774,000 children and youth of the Cuban system K-12, with an infrastructure equipped with modern computers, a student/PC twelve to twenty, depending on the education subsystem and the territory. Its general objectives are [12]:

- To support informatics training for students, starting in stages from adaptation level until mastering and application of these technologies to solve problems and to promote interest in their study.
- To develop practice and skills to work with computers and assimilate a set of basic computer concepts and procedures that will enable them to solve problems.

To guarantee the success of this educational informatics strategy, they developed several ongoing specialized programs that included educational software development and production organized as projects and collections such as the interesting "Multi-Know How" project. In those projects, coordinated by the education ministry, the UCI plays a protagonist role, in cooperation with prestigious Cuban pedagogical and software industrial institutions.

3.4 Continuous Education and Training for All

After studying linear algebra and operations research on his own in late 1964, the minister of industry Ernesto Che Guevara explained to the ministry council board the importance and need of such studies for the implementation of the computer application. He taught them an expeditious course himself, thereby heavily influencing them early in sectors such as the sugar industry, mining and geology, construction, poultry, and other areas [4].

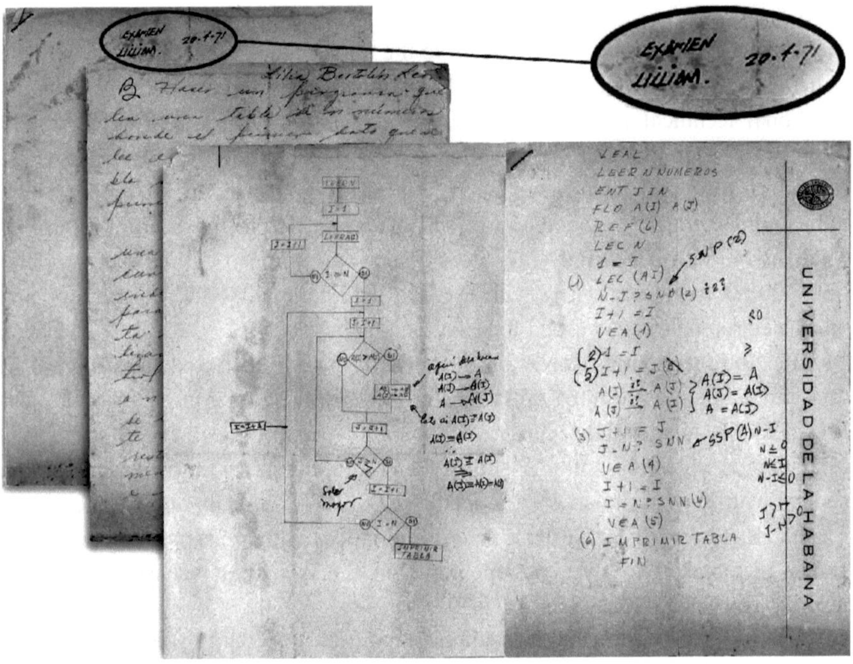

Figure 4 Copy of a LEAL 201A programming exam, made by a worker at Camilo Cienfuegos sugar factory, on April 20th, 1971.

The training department from CID was one of the pioneers in this education, starting in 1970 to offer courses to workers and specialists from the organizations that will operate Cuban computers, training operators, programmers, and analysts. They offered these courses on an optional basis in its central headquarters or in the client's sites. Figure 4 shows a copy of a LEAL 201A exam, made by a worker at Camilo Cienfuegos sugar factory headquarters, on April 20, 1971, who was being trained for developing future applications with the first Cuban minicomputer installed in that sugar enterprise on February 2, 1971.

Continuous education in Cuba includes a system of specialized schools by economy and society sectors for the instruction and training of workers and specialists; some of them are true high-level business schools. This system gradually incorporated computing and informatics teaching by the late 1970s.

The Computing Youth Club created in 1986, a result of the Fourth National Exhibition of the Builders of the Future, became the first Computing and Electronics Youth Club in July 1987 (CEYC, JCCE as in Spanish) [13]. On September 8, 1987, President Castro announced that the JCCE had become a national program; institutions were free and offer open access to the study of computing and its basic electronics. Since its beginnings, there were three areas: one for the introduction to computing, another for software and applications development, and the third for electronics and hardware in general. They promoted scientific and technical exchange activities, with increasing presence in national development, reaching also the most remote rural areas. In 1991, they launched the national network "Tinored" with international access, one of the first Cuban networks. There were 600 JCCE currently operating throughout the country, having an average of 3.5 clubs in each Cuban municipality; in June of 2006, they reached their first million graduates. The JCCE program continues to be a paradigm for the global population free access to computing and information on the conditions of a developing country, with a project of social justice and equality for all [14].

4 Conclusions

By this paper, we can see that in Cuba, in spite of being a small developing country having almost no natural resources in addition to the well-known adverse conditions, has reached an informatics development that surpasses the world average. Since 1959, the introduction and implementation of computing or informatics in the country had never been delayed for more than three or four years in comparison with the world advance level of basic platforms of software and hardware. To say it in another way, after 1970, this gap systematically decreased to not more than two years. In some instances, they developed original novelties many years before they appeared in publications abroad. Examples include the use of audio compact cassettes, the creation and implementation of a virtual machine, fast algorithms for binary to decimal conversion in different numerical formats, and other examples.

The local development has played an important role in the teaching and implementation of this discipline. It is quite possible that there is no other country in the world that had an education system similar to the K-12 system where all the students had plenty and free access to study and use modern informatics, supported by an official and advanced educational program. We can say the same for the rest of the educational levels and modalities on education and training of informatics as a science and technology by and for itself. The visionary and enduring priority and attention given to these matters have been essential to accomplish these goals.

Yet, we were compelled to illustrate that the fundamental strategy followed while setting the use and implementation of computing has been "*social inclusion*", which we can easily see when reading the given information about specialized and general education. We address these statements in a positive manner to demonstrate the existence and necessity of some of the scientific problems mentioned in the introduction.

References

1. Wang, Y.: The Theoretical Framework of Cognitive Informatics. Int'l J. of Cognitive Informatics and Natural Intelligence - 1(1), 1-27, University of Calgary – Canada. January-March (2007)
2. López J., T., Gil M., M. F.: Accomplishments of a Joint Cooperation Work between the Institutions of the Soviet Union and Cuba 1972-1990, Karelia – FR, Proc. SoRuCom'2006 (2006).
3. Sáenz, T. y Capote, E.: Ciencia y tecnología en Cuba, La Habana Editorial de Ciencias Sociales, La Habana (1989).
4. Figueras, M. A.: Oral Interview by a CHC61 contest team, UCI Collections Archive, La Habana – Cuba, (2007).
5. Lodos, O.: Oral Interview by a CHC61 contest team, UCI Collections Archive, La Habana – Cuba, (2007).
6. López J., T.: Los cubanos tenemos una inteligencia especial para dominar la Computación Periódico Juventud Rebelde – La Habana, March 23, (2006).
7. Ball-llovera D., A.: – Reporte interno del CID y comunicaciones posteriores, La Habana, (1970).
8. CEIS: http://www.cujae.edu.cu/centros/ceis/index.htm CEIS. Accessed April 18, 2006.
9. ISPJAE: Historia. Quienes Somos, La Habana, http://www.cujae.edu.cu/wwwcujae/quienes_somos/historia.html Quienes Somos. Acceded April 18, 2006.
10. O'Farril, E., Colunga, C.: La enseñanza de la informática médica en Cuba 1993 vol. 7(2):129-35 –La Habana – Cuba.
11. Castro R., F.: Discurso la inauguración de la EV "Vladimir I. Lenín", La Habana, Periódico Granma, January 31 (1974).
12. MINED: Informática Educativa, www.rimed.cu/computacion/web/computacion-educacionalbien.html Programa de Informática Educativa, Accessed January 9, 2006.
13. Labrada, M.: Oral Interview by a CHC61 contest team, Havana – Cuba, UCI Collections Archive (2007).
14. JCCE: La Computadora de la Familia Cubana, http://www.tribunaantimperialista.cu/Index.php?act=sn&id=607 La Habana – Cuba (2007).

15. Nitusov, A.: Computing Technique of the COMECON countries. www.computer-museum.ru/histussr/sev_it.htm Computing Technique of the COMECON countries. Accessed Nov 11, (2005).
16. Guerrero P., J.C. et al: Tecnología, tecnología médica y tecnología de la salud: algunas consideraciones básicas. La Habana – Cuba. http://bus.sld..cu/revistas/aci/vol12_4_04/aci07404.htm Tecnología, tecnología médica y tecnología de la salud. Accessed January 15, 2008.
17. ISPJAE: Ver en www.cujae.edu.cu/esp/paginas/facultades/electrica.html (Consultado en enero del 2008).
18. National Statistic Office: Panorama Económico y Social. Cuba 2007 La Habana – Cuba (2008).
19. Calzadilla R., I.: Ofrecerán 52000 plazas para el ingreso a la educación superior. La Habana – Cuba, Periódico Granma, marzo 18, (2005).

Computer Education in Spain: From Early to Recent Times

Ramon Puigjaner

Univeristat de les Illes Balears, Ctra de Valldemossa, km 7.5, 07122 Palma (Spain)
putxi@uib.cat

Abstract: This paper intends to present a short overview of the evolution of computer education in Spain since the initial teaching in this domain to the current works to adapt it to the European Higher Education Space (EHES) from the point of view of somebody that has been involved has directly participated in most of the this evolution.

Keywords: Computer science education history, Computer science curricula, Computer science in Spain

1 Remote Precursors

Here is not the proper place to talk about the precursors of computing machines. However, at least it is convenient to mention Ramon Llull (Raimundus Lullius) who in the XIII century invented several logical machines oriented to convert the Muslims to the, for him, truth religion, and Leonardo Torres Quevedo and Esteve Terrades who in late XIX and early XX centuries built several analogical machines to solve complicated analytical calculations.

2 Early University Courses: Decade of 1960

At university level just the *Universidad Complutense de Madrid* had an Automatic Computation specialty with some courses on the basic computer architecture and on programming, common to the curricula on Mathematics and Physics, and the Industrial Engineering Schools had a course on Computers in which was mainly explained the basic von Neumann architecture and the FORTRAN language.

In March 1969, the Ministry of Education created the *Instituto de Informatica*, [5] a strange organization, without any contact with the university and giving a

Please use the following format when citing this chapter:

Puigjaner, R., 2008, in IFIP International Federation for Information Processing, Volume 269; *History of Computing and Education 3*; John Impagliazzo; (Boston: Springer), pp. 79–98.

strange curriculum: the students earned a different title after each one of the five years of studies. With these degrees, it was intended that people who earned them were ready to develop professional tasks in industry and companies. It is easy to understand the difficulties of simultaneously giving a solid background and the practical knowledge associated to each degree.

In October 1967, the *Asociación de Técnicos de Informática* was created in Barcelona that developed an important educational task (mainly courses on data structures, basic computer organization, programming languages, operating systems, etc.) oriented to give a computer science background to the people working with computers at that time without any formal education in computer science.

3 Computer Science Arrives to the University: Decade of 1970

The *Instituto de Informática* started its regular courses in 1970 according to the above commented curriculum. It created a delegation in Donostia in 1971 and in 1972, the *Universitat Autònoma de Barcelona* created a Department of Informatics in its Faculty of Sciences. This Faculty was obliged to follow the same curriculum of the *Instituto de Informática.* The team that started to teach computer Science in this University was a mixture of good professionals and people having followed some university computer courses, mainly in France (Paris and Grenoble); they kept the titles of the official curriculum but they tried to transform the contents into a more reasonable structure according the university spirit.

In 1974, the Spanish Ministry of Education considered that Informatics should be included in the regular university structure. A commission was created to study how to pass the *Instituto de Informática* and its satellites to the university. Several universities fight in this commission to get the computer studies. Finally by the end of 1975 was decided that three Faculties of Informatics had to be created: Barcelona (in the *Universitat Politècnica de Catalunya*), Donostia (in the *Euskal Herriko Unibertsitatea*) and Madrid (in the *Universidad Politécnica de Madrid*), and that the previous institutions giving informatics studies had to stop to teach informatics [6]. This was true in Madrid and Donostia because the *Instituto de Informática* and its delegation were incorporated at the corresponding universities and their denomination changed. In Barcelona, the situation was more complicated because it was necessary to passing studies from one university to another (unbelievable in Spain at that time). Finally, both universities kept their studies. The new Faculties started to work in October 1977 with a five-year curriculum that, for the first time in Spain, was different for each university. In addition, in the Faculty of Barcelona the classical curriculum structure of a set of courses per academic year was broken. The curriculum was organized by courses with their corresponding pre-requisites in such a way that the student was able to organize his/her own curriculum choosing courses among those offered by the Faculty but respecting some compulsory courses [7]. In all cases, curricula were planned for five years of studies. Curricula of the Madrid and Donostia Faculties followed the traditional structure. In all cases, but especially in the Faculty of Barcelona, curricula were inspired by the ACM Computer Curriculum 1968 [1]. The students that successfully followed the studies in one of these universities obtained the title of *Licenciado en Informática* (Licensed in Informatics).

For its novelty at that moment, the structure of the Faculty of Barcelona and its curriculum follows: The Faculty was organized around eight departments: Mathematics, Theoretical Computer Science, Computer Programming, Computer Architecture, Physical Systems, Automatic and Hybrid Systems, Statistics, and Information Systems. Students arriving to the Faculty had a first year with the following courses:

- Computers and programming
- Algebra
- Mathematical Analysis I (Infinitesimal calculus)
- Representation techniques
- Physics

To get the first cycle of this License it was compulsory to succeed in the following courses:

- Mathematical analysis II
- Computer structure
- Information structure
- Programming technology
- Statistics
- Operating systems

Each course has assigned a number of credits (1 credit was 1 hour of course during an academic year) and to earn the first cycle a student should get courses for an amount of 75 credits and to earn the second cycle (*Licenciado en informática*) a student should get courses for an amount of 50 supplementary credits.

Each course had some pre-requisites, could be compulsory (C) or optional (O) and be valid for just the first cycle (F) or for both (B). A (C) besides some pre-requisite means that both courses can be followed in parallel. Appendix A shows tables that describe courses for different departments.

4 General Restructuring of University Studies: Decade of 1980

Around 1980 a new three years study in Informatics was created and started in Madrid (*Universidad Politécnica de Madrid*) and Valencia (*Universitat*

Politècnica de València). The students that successfully followed these stdies obtained the title of *Diplomado en Informática* (Diplomat in Informatics). Few after the *Universidad de Las Palma de Gran Canaria* and the *Univeristat de les Illes Balears* (Palma de Mallorca) created three years studies in Informatics. When these studies in Valencia, Las Palmas, and Palma arrived to the third year, extensions to five years were implemented in Valencia, Las Palmas and Palma de Mallorca. These three years studies had two orientations or intensifications:

- Computer systems, mainly devoted to a vision of the computer under the user interface
- Business management applications

In the last years of this decade the Spanish Ministry of Education started a general reorganization of all university studies creating a catalogue of official titles (those delivered by the Ministry itself based on the studies done in some university)reorganizing the existing titles and creating new ones. To get the official acceptance by the Ministry each one of these titles should respect a set of contents established by the Ministry (main topics). To describe the relative importance of each of these topics a measure was invented: the credit equivalent to a ten hours of teaching (including all kind of activities driven by the university teaching staff: theoretical classes, practical classes, etc.) received by the students. An academic year was estimated to have thirty weeks.

In the case of informatics, three new titles were created and disappeared those existing until that moment:

- *Ingeniero en Informática* (Informatics Engineer): five years divided in two cycles and between 300 and 400 credits [8].
- *Ingeniero Técnico en Informática de Sistemas* (Technical Engineer in Informatics: Computer systems orientation): three years and between 180 and 225 credits [9].
- *Ingeniero Técnico en Informática de Gestión* (Technical Engineer in Informatics: Computer business management orientation): three years and between 180 and 225 credits [10].

The main contents of these new careers appear in Appendix B. In addition, it was stated that the students having earned one of the two three-year degrees were allowed to follow the second cycle of *Ingeniero en Informática.*

5 Setup of the New Careers: Decade of 1990

In the early years of this decade, all universities giving the old degrees in informatics adapted their curriculum to the new characteristics. This adaptation took different solutions:

- Universities that delivered the three degrees separately: the five-year degree in a faculty or school and the three-year degree in a different school.

- Universities that delivered the three degrees in the same faculty or school with a complete implementation of the three degrees.
- Universities that delivered the three degrees in the same faculty or school but without the implementation of the first cycle of *Ingeniero en Informática* and using both three-year degrees as the first cycle.
- Universities that had just the five-year degree.
- Universities that had both three-year degrees.

However, soon several problems appeared:

- The fact that three different first cycles gave access to the second cycle introduced difficulties in different topics like networks, computer architecture and software engineering. The reasons were that sometimes the same main topic with the same descriptors had assigned different number of credits or that the student coming from some first cycle had a previous knowledge of some topic unknown for the students coming from other first cycles.
- The low number of credits assigned to operating systems that obliged to most of universities to create supplementary courses in this topic.
- The growing importance of networking and it was possible that an *Ingeniero Técnico en Informática de Gestion* could earn his/her title with no knowledge on this topic.
- The inconvenience of having automata theory as a compulsory topic in the first cycle of *Ingeniero en Informática* (too theoretical for beginners) and in *Ingeniero Técnico en Informática de Sistemas* (too theoretical for the applied orientation of the three years studies).

During this period, the number of faculties and schools delivering these degrees was continuously increasing (and currently there are approximately 80 in Spain). This fact and the need of exchanging information about experiences and discussing about the difficulties in the implementation of their curricula provoked the need of discussion meetings with the participation of all faculties and schools teaching informatics careers. These annual meetings started in 1995. However, as the number of schools and faculties was continuously increasing, in 1998 it was decided to set up a minimal organization: a president and a secretary, and a title: *Conferencia de Decanos y Directores de Centros Universitarios de Informática*, CODDI (Conference of Deans and Directors of Inforamtics University Centres). The first task assigned just after this designation was the review of the main topics of the informatics careers in order to correct the detected inconveniences. In 1999 this task was completed and the result was [4]. Appendix C shows the results.

This new definition of the main topic for the three degrees corrected the main defaults of the previous one:

- The same topic had the same description and the same number of credits.
- Networking was compulsory in the three first cycles.
- Too theoretical topics disappeared from the first cycles.
- Mathematics was split between Algebra and Analysis.

- Operating systems had a greater number of compulsory credits.

CODDI submitted this proposal to the Ministry of Education. However, it was not accepted because its acceptation would have allowed other careers to request also the modification of their compulsory main topics. Moreover, this would have introduced a high degree of discussions between universities and between these and the Ministry. Nevertheless, it was accepted as guidelines for the analysis and acceptation of future curricula submitted to the Ministry by the universities.

6 Towards the European Higher Education Space (EHES): Current Decade

In coincidence with the change of millennium, the European Union decided ask the member states to reorganize their university systems in such a way that a convergence was reached around 2010 in two main points:

- University studies should be organized in three levels: bachelor, master, and doctorate.
- University studies should define for each course the effort required to the student, the ECTS credit, equivalent, approximately to 25 to 30 hours of work for the student including all his/her activities (theoretical courses, practical courses, seminars, personal study, etc.).

This convergence was named as the Bologna process because the agreement of all the member states was reached in a meeting held city where the first European university was created.

In 2001, CODDI started to work on how to adapt the informatics studies to this convergence process. Initially a set of considerations showing mismatches either in the university studies structure or in the consideration by the society of the degrees delivered by the university [2]. These considerations were:

- It was observed that neither the market nor the universities have succeeded to clearly discern the professional and educational differences between the *Ingenierías Técnicas en Informática* and the *Ingeniería en Informática* due to the constant evolution of the informatics and the professional changes.
- The difficulties found at the second cycle of the *Ingeniería en Informática* due to coexistence of students coming from three different first cycles.
- The fact that the *Ingenieros Técnicos* have not a professional acknowledgement at European level as university graduates.
- The difficulty for defining competencies and responsibilities of the informatics professionals
- The great number of new activities with a fuzzy limit with other engineering branches (telecommunication engineers, industrial engineers, etc.).

- The consequences of the effort done to offer a higher non university education, public as well as private, oblige to reconsider the structure, contents and level of the informatics university studies

The main conclusions of these discussions were [3]:

- An initial premise says that the market will experience a strong growing of the demand in a near future. The strategic presence of the informatics suggests the need of a set of solutions considering all education levels (primary education, secondary education, vocational education) and not only the university one.
- In this sense a deep consideration about the University programming should be done to take into account the geographical distribution and the resources needed to attain the planned objectives.
- The university structure will be organized in two cycles: *Grado* (degree) and Master.
- There should be just a unique title of *Grado* whose name will be *Ingeniería en Informática* (informatics engineering).
- The title of *Ingeniero en Informática* will furnish full professional competencies for the exercise of the profession.
- The education furnished at the *Grado* level will general in the informatics domain.
- The *Grado* studies will have 240 ECTS credits organized en 4 years.
- Among the fundamental educational contents of the *Grado*, there should be an End of Studies Project, that will integrate the knowledge acquired by the student during his/her studies and that will make an approximation to real professional cases as well as to transversal contents that put in evidence his/her abilities for the exercise of engineering activities.
- The common educational contents of the *Grado* should represent about 60% of the total study load, including the End of Studies Project, leaving a 40% for topics to be freely decided by each university.
- Among the courses to be freely decided by the universities, it is recommended to have an enough large offer of courses oriented to give the students a solid knowledge of the current informatics technologies as well as its application domains.
- The Master will have as objective the professional specialization of the *Ingeniero en Informática* or his/her preparation for the research.
- The number of Master degrees should be large enough to cover the demand of specialized professionals at every moment.
- Master studies will have between 60 and 120 ECTS credits, depending on the previous degree earned and will include some effort allocated to a Master Thesis
- The Master degree will allow the access to the preparation of a doctoral thesis to obtain the Doctor degree.

The structure of the studies appears in Table 1.

Table 1 Current Structure of Studies

Contents			Min.	Max	
		Scientific base	10%	15%	Informatics mathematical fundamentals Informatics physical fundamentals
Common educational contents	60%	Informatics engineering specific contents	35%	40%	Programming Software engineering Information systems engineering Intelligent systems engineering Operating systems Distributed systems and networking Computer engineering
		General contents of engineering	5%	10%	Business management Ethical, legal and professional aspects Professional abilities
		End of studies project	6%	6%	
Contents freely decided by the university	40%				
Total effort		240 ECTS credits			

The students that earn the *Grado en Ingeniería en Informática* should be characterized by:

- To be prepared to exercise his/her profession, having a clear knowledge of the human, economic, social, legal, and ethical dimension.
- To be prepared to assume responsibility tasks in any kind of organization along his/her professional life, in technical and in managerial positions, and to contribute in the information and knowledge management.
- To have the required abilities in the professional practice of the engineering: to be able to manage projects, to communicate in a clear and effective way, to work in a multidisciplinary team as well as to manage it, to adapt himself/herself to the changes and to autonomously learn along with his/her life.
- To be prepared to learn and to use in an effective way techniques and tools that could appear in the future. This versatility is especially valuable in organizations in which a permanent innovation is needed.

- To be able to specify, design, build, verify, audit, evaluate, and maintain informatics systems giving answers to the user needs.
- To have the basic education to be able to continue his/her studies of Master and Doctorate in Spain or elsewhere.

7 The Future: Decade of 2010

Currently the Ministry of Education is setting up the framework for the implementation of the EHES [11]. Some points are clear but the framework is not yet complete:

- There will not be a catalogue of official titles. Each university must propose its own titles that will be validated by an independent agency (*Agencia Nacional de Evaluación de la Calidad del Sistema Universitario*, ANECA, National Agency for the Evaluation of the Quality of the University System) that will evaluate the appropriateness of the proposed title (specially avoiding confusion to the society), the quality of the proposal and the sufficient amount of the human and material resources allocated.
- The grade, in our case of *Ingeniero en Informática*, will have 240 ECTS credits that will include the end of studies project.
- The master degree will have 60 or 120 ECTS credits depending on the coherence between the grade earned and the intended Master.

From this information, it is easy to see that the proposal of the CODDI, several years before the decisions of the Ministry, is fully in line with the framework in which the universities will work in a near future.

Currently the universities are preparing the curricula for all the studies they are planning to offer to the students and soon the ANECA will start its evaluation tasks.

What will the future be?

References

1. ACM Curriculum Committee on Computer Science, "Curriculum '68— Recommendations for Academic Programs in Computer Science," *Comm. ACM,* vol. 11, no. 3, pp. 151-197, Mar. 1968.
2. J. Campos, J. Casanovas, J. M. Colom, G. Martín, J Martínez, A. Pont, R. Puigjaner, A. Robles, M. R. Sancho: Informe sobre la adaptación de los estudios de TIC a la declaración de Bolonia. Unpublished document. 2002 (For getting it, contact the author of this article).
3. J. Casanovas et al.: Libro Blanco sobre las titulaciones universitarias de informática en el nuevo espacio europeo de educación superior. ANECA 2004.
4. Conferencia de Decanos y Directores de Centros Universitarios de Informática (CODDI): Nuevas directrices generales propias de los títulos de Ingeniero en Informática, de

Ingeniero Técnico en Informática de Sistemas y de Ingeniero Técnico en Informática de Gestión. Unpublished document. 1999 (for getting it, contact the author of this article).
5. Ministerio de Educación y Ciencia (BOE de 14/04/1969 - Sección I): Decreto 554/1969, de 29 de marzo (Educación y Ciencia), por el que se crea un Instituto de Informática, dependiente del Ministerio de Educación y Ciencia, con sede en Madrid, y se regulan las enseñanzas del mismo.
6. Ministerio de Educación y Ciencia (BOE de 26/03/1976 - Sección I): Decreto 593/1976, de 4 de marzo, por el que se crean Facultades de Informática en Barcelona, Madrid y San Sebastián.
7. Ministerio de Educación y Ciencia (BOE de 27/07/1977 - Sección I): Orden de 7 de junio de 1977 por la que se aprueba el plan de estudios de la FAcultad de Informática de Barcelona.
8. Ministerio de Educación y Ciencia (BOE de 20/11/1990 - Sección I): Real decreto 1459/1990, de 26 de octubre, por el que se establece el título universitario oficial de Ingeniero en Informática y las directrices generales propias de los planes de estudios conducentes a la obtención de aquél.
9. Ministerio de Educación y Ciencia (BOE de 20/11/1990 - Sección I): Real decreto 1459/1990, de 26 de octubre, por el que se establece el título universitario oficial de Ingeniero Técnico en Informática de Sistemas y las directrices generales propias de los planes de estudios conducentes a la obtención de aquél.
10. Ministerio de Educación y Ciencia (BOE de 20/11/1990 - Sección I): Real decreto 1459/1990, de 26 de octubre, por el que se establece el título universitario oficial de Ingeniero Técnico en Informática de Gestión y las directrices generales propias de los planes de estudios conducentes a la obtención de aquél.
11. Ministerio de Educación y Ciencia (BOE de 30/10/2007 - Sección I): Real decreto 1393/2007, de 29 de octubre, por el que se establece la ordenación de las enseñanzas universitarias oficiales.

Appendix A

Department of Mathematics

Course	Acronym	Credits	Pre-req.	Class	Validity
Algebra	AL	5	None	C	F
Mathematical analysis I	AM-1	5	None	C	F
Mathematical analysis II	AM-2	6	AN-1	C	F
Numerical calculus	CN	4	AL, AN-2, TR	O	F
Representation techniques	TR	3	None	C	F
Numerical analysis	AN	4	CN	O	B
Information and coding theory	TIC	4	AF, E	O	B

Department of Theoretical Computer Science

Course	Acronym	Credits	Pre-req.	Class	Validity
Finite automata	AF	6	AL, E	O	B
Computability theory	TC	4	AF	O	B
Language theory	TL	4	C, AF	O	B
Mathematical logic	LM	4	AL, CP	O	B
Artificial intelligence	AI	4	LM, TL, AD	O	B

Department of Computer Programming

Course	Acronym	Credits	Pre-req.	Class	Validity
Computers and programming	CP	7	None	C	F
Information structure	EI	4	CP	C	B
Programming languages	LP	4	AL, CP	O	B
Programming technology	TP	4	AL, CP	C	B
Compilers	C	4	EI, LP	O	B
Files and data bases	FBD	5	EI, LP	O	B

Department of Computer Architecture

Course	Acronym	Credits	Pre-req.	Class	Validity
Computer structure	EC	4	CP, AL	C	F
Operating systems	SO	4	EC, EI, TP	C	B
Computer architecture	AC	4	EC, AF	O	B
Design and evaluation of configurations	DAC	4	AC, SI	O	B
Communications and computer networks	CRC	4	SO, AC, SI	O	B
Operating systems design	DSO	4	SO, AC	O	B
Diagnostic and reliability	DF	4	AC, TIC	O	B

Department of Physical Systems

Course	Acronym	Credits	Pre-req.	Class	Validity
Physics	F	5	None	C	F
Electronics	EL	4	F, AN-1	O	F
Digital circuits	CD	4	EL, AF	O	B
Design of computers	DC	4	CD, AC, DAH	O	B
Peripheral equipments	EP	4	CD	O	B
Analogical and hybrid design	DAH	4	EL	O	B

Department of Automatic and Hybrid Systems

Course	Acronym	Credits	Pre-req.	Class	Validity
Systems and signals	SS	4	AN-2, ES (c)	O	B
System dynamics	DS	4	SS	O	B
Optimal control and filtering	COF	4	DS, PE	O	B
Analogical and hybrid calculus	CAH	4	AN-2, LP, EL	O	B
Architecture and design of control systems	ADSM	4	SS, CAH	O	B
Real-time operating systems	SOTR	4	SO, SS	O	B

Department of Statistics

Course	Acronym	Credits	Pre-req.	Class	Validity
Statistics	E	5	AL, AN-2	C	F
Simulation	SI	4	E	O	B
Data analysis	AD	3	E	O	B
Stochastic processes	PE	4	E	O	B
Optimization	O	5	AN-2, AL, E (c)	O	B
Optimization algorithms	AO	4	E, O	O	B
Operational research	OR	4	E, O	O	B

Department of Information Systems

Course	Acronym	Credits	Pre-req.	Class	Validity
Economy	ECO	3	None	O	F
Design and utilization of files and data bases	DUABD	3	EI, DT (c)	O	B
Technological design	TP	4	TP DUABD (c), SO (c)	O	B
Logical design of information and decision systems	DL	5	DT, DUABD, EO	O	B
Project methodology	MP	5	DL, TO	O	B
Organization structures	EO	3	ECO	O	B
Organization techniques	TO	3	EO	O	B
Organization administration	AO	4	EO	O	B
Computer centre management	GSI	2	DL, TO	O	B
Group dynamics	DG	2	TO, AO	O	B
Law	DE	2	AO	O	B

Appendix B

Ingeniero en Informática

First Cycle

Main Topic and Description	Credits
Statistics Descriptive statistics. Probabilities. Applied statistical methods.	6
Structure Data and Information Abstract data types. Data structures and manipulation Algorithms. Information structure: Files, Data bases.	12
Computer structure and technology Functional Units: Memory, Processor, Periphery, Machine and Assembly Languages, Functional schema. Electronics. Digital Systems. Peripheral device.	15
Informatics physical fundamentals Electromagnetism. Solid state. Circuits.	6
Informatics mathematical fundamentals Algebra. Mathematical Analysis. Discrete Mathematics. Numerical Methods.	18
Programming Methodology and Technology Algorithms design. Algorithms analysis. Programming Languages. Programmes design: Modular decomposition and documentation. Programmes verification and testing techniques.	15
Operating Systems Operating systems organization, structure and services. Memory and processes management and administration. Input/output management. File systems.	6
Automata and Formal Languages Theory Sequential machines and finite automata. Turing machines. Recursive Functions. Formals grammars and Languages. Neuronal networks.	9

Second Cycle

Main Topic and Description	Credits
Computer architecture and engineering Parallel architectures. Architectures oriented to applications and languages.	9
Software engineering Requirements analysis and definition. Software design, properties and maintenance. Configuration management. Planning and management of informatics projects. Applications analysis.	18
Artificial Intelligence and knowledge engineering Heuristics. Knowledge based systems. Learning. Perception.	9
Language Processors Compilers, translators and Interpreters. Compiling phases. Code optimization. Macroprocessors.	9
Networks Networks Architecture. Communications.	9
Informatics Systems Analysis methodology. Informatics systems configuration, design, management and evaluation. Informatics systems environments. Advanced technologies of information systems, data bases and operating systems. Projects of informatics systems.	15

Ingeniero Técnico en Informática de Sistemas

Main Topic and Description	Credits
Statistics Descriptive statistics. Probabilities. Applied statistical methods.	6
Structure Data and Information Abstract data types. Data structures and manipulation algorithms. Information structure: Files, data bases.	12
Computer structure and technology Functional units: Memory, processor, periphery, machine and assembly languages, Functional schema. Electronics. Digital systems. Peripheral devices.	15
Informatics physical fundamentals Electromagnetism. Solid state. Circuits.	6
Informatics mathematical fundamentals Algebra. Mathematical analysis. Discrete mathematics. Numerical methods.	18
Programming Methodology and Technology Algorithms design. Algorithms analysis. Programming languages. Programmes design: Modular decomposition and documentation. Programmes verification and testing techniques.	12
Networks Networks Architecture. Communications.	6
Operating Systems Operating systems organization, structure and services. Memory and processes management and administration. Input/output management. File systems.	6
Automata and Formal Languages Theory Sequential machines and finite automata. Turing machines. Recursive Functions. Formals grammars and Languages. Neuronal networks.	9

Ingeniero Técnico en Informática de Sistemas

Main Topic and Description	Credits
Statistics Descriptive statistics. Probabilities. Applied statistical methods.	9
Structure Data and Information Abstract data types. Data structures and manipulation algorithms. Information structure: Files, data bases.	12
Computer structure and technology Functional units: Memory, processor, periphery, machine and assembly languages, Functional schema. Electronics. Digital systems. Peripheral devices.	9
Business management software engineering Business management software design, properties and management. Planning and management of informatics projects. Analysis of management application.	12
Informatics mathematical fundamentals Algebra. Mathematical analysis. Discrete mathematics. Numerical methods.	18
Programming Methodology and Technology Algorithms design. Algorithms analysis. Programming languages. Programmes design: Modular decomposition and documentation. Programmes verification and testing techniques.	15
Operating Systems Operating systems organization, structure and services. Memory and processes management and administration. Input/output management. File systems.	6
Organization techniques and business management Economic system and business. Administration and accounting techniques.	12

Appendix C

Ingeniero en Informática

First Cycle

Main Topic and Description	Credits
Algebra and discrete mathematics Basic algebraic structures. Lineal algebra. Combinatory. Discrete structures: graphs, trees. Logic. Coding. Numerical applications.	12
Mathematical analysis Successions and series. Integration. Differential equations. Numerical applications.	6
Data bases Data models. Data base management systems.	6
Statistics Probabilities. Applied statistical methods. Statistical inference.	6
Computer structure Functional units: memory, processor, input/output. Machine and assembly languages. Running schema. Microprogramming.	12
Informatics physical fundamentals Electromagnetism. Electronics. Circuits.	6
Software engineering fundamentals Software systems analysis and design. Software properties and maintenance. User interfaces.	6
Programming and data structure Algorithms design and analysis. Programming paradigms and languages. Basic techniques of programmes design, verification and testing. Object oriented programming. Abstract data types. Data structures and manipulation algorithms.	21
Computer networks Communication elements and systems. Hierarchical structure of networks. Usual types of networks: local area networks and wide area networks. Network interconnection. Security.	6
Operating systems Operating systems organization, structure and service. Memory, processes and resources management and administration. Input/output management. File systems	9
Computer technology Electronic components and systems of computers. Digital Systems. Microprocessors. Peripherals structure and functioning.	6

Second Cycle

Main Topic and Description	Credits
Computer architecture Speed increasing techniques. Parallel architectures.	9
Automata theory, formal languages and language processors Sequential machines and finite automata. Turing machines. Complexity theory. Recursive functions. Formal grammars and languages. Compilers. Translators and interpreters. Compilation phases. Macroprocessors.	15
Software Engineering Requirements analysis and definition. Software properties and maintenance. Software quality assurance. Software projects planning and management. Methodologies. Human-machine interfaces.	15
Artificial intelligence Heuristics. Knowledge representation techniques. Knowledge based systems. Perception.	6
Networks and distributed systems Network configuration, administration and management. Interconnection. High performance networks. Quality of service. Security. Information compressing. Distributed systems.	9
Informatics systems Analysis methodology. Informatics systems configuration, design, management and evaluation. Informatics systems environments. Advanced technologies of information systems, data bases and operating systems. Projects of informatics systems. Audit. Security.	12

Ingeniero Técnico en Informática de Sistemas

Main Topic and Description	Credits
Algebra and discrete mathematics Basic algebraic structures. Lineal algebra. Combinatory. Discrete structures: graphs, trees. Logic. Coding. Numerical applications.	12
Mathematical analysis Successions and series. Integration. Differential equations. Numerical applications.	6
Data bases Data models. Data base management systems.	6
Statistics Probabilities. Applied statistical methods. Statistical inference.	6
Computer structure Functional units: memory, processor, input/output. Machine and assembly languages. Running schema. Microprogramming.	12
Informatics physical fundamentals Electromagnetism. Electronics. Circuits.	6
Software engineering fundamentals Software systems analysis and design. Software properties and maintenance. User interfaces.	6
Programming and data structure Algorithms design and analysis. Programming paradigms and languages. Basic techniques of programmes design, verification and testing. Object oriented programming. Abstract data types. Data structures and manipulation algorithms.	21
Computer networks Communication elements and systems. Hierarchical structure of networks. Usual types of networks: local area networks and wide area networks. Network interconnection. Security.	6
Operating systems Operating systems organization, structure and service. Memory, processes and resources management and administration. Input/output management. File systems.	9
Computer technology Electronic components and systems of computers. Digital Systems. Microprocessors. Peripherals structure and functioning.	6
Informatics systems Management, planning and development of computer systems projects.	6

Ingeniero Técnico en Informática de Gestión

Main Topic and Description	Credits
Algebra and discrete mathematics Basic algebraic structures. Lineal algebra. Combinatory. Discrete structures: graphs, trees. Logic. Coding. Numerical applications.	12
Mathematical analysis Successions and series. Integration. Differential equations. Numerical applications.	6
Data bases Data models. Data base management systems.	6
Statistics Probabilities. Applied statistical methods. Statistical inference..	6
Computer structure Functional units: memory, processor, input/output. Machine and assembly languages. Running schema. Microprogramming.	12
Software engineering fundamentals Software systems analysis and design. Software properties and maintenance. User interfaces.	6
Programming and data structure Algorithms design and analysis. Programming paradigms and languages. Basic techniques of programmes design, verification and testing. Object oriented programming. Abstract data types. Data structures and manipulation algorithms.	21
Computer networks Communication elements and systems. Hierarchical structure of networks. Usual types of networks: local area networks and wide area networks. Network interconnection. Security.	6
Operating systems Operating systems organization, structure and service. Memory, processes and resources management and administration. Input/output management. File systems.	9
Informatics systems Management, planning and development of computer business application projects.	6
Business structure and functions Business as a system. Management and administration techniques. Organization structures.	6
Information systems Evaluation and management of information systems development. Strategic planning of information technologies and systems de. Applications.	6

The Emergence of Educational Technology

Elizabeth Koh[1] **and John Lim**[2]

1 Department of Information Systems, School of Computing, National University of Singapore; diskre@nus.edu.sg
2 Department of Information Systems, School of Computing, National University of Singapore; jlim@nus.edu.sg

Abstract: This paper traces the emergence of Information Technology (IT) for educational purposes. It begins with a discourse on the relationship between culture and educational technology. A key premise is that culture is an important influence in education. Similarly, the evolution of educational technology is very much intertwined with culture. This paper traces educational development from the traditional times to modern times. Educational technology was initially viewed as technology *in* education, a sole focus on IT tools. Subsequently, a holistic perspective of the educational system was adopted, termed the technology *of* education. In this larger view, educational technology is informed by research from learning theories and other educational research. The paper elaborates on these theoretical underpinnings with some examples of educational technology before concluding with implications for practitioners and researchers.

Keywords: Educational technology, E-learning, Online education, Culture, History of education

1 Introduction

Computing power and technologies have been developing rapidly in the present century. Fuelled by the knowledge economy, IT and education are forecast to become one of the biggest sectors in the world. We can see this rise in computing and education as originating from its cultural roots. To understand educational technology, we first have to realize what education is. In this article, we trace the history of educational technology. We premise that culture is an important influence in education. Following which, we describe the evolution of educational thoughts and pedagogy. The next section surmises the history of educational technology with examples. The paper then concludes with implications for practitioners and researchers.

Please use the following format when citing this chapter:

Koh, E. and Lim, J., 2008, in IFIP International Federation for Information Processing, Volume 269; *History of Computing and Education 3*; John Impagliazzo; (Boston: Springer), pp. 99–112.

2 Cultural Basis of Education

Since the beginning of civilization, education has been the inculcation of wisdom and knowledge, the passing down of traditions and values from one generation to the next. Since culture is the totality of socially transmitted behavior patterns, arts, beliefs, institutions, and all other products of human work and thought (Ferrante 2003), education is actually the process of transmitting culture. Education and culture are "interwoven and inseparable" (McLoughlin 1999, p.232). Culture influences the course of education. We now trace the developments of education and culture from ancient times to the modern day.

2.1 Cultural Underpinnings of Ancient Education

To educate, in Latin stems from the term "educare" with its root meaning to "lead forth" (Oxford English Dictionary 1989). The Latin word also implies a change brought about by practice or usage (Sharma 1987). The leading out of an individual has been formalized by society through educational systems and the induction of a curriculum. The earliest known educational systems originate from the ancient cultures of Greece, China and India. The structure of each educational system is based on each country's educational philosophies at that time.

In ancient China, education was a means of social unity and harmony (Cleverly 1991). In particular, the teachings of the sage Confucius heavily influenced educational ideals. He encouraged the learning of subjects through a long, detailed study with a good teacher. Good education should be open to all who will gain from it. The aim was not to impart knowledge or transmit skills but to improve the character of students (Cheng & Wong 1996). Students were produced to be full of grace and integrity, conscientious and altruistic, and to serve the society.

Since the Han dynasty (206BC-AD220), the Chinese instituted examinations for scholars wanting to enter the civil service. They rewarded greatly scholars who fared well in these examinations in terms of social standings and social mobility. This has led East Asians to have a high reverence for examination and competition (Cheng & Wong 1996). Ancient Chinese philosophy also emphasized self-instruction and learning from others; however, critical thinking was absent (Turner & Acker 2002). In fact, conformity was the norm and traditional scholars were taught to "compile rather than to compose" (Cheng & Wong 1996, p.42). These educational philosophies from ancient China have influenced how many East Asian countries view education.

On the other hand, educational philosophy in olden India was a spiritual affair as it was shaped by religious ideals. Indian culture regards divinity as the ultimate level of development (Sharma 1987). Education is regarded as a source of illumination. It is an inner discipline to gain the emancipation of the soul (Pathak 2002). The educational system was called Gurukul in which a student would live with his guru and learn from him through rigorous self-discipline over a long period of time (Sharma 1987). The goal was to develop a disciple that was physically, mentally, and spiritually equipped – and a good citizen.

The ancient Greeks were the "first real educators" of the western world (Castle 1965, p.11). The Greeks founded gymnasiums that became both a place for athletics, military training, and a centre for learning (Camp & Fisher 2002). Schools were recognized synonymously with their teachers (Cribiore 2001). The teachings of early Greek philosophers such as Socrates, Plato and Aristotle, have shaped Western aims in education. For example, from Plato, education is the imparting of information and redirection of the student to the knowledge of good; for students to be truth seekers (Gutek 1997). He viewed education as a means of developing the natural abilities of students. Moreover, these abilities would enable students to find satisfaction in their work and serve the needs of the state (Ellis, Cogan & Howey 1991). However, since education was privatized, only the rich and powerful could afford to receive a full education (Castle 1965). Poorer pupils only went to school for a few years (Castle 1965). Cribiore (2001) adds that the education system in ancient Greece was a "steep hill" that students climb to reach the summit. Many were unable to overcome obstacles and thus only a handful of pupils make it to the top.

Despite the different educational goals and subject matter, the ancient educational systems typically followed the master-disciple model (Cochrane 1998) or the apprentice model (Honebein, Duffy & Fishman 1993). The disciple or the apprentice learns a task like masonry or "thinking" under the instruction of an expert (Honebein et al. 1993). Honebein et al. (1993) observes that the driving force in these ancient cultures is to obtain work. Similarly McPherson and Nunes (2004) add that students of ancient times learned tasks and skills not for distant or symbolic goals (such as an educational certificate), but for its immediate value in getting the work done. These ancient educational structures were also alike in that only select pupils were privileged enough to be educated by a small number of available teachers (Cochrane 1998). In other words, the elite such as the wealthy and powerful in these nations were usually much more educated than the poor were.

The next section describes the changes to ancient educational structures primarily due to the invention of modern technology such as the printing press.

2.2 Traditional Education

The invention of the printing press led to massive changes in the education system (Cochrane 1998; McPherson & Nunes 2004). People could learn about the real world from an intellectual distance through the written word (McPherson & Nunes 2004). Moreover, the Industrial Revolution and widespread migration led to the creation of mass education (Cochrane 1998; Ferrante 2003) and the demise of the apprenticeship model (Honebein et al. 1993). It was first introduced by the United States in 1852 in the state of Massachusetts (Ferrante, 2003). By 1910, elementary school education was compulsory for all U.S. states.

Moreover, a new set of educational ideas started to influence education. Western educational philosophies originating primarily from America and parts of Europe can be classified into five schools of thoughts – perennialism, essentialism, progressivism, reconstructionism, and existentialism. An overview of these five educational philosophies appears in Table 1 (Ellis et al. 1991, p.103). A full discourse of these western philosophies is too wide for the scope of the paper. Refer to Ellis and colleagues (1991) for further information. These educational philosophies from Western cultures have dominated the research of education and learning.

Table 1 Overview of Educational Thought

Educational Viewpoint	Philosophic Base	Role of Teacher	Purpose
Perennialism	Idealism/Realism	Teacher as an example of values and ideals	Absorption of ideas
Essentialism	Neo-Thomism	Teacher as mental disciplinarian and moral/spiritual leader	Absorption and mastery of facts and skills
Progressivism	Experimentalism/Pragmatism	Teacher as challenger and inquiry leader	Problem solving and social experience
Reconstruc-tionism	Experimentalism/Pragmatism	Teacher as project director and research leader	Problem solving and rebuilding the social order
Existentialism	Existentialism	Teacher as non-interfering sounding board	Searching for self

Modern developments such as the establishment of the scientific inquiry, led to the study of higher mental processes of how people learn. Research in educational psychology produced theories of learning which have perpetuated into many cultures. Unlike philosophies that specify learning goals, learning theories focus more on the process of learning. There is a whole spectrum of learning theories and their derivations but the primary ones in traditional education are the behaviorist learning theory and cognitive information processing.

The earliest learning theory is the behaviorist learning theory. Also called objectivism, it is based on "Thorndike's connectionism, Pavlov's classical conditioning and Skinner's operant conditioning" (Williams 2002, p.134). It was the traditional belief system around the world. The central tenet is that we can learn or enforce target behavior through repetition and correction. Three other core principles are the need for objectives, learning through activity and reinforcement through rewards or punishments (Taylor & Furnham 2005). Education is a process of knowledge transfer from the expert teacher to the novice student.

While behaviorism concentrates on external stimuli, a new model was developed, known as cognitivism or cognitive information processing. Among its proponents are Jean Piaget and Jerome Bruner (Driscoll & Carliner 2005). Cognitivism holds that learning is a change in the cognitive structures of the mind and occurs when informational input is received and processed (Boettcher & Conrad 2004). Students learn better through linking prior knowledge, relationships between concepts, well-categorized materials, feedback, catering to the students' learning style and the engagement of many perceptions as possible (Taylor & Furnham 2005; Leidner & Jarvenpaa 1995).

Traditional education is hallmarked by its face-to-face component in classroom settings. Students tend to learn by themselves (Garrison & Anderson 2003) and absorb information passively from the teacher (Gillespie 1998). Moreover, the instructional approach is focused on the teacher who is the main source of knowledge. The teacher engages in didactic teaching and assesses students on their memory and knowledge (Gillespie 1998).

2.3 Modern Education

While traditional education is based on behaviorist learning theory and cognitive information processing, modern education is evolving to a new paradigm, termed constructivism. It is heavily influenced by Dewey's ideas of self-directed learning (Strijbos et al. 2004). Constructivism perceives learning from the locus of learners rather than educators (Tomei 2005). Constructivism holds that the creation of knowledge is based on the learner reflecting on his own experiences (Driscoll & Carliner 2005). Besides meaning making, another facet of constructivism is the need for authentic contexts (Duffy & Jonassen 1992) which is also called situated or distributed cognitions (Jonassen, Hernandez-Serrano & Choi 2000). It emphasizes that the social world around them, their culture, and community influence people's beliefs. Lastly, the constructivist theory of learning is a social nature of knowledge construction (Jonassen et al. 2000). Some theorists have extended the model to become the collaborative learning model that stresses on the role of peer relationships in a learning community as a key component of educational success (Leidner & Jarvenpaa 1995). As people cooperate, they discuss and share, contributing different understandings that lead to new, shared understandings.

The emergence of constructivism paralleled with the radical changes in educational technology. In addition, the growth of the knowledge economy and the need for new skills is "fueling a transition in modern learning in the era of the Internet" (Zhang et al 2004, p.75). Education in this modern era contains elements of traditional learning – the face-to-face component and virtual learning – learning through electronic means. In fact, some term this modern education to be blended learning, mixed mode learning, or hybrid learning (Ausburn 2004). The following table charts the difference between traditional education and modern education with information adapted from Kinder (2002, p.392) and Zhang et al (2004, p.76). (See Table 2).

Modern education is rife with the use of educational technology. A key issue in the development of educational technology is how one can effectively employ it in education. Before looking into this issue, we trace the emergence of educational technology and delve into the function of pedagogy for its theoretical foundation and as a possible solution to determine the effectiveness of educational technology.

Table 2 Differences in traditional and modern education

Characteristics of traditional learning	Characteristics of virtual learning
• Teacher control • Structured content • Errorless performance sought • Small steps • Liners, limited branching • Local • Transfer of knowledge and specific skills • Teach procedures • Control the learner • Immediate feedback • Familiar to both instructors and students • Motivating students	• Learner options or control • Exploration (negotiation) of content • Learn from errors • Large jumps • Linking • Global • Learn problem solving • Practice critical thinking skills • Empower the learner • Time and location flexibility • Cost-effective for learners • Unlimited access to knowledge • Archival capability for knowledge reuse and sharing
Traditional instructional approach	**Modern instructional approach**
• Teacher-directed • Didactic teaching • Short blocks of instruction on single subject • Passive or one-way instruction • Individual, competitive work • Teacher as knowledge dispenser • Ability grouping • Assessment of knowledge, specific skills	• Learner-directed • Student exploration • Extended blocks of multidisciplinary instruction • Action and interactive instruction modes • Collaborative, co-operative work • Teacher as guide and facilitator • Heterogeneous grouping • Performance-based assessment

3 Emergence of Educational Technology

IT has been used in many diverse and innovative ways in education contexts, ranging from a simple printing tool to an educational experience via virtual reality. There are two distinct functions of educational technology use – termed the technology *in* education and technology *of* education. The first term refers to the tools used in education such as instructional media, hardware and software used to present information (Ellington et al. 1993). The technology in education concept views IT as a silver bullet that will increase the learning of students just by applying educational technology. However, the second term, the technology of education, views the educational system as a whole. It encompasses the intangible features from research and learning theories together with the hardware and software portions. The technology of education aims to improve the effectiveness of the teaching and learning process (Ellington et al. 1993). We briefly summarize the manifestation of IT in education.

3.1 Historical Development of Educational Technology

Four key technologies - film, television, computers, and the Internet have enabled the utilization of IT for education. Beginning with film, this was utilized in education since the 1940s. For instance, the US military used movies to train its troops (Rosenberg 2001). Soon after, television was used to instruct students. Instructional videos were a central part of the US public school's education in the 1950s and 1960s (Ellington et al. 1993).

In the 1970s, researchers invented the microcomputer that began a new phase for educational technology. Parallel to the widespread usage of IT, the usage of educational technology grew (Matta & Kern 1989). It also prompted the growth of the educational software industry. The use of computers for education was termed computer-aided instruction (CAI). The development of word processing software and spreadsheet software has enabled computers to become a tool to create educational lessons. Individuals could express their knowledge using these applications. Another development was the commercialization of instructional material. Professionals developed complex and rich instructional materials and these required support staff. Technology became a black box to users. These educational technology integrated text, images, sound, and video into one whole package. Multimedia CD-ROMs proliferated into the market. An example is Microsoft's Encarta. This computerized encyclopedia could possibly be the most well known educational software product during our time (Adelsberger, Collis, & Pawlowski 2002).

The Internet explosion in the late 1990s has had a tremendous impact on educational technology. Users could use computers to contact other computers and persons through computer-mediated communications (CMC) like email and chat rooms. Two movements have arisen regarding the creation of instructional media. The first being the new iteration of the creative individual producing his own resources and maintaining it on the web while the other being the industrial track where professionals engage in educational web environments.

The Internet has facilitated a new type of electronic learning, simply termed e-learning. E-learning can be seen as the latest extension of technology in education and includes earlier computer-based technologies. There are many facets of e-learning. A glimpse of an e-learning system could contain courseware, a learning management system, library and digital resources and learner support services (Davis 2004). Indeed, e-learning consists of collaborative technology, Internet technology, human computer interaction, multimedia technology, accounting, knowledge management, security, and telecommunication technology (Zhang & Nunamaker 2003).

E-learning extends CAI by adding the communication element to the previously individualized experience (Piccoli et al 2001). A highly embraced strength of e-learning is the capacity for increased interaction. Not solely an interaction between the student and the system, e-learning allows communication between peers and instructors and even collaborative learning communities. E-learning also provides high levels of student control and supports participant contact and interaction continuously during the learning process.

As educational technology progressed, the goals in using IT changed too. As mentioned, the initial idea of educational technology was that it was an effective tool for learning. Later on, researchers realized that IT was not beneficial unless it was designed and used in ways that enhanced learning. The emphasis of educational technology has thus shifted away from the equipment. The focus is now on the technology *of* education where the goal is to improve learning and teaching based on educational psychology and pedagogy.

The Internet has facilitated a new type of electronic learning, simply termed e-learning. E-learning can be seen as the latest extension of technology in education and includes earlier computer-based technologies. There are many facets of e-learning. A glimpse of an e-learning system could contain courseware, a learning management system, library and digital resources and learner support services (Davis 2004). Indeed, e-learning consists of collaborative technology, Internet technology, human computer interaction, multimedia technology, accounting, knowledge management, security, and telecommunication technology (Zhang & Nunamaker 2003). These various aspects of e-learning are shown in Figure 1 (Zhang & Nunamaker, 2003, p.212).

E-learning extends CAI by adding the communication element to the previously individualized experience (Piccoli et al 2001). A highly embraced strength of e-learning is the capacity for increased interaction. Not solely an interaction between the student and the system, e-learning allows communication between peers and instructors and even collaborative learning communities. Figure 2 illustrates the various ways of interaction (adapted from Shale & Garrison 1990). E-learning also provides high levels of student control and supports participant contact and interaction continuously during the learning process.

As educational technology progressed, the goals in using IT changed too. As mentioned, the initial idea of educational technology was that it was an effective tool for learning. Educators concentrated on teaching discrete knowledge and basic skills to students through drill-and-practice applications of computers (Stites 2004). Also, educators transported teaching practices from the face-to-face classroom to the virtual classroom. Later on, researchers realized that IT was not beneficial unless it was designed and used in ways that enhanced learning. Moreover, IT had the potential to facilitate higher-order learning, problem solving, creativity, and integrated skills development (Stites 2004). Besides regarding IT as merely a tool, more and more educators and developers have realized the advantage of using technology as a learning strategy. Schunk (2004) suggests that IT should be implemented with learning goals in mind. The emphasis of educational technology has thus shifted away from the equipment. The focus is now on the technology *of* education where the goal is to improve learning and teaching based on educational psychology and pedagogy.

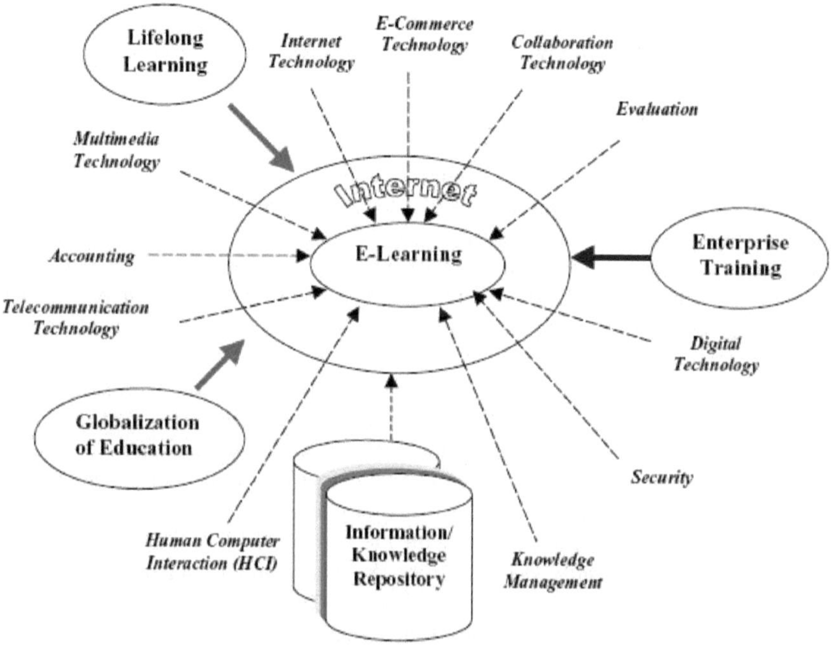

Figure 1 A framework of enabling technologies in e-learning

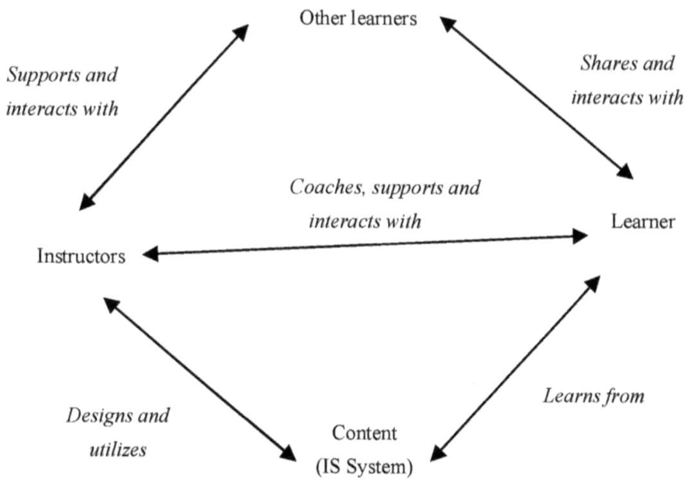

Figure 2 Elements of an e-learning system

3.2 The function of Pedagogy in Educational Technology

Pedagogy or learning theories dovetail the educational systems in many cultures. These pedagogies are important factors that improve the effectiveness of educational technology. For example, Leidner and Jarverpaa (1995) and Piccoli and colleagues (2001) show support for improved learning outcomes when learning theory was incorporated in the design and application of e-learning systems. As mentioned earlier, three influential theories of learning have arisen - behaviorism, cognitivism and constructivism. These theories are summarized in Table 3 (adapted from Driscoll & Carliner, 2005).

These learning theories have been utilized in educational technology for better learning. A conceptualization of the use of these pedagogies in educational technology is termed the generations' view (Garrison & Anderson 2003). Originally a scheme to classify distance education technologies, it can also be used as a general framework to trace the intertwining of pedagogy and educational technology.

The first generation is based on the behaviourist model of learning. This generation of educational tools created instructional material that had high standards that "could be delivered cost effectively to many thousands of students" (Garrison & Anderson 2003, p.37). Students learn from preconceived educational objectives. Educational technology of this first generation are mostly independent study types – that is, students work with the computer alone at their own time. However, content is totally derived from the instructional material and do not make use of resources available on the Internet. These tools are known simply as CAI and were the most used application in schools in the 1990s (Schunk 2004). It provides drill and practice programs which reinforce lessons for students, simulation activities for them to improve their decision-making or problem-solving skills and tutorials to teach new subject materials (Tomei 2005). CAI that is developed with behaviorist principles is able to command learners' attention, provide immediate feedback, and improve their learning (Schunk 2004).

The learning theory of cognitivism was prevalent in second-generation educational systems. These included broadcast media, advanced organizers, summary reflections, and self-paced tutorials. This generation reiterated the need for independent study. Often, these technologies were expensive which drove the need for large student populations to lower average costs and limited the reach of such second-generation courses. The higher costs of production and problems of distribution resulted in "the development of centralized and distributed libraries of educational objects, such as MERLOT (http://www.merlot.org)" (Garrison & Anderson 2003). E-learning based on the cognitive model of learning imitated the way the brain thinks, i.e., cognitive development through the layout, presentation, sequencing, and delivery of new knowledge (Tomei 2005). Programs also proceed deductively from the general to the specific.

Table 3 Summary of Learning Theories

	Behaviorism	Cognitivism	Constructivism
How is learning described?	Change in probability of particular behavior occurring in particular situation	Change in knowledge is stored in memory	Change in meaning constructed from experience
What is the role of the instructor?	Provide a highly structured environment in which to practice behaviors	Structure and organize information to make the processing more efficient and effective	Guide and provide materials from which learners can construct knowledge
What is the role of the learner and the nature of knowledge?	Learner is passive, an empty vessel and knowledge exists independent of the learner	Learner is active but knowledge is still independent of learner	Learners are active participants who construct their own knowledge
How does transfer happen?	When a correct response is demonstrated following the presentation of a specific environment stimulus. Emphasis is on observable, measurable behavior.	When the learner encodes and stores information in memory in a meaningful way	When the learner builds a personal interpretation of the world based on his or her experiences and interactions
What types of learning are best explained?	Teaching behaviors that can be observed or demonstrated	Problem solving, deep processing, exploring, organizing and synthesizing content	Higher order thinking skills such as analysis, synthesis, and evaluation
What principles are relevant?	Reinforcement, shaping, stimulus and response	Events of instruction, types of learning, learning hierarchies	Collaborative learning, learner-centered instruction, scaffolding, problem-solving

The third generation educational system marks a change in direction to focus on interactivity. This was materialized either by means of asynchronous and synchronous communication technologies. Constructivism was the base pedagogy and through CMC, students were able to construct shared realities and knowledge individually and in group settings. Weller (2000) developed an introductory course to the Internet embracing third generation principles for the Open University in the UK. Another initiative is the WebQuest model, an inquiry-oriented activity in which students search and evaluate information from the web (Jonassen et al. 2000). Through the ability to click on a wide array of links, it allows learners to construct their own learning experiences and encourage the individualized leaning of the student. Moreover, groups are able to collaborate and learn through online collaborative tools like chatrooms, electronic forums, wikis, and other collaborative systems.

Lastly, the fourth generation is a coalescence of the three key attributes of the Internet – "information retrieval of vast amounts of content, interactive capacity of CMC and the processing power of locally distributed processing via computer-assisted programming" (Garrison & Anderson 2003, p.38). Fourth generation types of educational systems include powerful packages and fully integrated learning systems such as Blackboard and Lotus Notes. In this generation, no dominant pedagogy exists but learning theories from behaviorism, cognitivism and constructivism are integrated to develop specific learning goals.

This generation view shows the utilization of pedagogy in educational technology. The function of learning theories in technology is then to provide sound principles to effectively teach and increase the learning of students. Combining the strengths of learning theories and IT is core to the mindset of the technology *of* education. In fact, this approach is prevalent among educators and instructional designers currently. Depending on the type of learning and learning goals, educators are designing educational software and e-learning systems that will enhance learning for learners based on pedagogy.

4 Concluding Remarks

In sum, this paper has traced the emergence of educational technology. It first proposes that culture has influenced what we understand in education and this development of educational technology is very much intertwined with culture. It goes on to describe the evolution of educational technology and the theoretical underpinnings alongside its development. This discourse has the following implications for practitioners and researchers. First, the importance of culture should not be ignored in the design and understanding of educational technology. As seen from the cultural basis of education and subsequently modern theories about educational technology, cultural roots do have an influence. Second, learning theories are crucial for the implementation of technology. Simply applying technology in education will not be beneficial for education. Rather, it is essential that supporting theories and frames of references are considered together with the technology. An example of such a framework is seen in Conole et al. (2004). It is hoped that educators and researchers will be cognizant of culture and learning theories as they continue to improve and gain new experiences from using IT in education.

References

1. Adelsberger, H, H., Collis, B. and Pawlowski, J. M. (2002). Handbook of information technologies for education and training. Springer, New York
2. Ausburn, L. (2004). Course design elements most valued by adult learners in blended online education environments: an American perspective. Educational Media International, 41(4), 327-337.
3. Boettcher, J. V., and Conrad R-M. (2004). Faculty guide for moving teaching and learning to the Web. League for Innovation in the Community College, Phoenix, AZ.

4. Camp, J. and Fisher, E. (2002). Exploring the world of the ancient Greeks. Thames & Hudson, London.
5. Castle, E.B. (1965) Ancient Education and Today. Penguin Books Ltd, England.
6. Cheng, K. & Wong, K. (1996) School effectiveness in East Asia: concepts, origins and implications. Journal of Educational Administration, 34(5)
7. Cleverly, John. (1991) The Schooling of China, Allen and Unwin, North Sydney, Australia.
8. Cochrane, P. (1998). Exponential education. In M. Henry (Ed.), Using IT effectively: a guide to technology in the social sciences(pp.3-16),.UCL Press, London,.
9. Conole, G. M., Dyke, M. O., Seale, J. (2004) Mapping pedagogy and tools for effective learning design, Computers & Education, 43(1-2), 17-33,
10. Cribiore, R. (2001). Gymnastics of the mind: Greek education in Hellenistic and Roman Egypt. Princeton University Press, Princeton, N.J.
11. Davis. A. (2004). Developing an Infrastructure for Online Learning. In T. Anderson and F. Elloumi (Ed), Theory and Practice of Online Learning (pp. 97-114). Athabasca University, Canada.
12. Driscoll, M. and Carliner, S. (2005). Advanced Web-based training strategies, Pfeiffer Publishing, San Francisco.
13. Duffy, T.M. and Jonassen, D.H. (1992) Constructivism and the technology of instruction: a conversation. Lawrence Erlbaum Associates Publishers, Hillsdale, N.J.
14. Ellington, H., Percival, F. and Race, P. (1993). Handbook of educational technology, Kogan Page, London.
15. Ellis, A. K., Cogan, J.J., and Howey, K.R. (1991). Introduction to the foundations of education. 3rd Edition, Prentice-Hall, New Jersey.
16. Ferrante, J. (2003) Sociology: A Global Perspective. Wadsworth/Thomson Learning, Belmont.
17. Garrison, D. R. and Anderson, T. (2003). E-learning in the 21st Century: A framework for research and practice. RoutledgeFalmer, London.
18. Gillespie, K.H. (1998) The Impact of Technology on Faculty Development, Life and Work. Jossey-Bass, San Francisco.
19. Gutek, G. L. (1997) Philosophical and ideological perspectives on education. Allyn and Bacon, Boston.
20. Honebein, P.C., Duffy, T.M. and Fishman, B.J. (1993). Constructivism and the Design of Learning Environments: Context and Authentic Activities for Learning. In T.M. Duffy, J. Lowyck, and D.H. Jonassen (eds.) Designing Environments for Constructivist Learning (pp. 87-108). bSpringer-Verlag, Berlin.
21. Jonassen, D.H., Hernandez-Serrano, J. and Choi, I. (2000) Integrating Constructivism and learning technologies. In J.M. Spector and T.M. Anderson (eds.) Integrated and Holistic Perspectives on Learning, Instruction and Technology (pp. 103-128). Kluwer Academic Publishers, Dordrecht, Netherlands.
22. Kinder, T. (2002) Are schools learning organizations. Technovation, 22(6), 2002, 385-404.
23. Leidner, D. E. and Jarvenpaa, S. L. (1995) The Use of Information Technology to enhance management school education: a theoretical view. MIS Quarterly,19(3), 256-291.
24. Matta, K.F. and Kern, G.M. "A framework for research in computer-aided instruction: challenges and opportunities," Computers and Education 13(1), 1989, pp. 77-84.
25. McLoughlin, C. (1999) Culturally Responsive Technology Use: Developing an On-line Community of Learners. British Journal of Educational Technology, 30(3), 231-243.
26. McPherson, M. and Nunes, M. B. (2004) Developing Innovation in Online Learning: An Action Research Framework. Routledge Falmer, London.
27. Pathak, A. (2002) Social Implications of Schooling: Knowledge, Pedagogy and Consciousness. Rainbow Publishers, India.
28. Piccoli, G., Ahmad, R. and Ives, B. (2001) Web-based virtual learning environments: A research framework and a preliminary assessment of effectiveness in basic IT skills training. MIS Quarterly, 25(4), 401-426.
29. Rosenberg, M.J. (2001) E-learning: Strategies for Delivering Knowledge in the Digital Age. McGraw-Hill, New York.

30. Schunk, D. H. (2004) Learning theories: an educational perspective. Pearson Education, Upper Saddle River.
31. Sharma, G. R. (1987) Trends in contemporary Indian philosophy of education: a critical evaluation. Nirmal Publishers, New Delhi.
32. Stites, R. (2004) Implications of New Learning Technologies for Adult Literacy and Learning. In J. Comings, B. Garner and C. Smith (eds.) Review of adult learning and literacy, Vol. 4, Connecting research, policy, and practice. Lawrence Erlbaum, New Jersey.
33. Strijbos, J., Kirschner, P. A. and Martens, R. L. (2004) What we know about CSCL and implementing it in higher education. Kluwer Academic Publishers, Boston, Mass.
34. Taylor, J. and Furnham, A. Learning at Work: Excellent practice from best theory, Palgrave Macmillan, Great Britain, 2005.
35. Tomei, L. A. (2005) Taxonomy for the Technology Domain, Idea Group, Hershey, PA.
36. Turner, Y. and Acker, A. (2002) Education in the new China: shaping ideas at work. Ashgate Publishing Limited, Aldershot, England.
37. Weller, M. J. (2000) Creating a Large-scale, Third Generation, Distance Education Course. Open Learning, Volume 15, Number 3, 1 November 2000, 243-252
38. Williams, S. W. (2002) Instructional Design Factors and the Effectiveness of Web-Based Training/Instruction, ERIC, ED474156.
39. Zhang, D. and Nunamaker, J.K. (2003) Powering E-learning in the new millennium: an overview of e-learning and enabling technology. Information Systems Frontiers, 5(2), 207–218.
40. Zhang, D., Zhao, J. L., Zhou, L. and Nunamaker Jr, J. F. (2004) Can e-learning replace classroom learning? Communication of the ACM, 47 (5), 75-79.

History of Computing Education Trends: The Emergence of Competitive Intelligence

Kevin R. Parker[1], Philip S. Nitse[2], and Bill Davey[3]

[1] College of Business, Idaho State University, Pocatello USA: parkerkr@isu.edu
[2] College of Business, Idaho State University, Pocatello USA; nitsphil@cob.isu.edu
[3] School of Business Information Technology, RMIT University, Melbourne, Australia; billd@rmit.edu.au

Abstract: Several studies have shown that new curriculum initiatives such as enterprise systems have a predictable lifecycle [1]. This paper looks for trends in competitive intelligence (CI), a relatively new area of study that is beginning to infiltrate curricula around the world. We first examine existing research concerning CI and academia, listing the various approaches through which CI's role in educational curricula is considered and tracing the history of its emergence. A survey of CI course offerings throughout the US and Australia was conducted in an attempt to identify trends outside a single culture or education system. It shows that CI is an emerging discipline and often appears as an independent degree program rather than just a component of other programs. The methodology used in this study demonstrates how a historical perspective can be used to identify new issues to be considered by curriculum planners.

Keywords: Curriculum trends, Competitive intelligence, Computer education, Computing history

1 Introduction

The curriculum planner in technology-dominated areas is often faced with a rapidly moving target and very few planning tools. This paper looks at a new discipline that is emerging and attempts to plot the trend of its emergence. The process of looking at the introduction of a new role for technology as a topic for courses and programs in two countries should help the curriculum planner see the utility of considering a historical perspective when planning for new trends. Competitive intelligence (CI) is a systematic program for gathering and analyzing information about key stakeholders, such as competitors, customers, and suppliers,

Please use the following format when citing this chapter:

Parker, K.R., Nitse, P.S. and Davey, B., 2008, in IFIP International Federation for Information Processing, Volume 269; *History of Computing and Education 3*; John Impagliazzo; (Boston: Springer), pp. 113–127.

in order to find new opportunities and stay competitive [2]. CI is based on the premise that through analysis of data, companies can predict the probable future actions of these stakeholders. Organizations use the CI process to gather information, to add value to it through analysis, and to report the findings to managers to assist them in making tactical or strategic decisions or satisfy requests for information. CI projects range from obtaining competitive information about competitors or customers to information on recruiting or mergers and acquisitions. The types of information needed for such projects may include financial information, demographics, biographies, economic indicators, news articles, and customer and competitor information. With the vast amount of information that is available on every topic imaginable, it is vital that the knowledge gained from CI activities be managed in a systematic manner. Once the information is secured, it must be analyzed and proper reports must be generated and disseminated to the appropriate individuals within the organization.

CI provides a means of gathering and analyzing information for use in developing global strategies. It is critical to get the right information into the hands of the appropriate people at the time they need it to make decisions [3]. Identification of key economic, social, and technological issues that affect the organization, its life cycle stages, and their relevance to each other helps managers allocate attention and resources to them [4]. Organizational adaptation, survival, and competence in the face of discontinuous environmental change require access to timely and accurate information, as well as tools to constantly monitor, analyze and interpret that information [5]. CI is a fundamental, early step in the chain of perceptions and actions that permit an organization to adapt to its environment [6]. CI must be able to uncover and provide information that will allow management to identify and fill gaps in consumer or business demand curves that are unfulfilled by the products and services that are currently available [7].

2 CI Education Research

2.1 The Development of CI

Facets of competitive intelligence gathering have been a part of business for many years, but Prescott [8] states that the systematic orientation towards CI is a fairly recent phenomenon, citing Ecells and Nehemkis [9]. Other sources point to Porter's [10] work as the foundation of modern CI. However, Underwood [11] maintains that business-related intelligence came into use in the 1960s. [12], [13], [14], and [15] all published intelligence research during this period [16]. The 1980s saw the introduction of formal intelligence gathering functions and in 1986, the Society of Competitive Intelligence Professionals (SCIP) was founded. Juhari and Stephens [17] note that the technology explosion of the 1990s probably stimulated the notion of CI being something new or revolutionary. The emergence of the Internet and online databases offered an almost overwhelming supply of information.

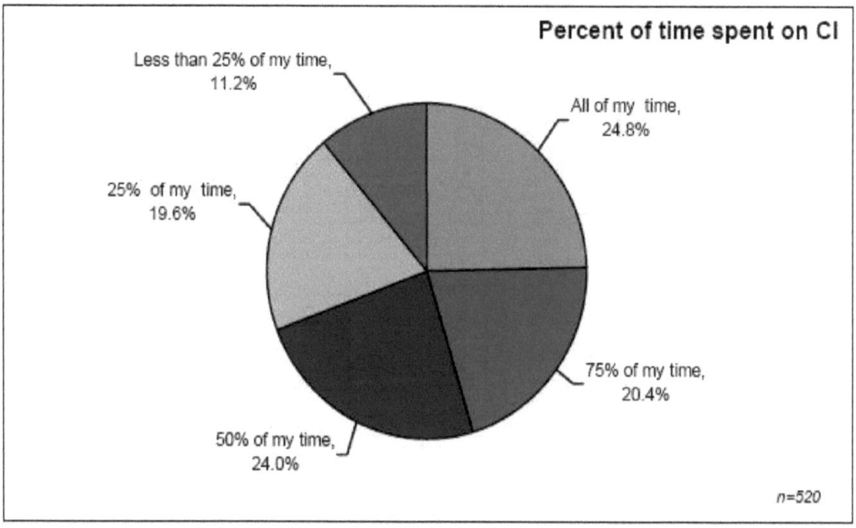

Figure 1 Time spent on CI (from [18])

2.2 CI in Industry

It is possible for issues in education to be self-sustaining and independent despite having no real use. Sometimes an issue will be seen as demonstrating some underlying principle that is not yet used in industry. CI is not one of those issues and much evidence can be found of its use. The Competitive Intelligence Institute [18] conducted a survey of over 500 practitioners in 2005 and 2006 and found "Awareness is high and CI visibility has increased in many organizations. Most CI practitioners create exposure to senior management through distribution of their deliverables. They present an excellent opportunity for CI practitioners to demonstrate the value competitive intelligence provides to the organization." This survey showed that CI was mostly a part time activity, but that many practitioners spend much of their time in CI dedicated activities (Figure 1).

This same survey [18] showed that a wide range of activities in business are supported by CI (see figure 2). We can see, from the existence of the group supporting CI and the way in which practitioners can identify their CI activities, that CI is a part of the industrial landscape.

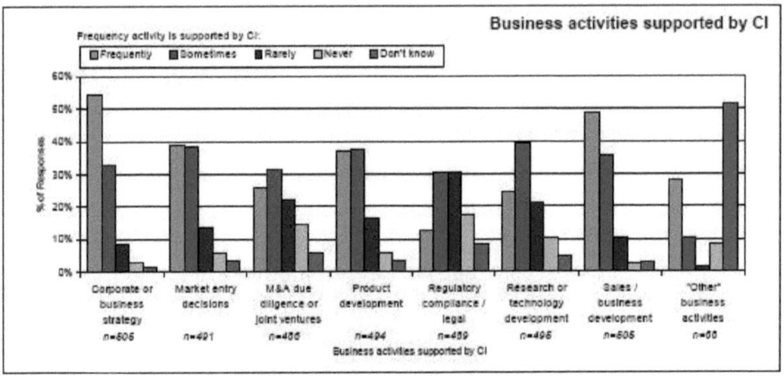

Figure 2 Business activities supported by CI (from [18])

2.3 CI and Education

CI education research can take a variety of paths. While some authors focus on what topics are critical to a CI education or the best fit for a CI program, others take different approaches. Some authors focus on the best teaching approaches to use when teaching CI courses. Others prefer to describe what their university has done with their particular CI program. Still others view CI from the context of library science.

2.4 Overviews of CI

A good starting point for an analysis of CI education research is McGonagle's [19] bibliography of publications that deal with university education and professional training. Prescott [20] presents an informal sampling of CI programs across the globe. Davis, Kohun, and Woratschek [21] also present a table of U.S. Universities and Colleges with offerings in CI/BI, breaking them down by those that have a degree program, those that offer a professional certificate, and those that offer courses only.

2.5 The Dispersion of CI Into Schools

Merritt [22] laments that most educational institutions have not incorporated CI into their academic programs. He points out that many teach only business research techniques that follow time-insensitive methodologies, ignoring current business requirements. He speculates that a major obstacle to the development of CI courses is a combination of inexperienced instructors and limited teaching materials. He then prescribes a course of action that involves developing suitable instructional materials, training faculty members, and making career placement centers aware of intelligence internships and entry-level CI positions. Fleisher [23] agrees that formal educational offerings in CI have been constrained by a variety of factors including a dearth of CI offerings at the post-secondary level, confusion about the proper placement of CI studies, and a lack of an agreed upon body of knowledge, core texts, and case studies.

Prescott [8] offers a different perspective. He observes that while business schools may not be teaching dedicated CI courses, most universities offer a wide range of courses that include CI content. With that as a basis, he contends that most schools are already positioned to offer business majors in CI. He ponders that the barrier to implementing a CI major is political rather than economic. Fleisher [23] reflects that educational offerings will likely grow slowly and that prospective and current CI practitioners may have to fall back on formal and self-directed learning opportunities.

2.6 Where Does CI Fit In?

Calof [2] discusses the best fit for a CI course or program using SCIP's CI skills checklist as a yardstick. He stresses the importance of the integration of multiple techniques to understand how the firm should react to various situations. He complains that few schools of business teach interview methodology, revealing his unfamiliarity with the course content of many systems analysis and design courses in information systems programs. He then points out that most universities that offer CI include it in with strategy (his recommendation), although some include it in IS or marketing. He concludes that three approaches should be considered if a school is serious about CI: integration into existing courses, an intelligence capstone course, or a dedicated intelligence program.

Fleisher [23] notes several key trends that are discernible in CI education. They include integration with other disciplines and areas, horizontal education in which knowledgeable industry participants are trained about CI, the increasingly global emphasis of CI and its need to address global competition and competitors, and the fact that CI education now addresses technology in terms of both content and process. He points out that "it would be difficult to teach CI without discussing the importance of database management and structure, secondary data acquisition formats and processes, network formats, enterprise information systems integration, information security, and communication protocols." Miller [24] also stresses integration with other disciplines. He points out that a comprehensive curriculum includes strategy development, market research, primary research methods, statistics, information sources, and interviewing and communication techniques. These topics are drawn from multiple disciplines, including information science, business administration, statistics, communication, and journalism. The intricate relationships between CI and other academic disciplines were also a key theme at the SCIP/Drexel CI Academic Conference [25].

2.7 What Should Be in a CI Program?

Miller [24] points out that completing coursework is insufficient preparation for a career as an intelligence professional, especially since many professionals may find the trait-coursework-experience-mentoring sequence inappropriate for their training needs. SCIP/Drexel (2001) discussed the skill sets that CI managers look for in new recruits, such as forecasting, cultural analysis, and experience with analytical techniques. Teaching priorities include such things as the need for MBA capstone courses, forecasting, and training MBAs to be consumers of CI. Miller [26] states that "[a]n effective CI educational program must emphasize practical techniques and approaches for conducting CI rather than nebulous academic theories."

Some studies take a more narrow focus than general issues that impact CI education. Several reflect on the best teaching approaches to use when teaching CI courses. Blenkhorn and Fleisher [27] look at different teaching approaches that are best suited to the diverse groups that might be encountered in an academic setting, including undergraduates, MBAs, and executives. They conclude by specifying a set of goals that would facilitate teaching CI to the diverse groups, one of which is achieving consensus among CI educators about the scope of CI and what it entails. Hulnick [28] describes his experiences in developing a CI course for liberal arts students. Kinsinger [29] discusses how to better prepare MBA students to make better use of CI resources when they join (or rejoin) the workforce. The author first complains that MBA programs do not prepare students to understand the drivers to critical thinking: how they learn, think, and decide. He further generalizes that most MBA teaching is done in off-the-shelf formats. He then states that future executives must be trained to maximize the value that they receive from CI tools by learning to (1) understand the premium ingredients of a quality intelligence product, (2) assess the density and reach of the information source base and the features of the analytical frameworks and methodologies, and (3) understand the necessary logic flow between raw information and insight, and the conclusions and recommendations derived from them.

Some papers present what their university has done with their particular CI program. Davis, Kohun, and Woratschek [21] outline the conception, development, and implementation of the Master of Science in Competitive Intelligence Systems degree at Robert Morris University. They then compare their curriculum to three other universities that offer a graduate degree in CI: American Military University, Dominican University, and Simmons College. Although the RMU curriculum most closely resembles that of Simmons College, it has a stronger foundation in Information Systems. Miller [26] discusses the SCIP curriculum models, a resource that no longer seems to be available, and then describes the Competitive Intelligence Center at Simmons College and provides a summary of the program's course offerings. Prescott [8] examines the curriculum of the Katz Graduate School of Business, comparing the course offerings to the skills required for each component of the intelligence cycle.

2.8 CI in Library and Knowledge Management Settings

MacGillivray [30] discusses how her university chose to harness the interrelationships and mutual competencies of CI and KM. She asserts that "looking at the common ground and mutually supportive natures of CI and KM is more beneficial than carving out separate territories", contrary to McGonacle's [31] position that CI and KM have "almost nothing in common." The degree plan that is described is a graduate degree in KM with a CI component. Finally, Larrat [32] examines the Atelis Competitive Intelligence (CI) educational program. When developing the program they decided to focus on the synergies between intelligence, CI, and knowledge management. They also formed an alliance between the business school, research centers, consultants, and various business organizations. They discuss the required coursework, and then elaborate on a real-world practical group work section designed to provide hands-on training. They conclude that it is by applying techniques in the field that students achieve full awareness of the contribution of a CI approach.

Skills similar to those required of a CI professional are taught in library science or information science programs. Trimberger [33] contends that information and library science schools have been teaching CI-type courses, skills, and techniques for years. The paper goes on to consider how CI skills are taught to information and library science schools and applied by the information professional. In the process of making connections between disparate pieces of data, the information professional creates the CI product, a synthesis of that data. That CI product is the information that can be used to gain an advantage in the marketplace. Papik [34] draws parallels between CI educational requirements and those of library science. Davis [35] maintains that in their current form library science degrees are not adequate for prospective CI professionals. She notes that the skills learned in MLS/MLIS degree programs are not sufficient to equip individuals for careers in CI. Instead, training requires basic knowledge of business terminology and some industry knowledge. Further, formal business training and even an MBA are advisable, and therefore more and more library schools are incorporating business courses into their MLS programs to help graduates break into fields such as CI. Shelfer [36] identifies three primary multidisciplinary knowledge domains that contribute to CI: business, information management, and information science. She then goes on to describe the contributions made by each. Both Shelfer [36] and Shelfer and Goodrum [37] describe the various CI-related degrees offered by Drexel.

3 Current State of CI in Academia: U.S. and Australia

The next step in examining CI education is to identify the types of academic offerings currently available at institutions of higher education.

3.1 U.S. Programs

Table 1 lists U.S. schools that have been identified as offering courses or programs with a CI component. In the first column are the six schools that offer full degree programs at either the undergraduate or the graduate level. The second column shows the eleven schools that offer professional certification in CI. Three of these offer full degrees as well. The last column lists the sixteen schools that offer only a course (or courses) identified as having CI content. Again, these courses are offered at both the undergraduate and the graduate level. The schools in the first two columns of Table 1 offer formal programs and certificates, and therefore can be used to determine representative course offerings or sequences. The schools that offer only individual CI courses cannot be used in such an analysis and as a consequence only the first two columns will be considered.

A comparison of degree programs and certificate programs reveals that the major difference is that the certificate programs offer more CI-focused content than a traditional academic degree program. This is not unexpected since those seeking a certificate are generally professionals requiring a specialized program that restricts itself to core knowledge about a field such as CI. Degree programs normally require students to take a wide range of courses in addition to their specialization, and may therefore incorporate everything from liberal arts to business foundations. In addition, CI programs themselves will vary based on where the program resides. For example, if the CI degree program resides in the college of business the program places more emphasis on the role of CI in solving business problems, whereas if the CI degree program is associated with an information and library science program there may be an emphasis on finding and cataloging information. Because certificate programs are not representative of typical academic requirements, they will not be considered in our discussion of CI in academia.

Table 1 US CI Education Programs, Certificates, and Courses

Degree Program	Professional Certificate	Courses Only
American Military U.	American Military U.	Boston U.
Dominican U.	Babson College	Brigham Young U.
Johns Hopkins U.	Dominican U.	CalTech
Mercyhurst College	Drexel U.	Champlain College
Robert Morris U.	Marist College	Harvard U.
Simmons College	Notre Dame College	Hawaii Pacific U.
	Simmons College	Idaho State U.
	Trinity College	Indiana U.
	U. of Pennsylvania	Kent State U.
	U. of Tennessee	Rutgers
	U. of Washington	Thunderbird
		UCLA
		U. of Central Missouri
		U. of Hartford
		U. of Pittsburg
		U. of Texas at Austin

An examination of degree titles from the six schools in column one shows a variance across these offerings and shows how few "true" CI programs there are. Table 2 shows that only two of the six are actual master's degrees, three are degree concentrations, and the last is a master's degree in strategic intelligence rather than competitive intelligence. This indicates that the discipline is still in its nascent stages with regard to academia and as such, academia appears not to be meeting the needs of industry.

Table 2 CI Program Variance

Master's Degrees in Competitive Intelligence
Robert Morris University
Department of Computer and Information Systems
Master of Science in Competitive Intelligence Systems
Simmons University
Graduate School of Library and Information Science
Master of Science in Competitive Intelligence
Degree Concentrations in Competitive Intelligence
American Military University
Master of Arts in Intelligence Studies
Concentration in Competitive Intelligence
Dominican University
Brennan School of Business
Master of Science in Knowledge Management
Concentration in Information Science
Johns Hopkins University
Carey Business School
Master of Business Administration
Concentration in Competitive Intelligence
Degrees Specializing in Strategic Intelligence
Mercyhurst College
Institute for Intelligence Studies
Master of Science in Applied Intelligence

The next step is to examine the required courses in the six-degree programs. Table 3 shows little commonality across the degree programs. Although some of this may be attributed to the above issue regarding where the degree program is housed, there may be other reasons for the lack of a consistent set of courses. On the technical side CI programs offer courses in Database Management, Data Mining and Warehousing, Information Systems Analysis and Design, Informatics, Knowledge Management, and Metadata under a wide variety of titles. On the strategic side CI programs offer a variety of courses with a more managerial basis, such as Strategic Intelligence, Interagency Operations, Competitive Intelligence, Legal and Ethical Issues in Management, Industrial Espionage, Intelligence Theories and Applications, Managing Strategic Intelligence Analysis, Leadership and Organizational Behavior, Introduction to the Intelligence Function, and Organizational and Legal Issues in Technology. There may be some overlap in course content depending on how they are structured.

Table 3 CI Course Offerings in Graduate Programs

Robert Morris University	Simmons College	American Military University	Dominican University	Johns Hopkins University	Mercyhurst College
DS System Analysis & Design	Intro to the Intelligence Function	Research Methods in Intelligence Studies	Knowledge Management	Org. & Legal Issues in Technology	Intelligence Theories & Applications
Database Management Systems	Basic Analytical Tools & Techniques	Strategic Intelligence	Org. Analysis & Design	Competitive Intelligence	Topics In Intelligence
Cyberlaw & E-Commerce	Conducting CI Legally	Collection	Management Information Systems	Data Mining & Discovery Informatics	Strategic Business Intelligence
Computer Network Security	Conducting CI Ethically	Analytic Methods	Organization of Knowledge	Knowledge Management Systems	Managing Strategic Intelligence Analysis
CI Systems	Business Info. Sources & Services	Interagency Operations	Information Policy		Intelligence Commun.
Data Mining		Competitive Intelligence	Org. of Knowledge		Leadership & Org. Behavior
Data Warehousing		Legal/Ethical Issues in Mgmt	Database Management		Comparative History of Intelligence
		Industrial Espionage	Info Systems Analysis & Design		
			CI for Mgmt. Decision Making		

3.2 Australian Programs

Table 4 lists Australian schools that have been identified as offering courses or programs with a CI component. We were unable to locate any Australian universities that offer a degree program or certificate in CI. The last column lists the eight schools that offer only a course (or courses) identified as having CI content. Again, these courses may be offered at the undergraduate and/or graduate level. Because the schools that offer only individual CI courses cannot be used in an analysis of representative program content, it is difficult to draw any conclusions about CI educational offerings in Australia, other than the fact that CI education is not yet considered adequately significant to merit a specialized degree.

Table 4 Australian CI Education Programs, Certificates, and Courses

Degree Program	Professional Certificate	Courses Only
		Curtin U. of Technology
		Macquarie U.
		Monash U.
		RMIT U.
		Swinburne U. of Technology
		U. of South Australia
		U. of Technology Sydney
		U. of Western Sydney

4 Future Research

Future research will attempt to establish essential components of CI graduate education, as well as a set of IS courses that best complements a CI program. Additional research will consider the parallel between the development of CI and computer science (CS) programs. Most CS programs were originally founded in either Mathematics or Engineering departments, and many CI programs have their genesis in Information and Library Science programs or in a college of business. In the case of CS, the program was highly influenced by its host discipline, and it will be useful to see if the same holds true of CI programs.

One possible solution to the problem of slow infiltration of CI programs, one that will be elaborated on in a future paper, is the development of multiple CI tracks. These tracks, one with a technical emphasis and one with a managerial emphasis, will be designed with minimal overlap in order to complement each other. The availability of tracks will allow students to select that program that best fits their interests and skills. It will also allow the program to be developed and implemented in increments rather than all at once. A model curriculum will be proposed and made available so that it can be adopted by other schools, thus making more feasible somewhat faster growth of CI in academia.

5 Conclusion

The literature review establishes that over the last ten years there has been much discussion about the need for a cohesive CI educational program in academia. The examination of the offerings currently available clearly indicates that the need still exists even though some schools now offer degrees or certificates. Many more schools restrict their CI offerings to a single course or a few courses. These courses can, however, serve as a starting point for more detailed programs and help to indicate what will and will not work. Further, their very existence enhances the visibility of CI with both students and recruiters.

When viewing the deployment of CI courses in terms of the ERP Education Deployment Maturity Model [1], it seems that CI can be categorized as Stage 2 (Adaptive) or Stage 3 (Developing). In the adaptive stage curriculum from others is adapted to the environment of the school, and some integration across courses within disciplines is evident. In the Developing stage curriculum is developed within the school and is specific to courses within the school's environment. This stage is also categorized by integration across disciplines, which is not yet evident.

It is clear from the analysis of existing degree programs that CI educational programs, whether in the US or Australia, are still in their nascent stages. The presence of individual courses in Australia with the complete lack of full degrees or certificate programs shows that CI is in an earlier stage of evolution in this otherwise developed educational environment. Before they reach full maturity a developed curriculum, as the one described in the future research discussion, must be made repeatable across multiple school environments, and eventually shared with other schools. Finally, that curriculum must be extended to in-depth processes that cross functional silos. It will require time and effort before this is possible for competitive intelligence, but industry need for CI workers may eventually spur greater academic efforts.

References

1. Antonucci, Y.L., et al., *Enterprise systems education: where are we? Where are we going?* Journal of Information Systems Education, 2004. **15**(3): p. 227-234.
2. Calof, J.L., *Teaching CI: Opportunities and needs.* Competitive Intelligence Magazine, 1999. **2**(4): p. 318-324.
3. Petrash, G., *Managing knowledge assets for value.*, in *Knowledge-Based Leadership Conference*. 1996, Linkage Inc: Boston.
4. McCann, J. and L. Gomez-Mejia, *Going "online" in the environmental scanning process.* IEEE Transactions on Engineering Management, 1992. **39**(4): p. 394-399.
5. Malhotra, Y., *Deciphering the knowledge management hype.* Journal for Quality & Participation, 1998. **21**(4): p. 58-60.
6. Hambrick, D.C., *Specialization of environmental scanning activities among upper level executives.* Journal of Management Studies, 1981. **18**(3): p. 299-320.

7. Johnson, A., *Decisions, decisions; Competitive intelligence for predictive decision support and market risk management.* KM World, 2005. **14**(10): p. 8-11.
8. Prescott, J.E., *The evolution of competitive intelligence: Designing a process for action.* The Journal of the Association of Proposal Management Professionals, 1999 **1**(1): p. 37-52.
9. Ecells, R. and P. Nehemkis, *Corporate intelligence and espionage: A blueprint for executive decision making.* . 1984, New York NY: Macmillan.
10. Porter, M.E., *Competitive strategy: Techniques for analyzing industries and competitors.* 1980, New York NY: The Free Press.
11. Underwood, J., *Competitive intelligence.* 2002, Oxford: Capstone Publishing.
12. McGovern, W.M., *Strategic intelligence and the shape of tomorrow.* 1961, Seattle, WA: Vashon Island Books.
13. Green, R.M., *Business intelligence and espionage.* 1966, Homewood, IL: Dow Jones-Irwin.
14. Aguilar, F.J., *Scanning the Business Environment.* 1967, New York NY: Macmillan.
15. Kelley, W.T., *Marketing Intelligence: The Management of Marketing Information.* 1968, London: Staples Press.
16. Kent, S. *On the origins of competitive intelligence. Kent's Imperative, November 30.* 2007 [cited 11-1-2007]; Available from: http://kentsimperative.blogspot.com/2007_11_01_archive.html.
17. Juhari, A.S. and D. Stephens, *Tracing the origins of competitive intelligence throughout history.* Journal of Competitive Intelligence and Management, 2006. **3**(4): p. 61-82.
18. Fehringer, D., B. Hohhof, and T. Johnson, *State of the Art: Competitive Intelligence.* 2006, Competitive Intelligence Institute.
19. McGonagle, J.J., *Bibliography: Education in competitive intelligence.* Competitive Intelligence Magazine, 2003. **6**(4): p. 50.
20. Prescott, J.E., *Debunking the "academic abstinence" myth of CI.* Competitive Intelligence Magazine 1999. **2**(4): p. 22-27.
21. Davis, G.A., F.G. Kohun, and C.R. Woratschek, *Curriculum development: Developing a graduate degree program in competitive intelligence.* Issues in Information Systems, 2005. **VI**(1): p. 318-324.
22. Merritt, C., *Competitive Intelligence and the Higher Education Dilemma.* Competitive Intelligence Magazine, 1999. **2**(4): p. 19-21.
23. Fleisher, C.S., *Competitive intelligence education: competencies, sources, and trends.* Information Management Journal, 2004. **38**(2): p. 56-63.
24. Miller, J.P., *Educational programs for intelligence professionals - The Library in Corporate Intelligence Activities.* . Library Trends, 1994. **43**(2): p. 253-270.
25. SCIP/Drexel CI Academic Conference, *Academics and practitioners: Forging a partnership.* Competitive Intelligence Review., 2001. **12**(2): p. 32-36.
26. Miller, J., *A comprehensive CI curriculum.* Competitive Intelligence Magazine, 2003. **6**(4): p. 27-30.
27. Blenkhorn, D. and C. Fleisher, *Teaching CI to three diverse groups.* Competitive Intelligence Magazine, 2003. **6**(4): p. 17-20.
28. Hulnick, A.S., *Teaching CI in a liberal arts curriculum.* Competitive Intelligence Magazine, 2003. **6**(4): p. 56-57.
29. Kinsinger, P., *Building a better customer: teaching MBAs how to use CI.* Competitive Intelligence Magazine, 2003. **6**(4): p. 6-11.
30. MacGillivray, A., *Knowledge management education at Royal Roads University.* Competitive Intelligence Magazine, 2003. **6**(4): p. 37-40.
31. McGonagle, J.J., *Competitive intelligence is not knowledge management.* Competitive Intelligence Magazine, 2006. **9**(4): p. 26-27.
32. Larrat, P., *Educating or building awareness on Competitive Intelligence?*, in *Society of Competitive Intelligence Professionals 2006 Annual International Conference & Exhibition.* 2006: Orlando, Florida
33. Trimberger, K.K. *Preparing for the CI role: a student's perspective.* Information Outlook. 2000 [cited Feb Available from: http://www.sla.org/content/Shop/Information/infoonline/2000/feb00/trimberg.cfm

34. Papik, R. *Reasons for Competitive Intelligence Topics in Curriculum of Information and Library Schools.* in *Proceedings Bobcatsss 15th Symposium, Marketing of Information Services*. 2007. Prague.
35. Davis, G.A. *Competitive intelligence and librarianship. Suite101.com.* 2006 13-12-2006 [cited; Available from: http://www.suite101.com/article.cfm/9460/61236.
36. Shelfer, K.M., *CI education that advances CI practice.* Competitive Intelligence Magazine., 2003. **6**(4): p. 31-36.
37. Shelfer, K.M. and A. Goodrum, *Competitive Intelligence as an Extension of Library Education.* Journal of Education for Library and Information Science., 2000. **41**(4): p. 353-361.

An Open Adaptive Virtual Museum of Informatics History in Siberia

Victor N. Kasyanov

A.P. Ershov Institute of Informatics Systems / Novosibirsk State University, Novosibirsk, 630090, RUSSIA, kvn@iis.nsk.su

Abstract: In the paper, the SVM project, which is under development at the A.P. Ershov Institute of Informatics Systems and is aimed at development of an open adaptive virtual museum of informatics history in Siberia, is described. It is assumed that this museum can be used as accessible annals of the Siberian computer science history, which can be written by active users. As an open adaptive virtual museum, SVM is full of great teaching and learning opportunities for a wide audience, from schoolchild to professional researcher.

Keywords: Informatics history, Open adaptive virtual museum, Siberian School of Informatics

1 Introduction

The history of informatics (or computer science), as the history of any other science, is an important and inseparable part of this science. During previous years, the teaching of the history of computer science was introduced into the computing curriculum of many Western universities. A special IFIP Joint Task Group has published a comprehensive report containing a number of valuable methodological instructions [10].

At the same time, informatics history of the Eastern Europe and the USSR was practically unknown in the Western Europe, although some works on this problem have been published [5, 8]. In 1996, the IEEE Computer Society, in connection with the 50th anniversary of its founding, presented the Computer Pioneer Award (see Figure 1) to sixteen scientists from Central and Eastern Europe countries. Among those included the outstanding Russian scientist academician Alexej Lyapunov (see Figure 2) who "developed the first theory of operator methods for abstract programming and founded Soviet cybernetics and programming" [3].

Research in programming in Siberia has been started after Alexej Lyapunov and his disciple Andrei Ershov (see Figure 3) had arrived to the Novosibirsk

---

Please use the following format when citing this chapter:

Kasyanov, V.N., 2008, in IFIP International Federation for Information Processing, Volume 269; *History of Computing and Education 3*; John Impagliazzo; (Boston: Springer), pp. 129–146.

Academgorodok (at the beginning of the 60s of the last century). Academician Andrei Ershov and his disciples have founded the Siberian School of informatics that was the third one in the USSR, after Moscow and Kiev. Now, many years after its founder Andrei Ershov died [1], it keeps on playing an important role in spite of all these difficulties endured by the Russian science and education. This gives us an opportunity to investigate independently formation and development of informatics in Siberia, namely, in the Novosibirsk Scientific Centre, against the Russian and world scenes.

Figure 1 Computer Pioneer Medal

In the paper, our project SVM of the virtual museum of informatics history in Siberia is described [12, 14, 20].

During about fifty years, informatics as a science developed in Siberia very much, but for this period some active participants and witnesses of its development died, many facts have been forgotten and something is not known yet. So, it is very interesting to study and to represent in structural form, using some methods of informatics itself, the history of informatics that is a result of activities of the current generation of people. We assume that the SVM museum will be open and can be used as accessible annals of the Siberian computer science history, which can be written by active users.

Now the electronic or virtual museums available via the www are being widely developed along with traditional ones (see, for example, [9, 15, 17 – 22]). Moreover, there is a standard computer-to-computer protocol for information retrieval that specifies communications between a client and server for purposes of searching and retrieving of the cultural heritage information [16].

However, most of the museums presented now in www are traditional hypermedia systems and give the same information and navigation to all users.

At the same time, the SVM museum is intended for use by different categories of users, and museum visitors with different preferences, goals, knowledge and interests may need different information and may use different ways for navigation. Therefore, we give a particular attention to adaptation problems in our project.

SVM provides a free common access to pages of the true history of computer science in Siberia. As an open adaptive virtual museum, it is full of great teaching and learning opportunities for wide audience from schoolchild to professional researcher.

Figure 2 Alexej Lyapunov

The rest of the paper is as follows. In Section 2, we outline the history of informatics in Siberia. The conception of open adaptive virtual museums is discussed in Section 3. The structure of the virtual museum SVM and we briefly consider its content in Section 4. In Section 5, we describe the users of SVM. The user interface and interface adaptation of the SVM museum appear in Section 6 and 7. Section 8 is a conclusion.

2 Andrei Ershov and Siberian School of Informatics

Academician Andrei Ershov (19 April 1931 - 8 December 1988) was one of the Soviet pioneers in the field of theoretical and systems programming, a founder of the Siberian School of Computer Science.

His significant contributions to establishing informatics as a new branch of science and a new phenomenon of the social life are widely recognized in Russia and abroad. More than thirty years ago, he began to experiment with teaching programming in the secondary school. Initially unrecognized, these attempts evolved into the notion of computer literacy [6] and resulted in introducing a course on informatics and computing machinery in Soviet schools [7].

A.P. Ershov's fundamental research on program schematology and theory of compilation inspired a large number of his students and successors. He investigated a broad spectrum of systems programming problems: implementation of DO statement in programming languages; hash addressing with application to the common sub-expression elimination; program schemata over distributed memory; the theory and algorithms for global memory optimization, etc. His book "A Programming Programme for the BESM Computer" was one of the world's first monographs on automatic programming.

Figure 3 Andrey Erchov

In 1958, the Department of Programming was organized at the Institute of Mathematics in Novosibirsk and the late Academician Andrei Ershov was appointed its head.

The first project of the Department was a design and implementation of the Algol-like algorithmic language ALPHA [4]. The ALPHA system was the first in the world optimizing programming system (an optimizing compiler) for the languages more complex than FORTRAN. The Algol-60 system simultaneously developed by Hawkins and Huxtable in the UK, with functional capabilities similar to those of the ALPHA system, was never implemented. It is worth noting, because at that time many specialists contested the very possibility of constructing compilers for the languages more complex than FORTRAN. The ALPHA system turned out to be a constructive proof of this possibility, which essentially removed barriers on the way of designing new languages with more rich semantics.

Figure 4 Andrey Erchov with his disciples (from left to right): Viktor Sabelfeld, Igor Pottosin, Vadim Kotov, and Victor Kasyanov

In 1964, the Department was transferred to the newly organized Computer Center headed by Academician Gury Marchuk, former (and the last) President of the USSR Academy of Sciences. The Department was growing, extending research from the compiler design to broad aspects of system programming, theoretical informatics, experimental computer architecture, AI and educational informatics. As a result, the Siberian School of Informatics has been formed [1].

In 1990, on the basis of the Department, the Institute of Informatics System headed by Vadim Kotov (see Figure 4), a disciple of Andrei Ershov, was organized. In 1995, the Institute became A.P. Ershov Institute of Informatics Systems.

3 Conception of Open Adaptive Virtual Museum

With the advent of the digital age and the Web, museums and cultural heritage institutions are rethinking their roles [13].

An increasing number of museums make the decision to maintain a website (a *digital museum*) in order to provide useful information and attract new visitors. The advantage of digital museums is clear. The visitors of a digital museum can enjoy cultural relicts without a restriction of time and place, and complete safety of artifacts is guaranteed. The visitors have the opportunity to see precious cultural relicts that cannot be exhibited in a conventional way for reasons of safety or security. Furthermore, with the help of multimedia interaction, the visitors can even "touch" or "manipulate" the objects, which would be important for professionals.

Along with the "classic" digital museums, which are websites of real museums, there are so-called virtual museums [9, 15, 18-22]. A *virtual museum* in this context refers to a repository of digital cultural and scientific resources that can be accessed and used in any time from anywhere via the Internet. It means it is a website (a digital museum) that can but does not have to have any corresponding real museum and contains virtual exhibits being multimedia digital representations of any artifacts without a restriction on their nature or current state.

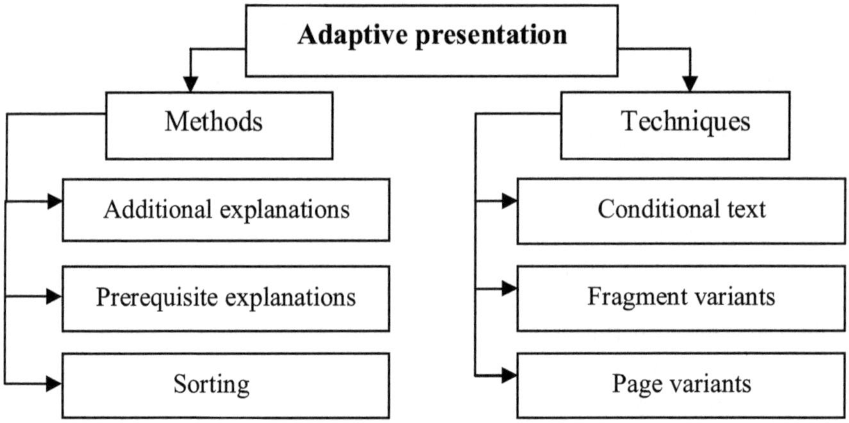

Figure 5 Adaptive presentation

From the viewpoint of museum visitors, a real museum is an environment for excursions and expositions. On the other hand, museums are cultural heritage institutions intended to support collecting, research, making catalogues and exhibiting artifacts, but museum visitors cannot take part in this important museum work. We believe that virtual digital museums can be "open museums" that allow extending this museum work to a wide range of virtual museum users. We assume that it is useful that a museum user can propose a presentation of some real artifact as a virtual exhibit to an open virtual museum. In addition, an open virtual museum may also have a facility to supply exhibits with author descriptions, to offer guided tours around the museum, and to make a curatorial exposition. These possibilities are very important for modern history museums.

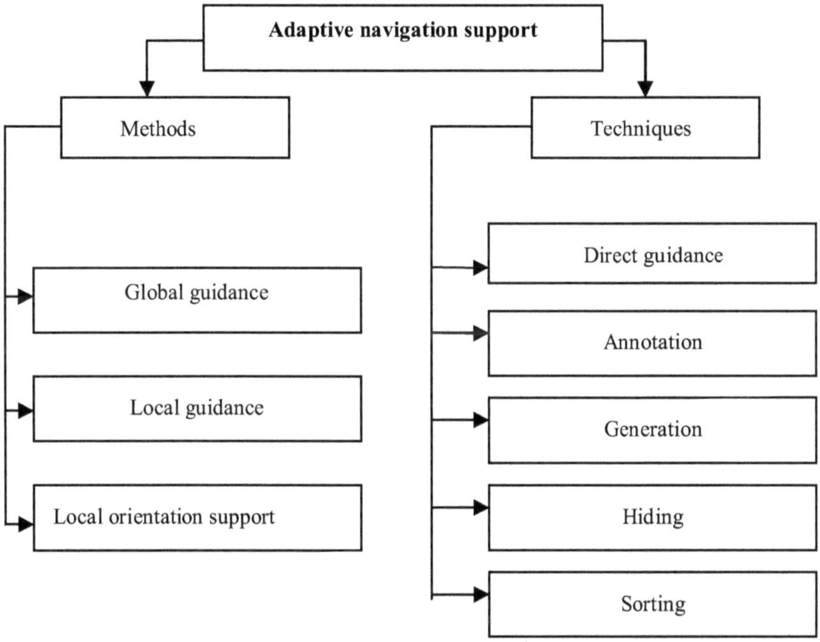

Figure 6 Adaptive navigation support

An *open virtual museum* [12] is a hypermedia system intended to be both an accessible repository for artifact collections and a cultural heritage institution supporting the collective work of many people, which are interested in collecting, annotating, organizing, research, making catalogues and exhibiting these artifacts.

Adaptive hypermedia is an alternative to the traditional "one-size-fits-all" approach in the development of hypermedia systems [2].

Adaptive hypermedia systems (AHS) are all hypermedia and hypertext systems, which reflect some specific features of the user, such as preferences, knowledge, and interests in the user model and use this model for adaptation of different visible system aspects to the user.

AHS provides adaptive presentation (adaptation of the hyper-document content) and adaptive navigation support (adaptation of the hyperlink structure).

The aim of adaptive presentation methods is adaptation of the page content that the user addresses to her/his knowledge, preferences, interests, goals and other characteristics. The main methods of adaptive text presentation are additional, prerequisite and comparative explanations, explanation variants and sorting

(Figure 5). They used the following techniques for implementation of these methods: conditional text, stretchtext, fragment and page variants, and frame-based technique.

The aim of adaptive navigation support methods is to help users to find the way in the hyperspace by adapting the hyperlink presentation to the goals, knowledge and other characteristics of the user. Adaptive navigation support methods are used to achieve the following adaptation goals: to provide global and local guidance, global and local orientation support, and managing personalized views (Figure 6). To implement these methods, the following techniques are used: direct guidance, link sorting, hiding, annotation, generation, and map adaptation.

At the abstract level, AHS consists of the three components: domain model, user model, and adaptation model.

The domain model (DM) describes the information content and link structure of application domain at the conceptual level (using a set of concepts and concept relationships represented as a directed acyclic graph).

The user model (UM) represents user's preferences, knowledge, goals, browsing history, and other relevant aspects. The system acquires user's information in two ways: explicitly (from the user) or implicitly (tracking the user interaction with the system). The main part of UM is representation of the user's domain knowledge using DM concepts (by means of the overlay model).

The base of adaptive functionality of AHS is the adaptation model (AM) consisting of adaptation rules that form connection between DM and UM and determine the representation of the generated information.

Open adaptive virtual museums can support accessibility and active use of digital cultural and scientific resources for everybody without a restriction on time and place. They can bring several benefits:

Collective work of many people that are interested in collecting, annotating, organizing, research, making catalogues and exhibiting any artifacts;

The museum is an arena where many physical constrains do not apply, where technology can allow each visitor to organize virtual artifacts into an individual exhibition or tour;

Virtual exhibitions that cannot be organized otherwise, e.g. a comprehensive exhibition of an artist whose works are distributed all over the world in public and private collections;

Private collections and artifacts can be made available for public, taking into account various levels of anonymity for the owner – anonymous, semi-anonymous (i.e. available for discussions under a nickname), non-anonymous, available for a visit, etc;

Exhibitions on demand can be organized for visitors;

Adaptive guided tours can be provided for each individual visitor taking into account her/his interests, preferences and constraints (like time).

4 Architecture of the SVM Museum

At present, databases (DBs) of our web-based museum SVM provide storage and processing of the information about the following objects: publications, archive documents, projects, data about scientists in informatics, scientific teams, various events concerning informatics history, conferences, and computers (see Figure 7). All the above objects are the *exhibits* of our virtual museum.

Every exhibit has the following main attributes: a Unique Universal Identifier (UUID) of an object, a name, sometimes a date, a brief description (or an annotation), a full description (or a file), a name of a person who presented this exhibit, the date of its addition, the possibility and permission of its modification and participation in exhibitions.

We can represent a set of exhibits united according to the thematic, chronological, or typological criteria as an *exhibition* or a *tour* (or an *excursion*). Both an exhibition and a tour have the following attributes: UUID, a name, a name of a person who created it, brief description, and reference(s) to the file(s) representing it contents. The main differences between an exhibition and a tour are the following:

- A tour is composed of one section (a file), while an exhibition can consist of several sections (exhibitions or sub-exhibitions).
- A tour is a story about the museum (elapsing in time) followed by demonstration of its exhibits in a definite order. A tour, for example, may be a clip or a presentation for MS PowerPoint and may be not only in the on-line mode but sometimes off-line. In contrast to a tour, an exhibition consists of exhibits that a visitor is looking at by himself and only on-line. Usually, they provide several ways of navigation, including a free movement among exhibits.

All exhibitions (and tours) are divided into *permanent* and *temporary* ones. They designed a *hall of exhibitions* and *a hall of tours* as accessible to all users of the museum.

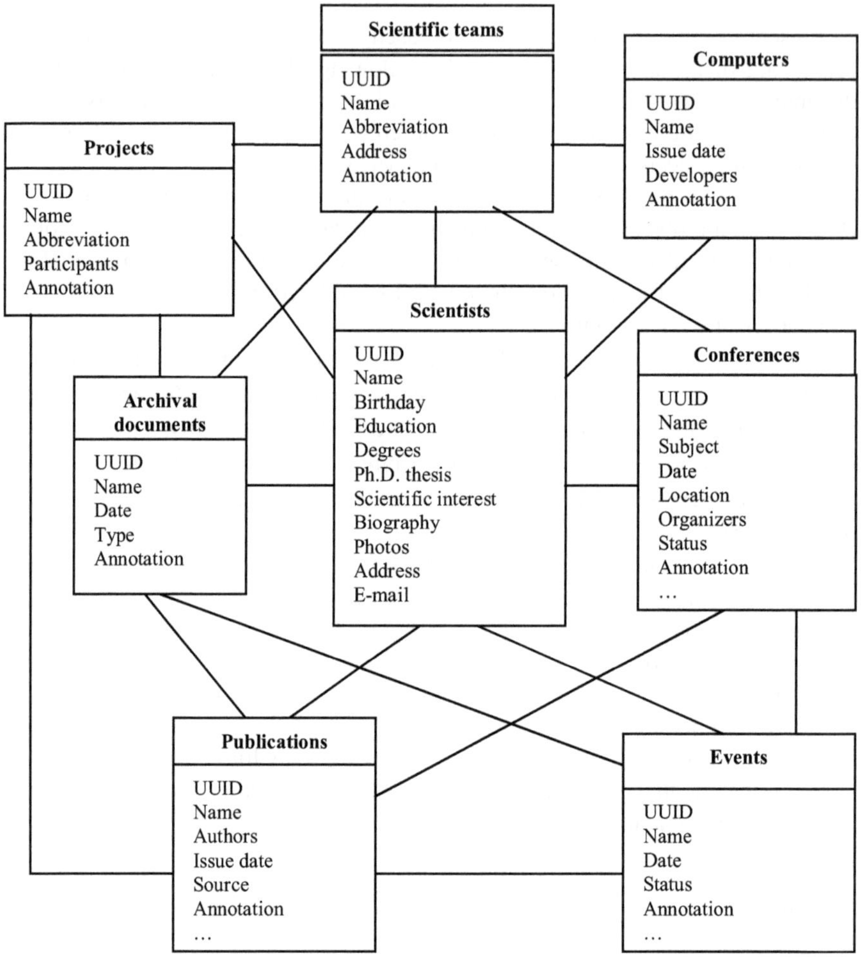

Figure 7 The net of exhibits

There are also restricted halls in our museum (see Figure 8): the library, the archive, the chronicle, the halls devoted to scientists in informatics, scientific teams, projects, computers, conferences, the hall of new exhibits and the hall of preparation of exhibitions and excursions. These halls are accessible only to registered users of the museum.

The *library* consists of books, articles and so on. In addition to the general exhibit attributes, each library exhibit has a list of authors and other attributes.

The *archive* consists of text, graphic, audio, and video materials. The *chronicle of events* contains a description of the most remarkable events of informatics history in Siberia.

The *hall of scientists in informatics* presents information about the prominent scientists in informatics. In addition to the general information, it provides the following data about scientists: their education, scientific degrees, titles and posts, scientific interests, the text of the biography, photos, the main publications, and projects.

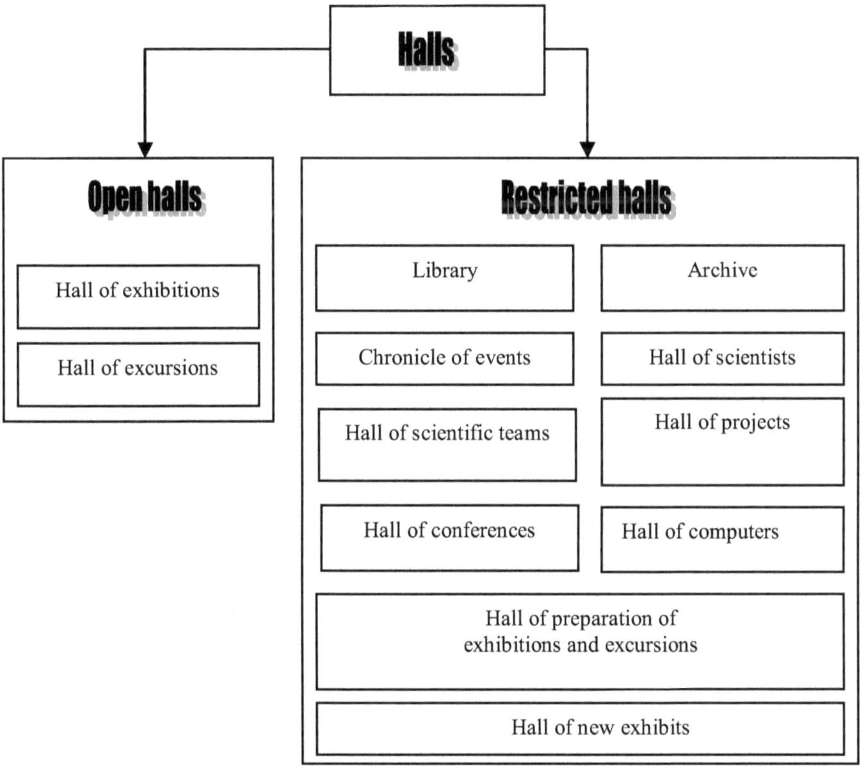

Figure 8 Architecture of SVM: halls

The *hall of scientific teams* presents information about groups, laboratories, and institutes. Along with the general attributes, each team has its address, etc.

The *hall of projects* provides information about projects in informatics, including the dates of its beginning and finishing.

The *hall of computers* shows the computers that the Siberian Division of the Russian Academy of Sciences used and created. In addition, each exhibit has the name of the designer and the photo.

The *hall of conferences* contains the following information about each scientific event: where and when it was held, its status, and the general exhibit information.

They place new entries to the museum (added by users) in the *hall of new exhibits*. Exhibitions and excursions created by users of the museum are being composed in the *hall of preparation of exhibitions and excursions*.

5 Users of the SVM museum

All users of our web-based museum are divided in two main categories: unregistered users (*visitors*) and registered ones (*specialists*) with different level of access to information resources (see Figure 9).

Visitors have access only to the part of museum information that is open for public access (e.g., in the form of excursions and exhibitions). In this case, all resources are accessible only for review and search. Visitors are divided in two subcategories depending on their level of knowledge in subject domain: *beginners* and *experts*. Beginners have an opportunity to look only at tours, and experts can also look at exhibitions and electronic conferences of users.

Specialists have access to reviewing all information resources of our museum, including restricted halls closed for public access; they can also take part in electronic conferences and write in a visitors' book. All specialists are divided in two main groups depending on their level of access to resources: *simple specialists* and *museum employees*.

A group of simple specialists consists of *volunteers*, *tour guides,* and *exhibition curator/designers*. Volunteers have permissions to add new exhibits of any type. Tour guides may create their own tours, and exhibition curators/designers can create new exhibitions. Simple specialists have no permissions to modify the museum databases.

They present a group of museum employees as a hierarchical structure, with a *director* (or the *senior manager*) at its very top. He has full authority to administrate the museum DBs, including DB of museum users.

The second level of the hierarchy consists of *managers* (or *administrators*) of the corresponding museum resources. The director appoints them – the head of exhibitions, the chief tour guide, the chief librarian, the chief archivist, the chief historian, the chief biographer, the chief expert on scientific teams, the chief planner, the chief engineer, the chief secretary. They have full authority to administrate DBs of the corresponding resource types. They also control specialists working with DBs of corresponding types of resources.

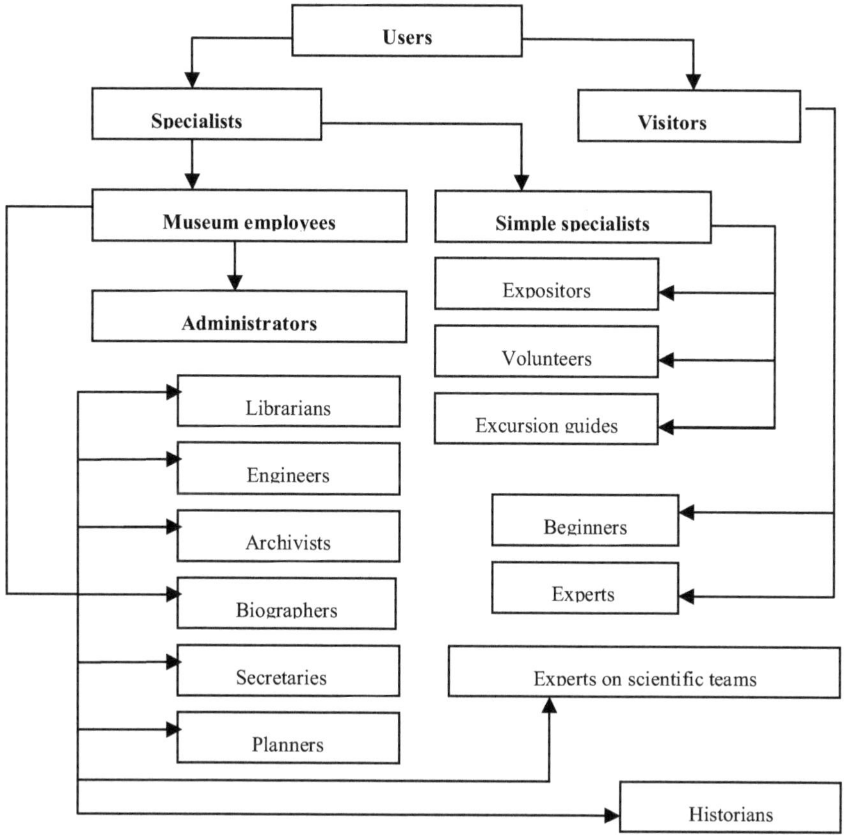

Figure 9 Users of the SVM museum

The third level of the hierarchical structure includes museum employees appointing by the managers of the corresponding types of resources: librarians, archivists, historians, biographers, experts on scientific teams, planners, engineers, and *secretaries*. They have limited rights to change DBs of the corresponding resource types.

6 User Interface

Current implementation of the DBs of our virtual museum provides storage and processing of data about the following objects: publications, archival documents, projects, events, scientific teams, informaticians, computers, and conferences. At present, the hypermedia interface of the DB for information filling of our virtual museum has been designed and implemented. It allows one to review, search, insert and update data on above objects and to link them together. An interface for registration and authentication of the museum users and for user electronic conferences has been implemented.

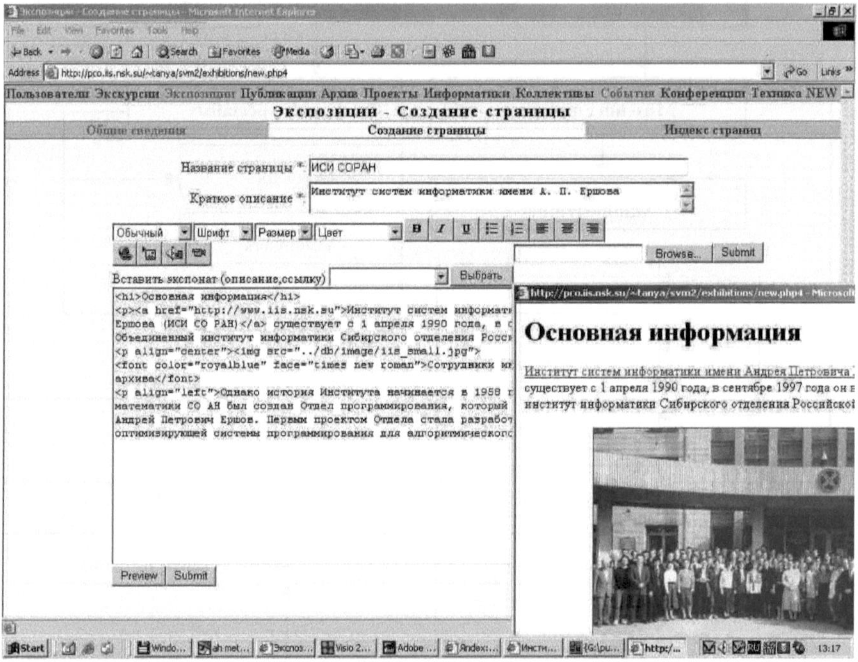

Figure 10 The interface for insertions and updates

The following main functions are supported by the interface: registration of a new visitor, search mechanism by key criteria, interface for insertion and update, interface for interconnection between objects, interface for holding a user electronic conference.

The registration of a new visitor consists in filling a special form. It contains obligatory (a user name, e-mail, a password for entry to a system) and supplementary (a country, an index, an address) fields. If users want to contribute information to the museum (to add exhibits, make up excursions or exhibitions), they should mark the corresponding points in the registration form. A login (a user name for entry to the system) is generated automatically by a special algorithm and sent to the user by email. The director or a corresponding administrator completes the registration of a new specialist.

A search mechanism by key criteria is implemented; there is an opportunity to carry out a pattern search over all DBs. It is possible to choose the form in which the search results are represented. Brief information about objects and a reference to complete one is put out as a search result.

An interface for insertion and update is implemented for all resource types of our museum (see Figure 10). Data input is realized with filling of the corresponding forms depending on the resource type: forms for input of the general and additional information, and forms for linking objects together. UUID is automatically generated and assigned for every new added object. The following information about added object is automatically stored in the DB: the name of a person who added the object, the date of addition, possibility of modification and taking part in exhibitions, modification permissions. An interface for data modification is implemented via data edition in the corresponding fields of the form.

An interface for interconnection between objects and linking them together is implemented. Interconnection between objects is implemented as a choice of corresponding objects (that are needed to connect with this object) from a list of all possible objects (for each object type). Information links between objects are generated as hyperlinks from the given object to objects connected with it.

An interface for holding a user electronic conference is implemented. Unregistered users can only view the conference information, while registered ones can send information to the conference. This interface supports all standard functions of electronic conferences: sending a new message, receiving an answer and search for messages according to some key criteria.

7 Interface Adaptation

For adaptive information, presentation in our museum SVM we use both the adaptive presentation methods, such as additional and prerequisite explanations and sorting, and the adaptive navigation support methods, such as direct guidance, link sorting, hiding, annotation, and generation. The model of a registered user of the SVM consists of tree parts: the model of categories, the model of knowledge and the model of preferences (see Figure 11).

The model of categories is supported for all registered users, the model of knowledge and preferences - for all categories of users except the group of museum employees. The model of categories represents the access permissions to the museum information resources. They implement it as a static stereotype model (a set of attribute-value pairs). The names of types of the DB resources are used as attributes of the model; the access permissions to these resources (view, insert, modify and their combinations) are the attribute values. A stereotype of the same name, characterized with specified attribute values, corresponds to each user category.

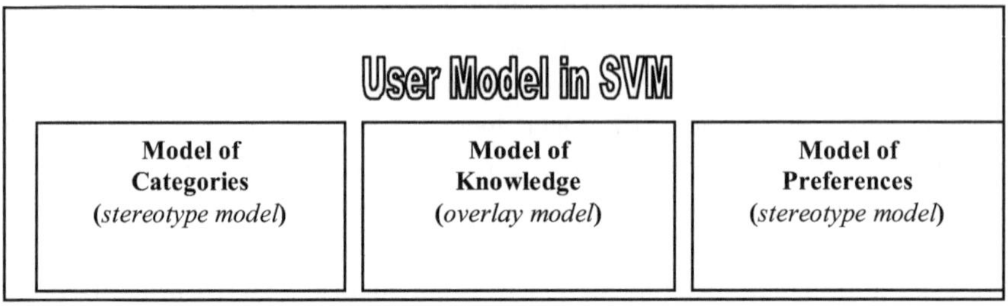

Figure 11 User model

They use the model of knowledge to model the user domain knowledge. It is supposed to implement a model of knowledge as an overlay model based on the structural domain model. They use a structural model for representation of presented by the museum information as a structure of interconnected concepts and relations between them (acyclic graph). The overlay model is intended to present the user knowledge as an overlay of the domain model. The overlay model for a user is a table structure. This structure determines the values of the following attributes: knowledge of concept (studied, not studied), reading (read, not read), ready for reading (ready, not ready) for each domain concept. The overlay model is a dynamic one: it is automatically updated when a user reviews the information.

The model of preferences represents different user preferences, in particular, a method of information presentation (using only a text, graphics, audio, video and so on). A static stereotype model implements it. The attributes of this model are the methods of information presentation mentioned above, and their values are true or false.

8 Conclusion

The conception of an open adaptive virtual museum that supports accessibility and active use of digital cultural and scientific resources for everybody without a restriction on time and place has been considered, and the SVM project of an open adaptive virtual museum of informatics history in Siberia has been presented.

The main purpose of creating SVM is to save historical and cultural heritage, the history of creation and development of computer science in Siberia. One may use it as accessible annals of the Siberian computer science history, which can be written by active users.

SVM is also intended to provide a free common access to pages of the true history of computer science in Siberia, and therefore to increase cultural and educational level of people. It can also serve as an important teaching and learning tool for a wide audience, from schoolchild to professional researcher. The museum is an arena where many physical constraints do not apply, where technology can allow each visitor to organize virtual artifacts into an individual exhibition or tour. For example, it can be an individual gallery and museum to every teacher, where that teacher is a curator.

The solutions here considered can be used in the development of other virtual museums related to modern history or needed in the collective work of people from different places. They can also be useful in the development of digital websites of real museums to support integration of knowledge and skills of museum workers from different museums.

Acknowledgments: The author is thankful to all his colleagues, taking part in works related to elaboration of the SVM museum. The SVM project is based on informatics history pages of the Web-system SIMICS [11] and is supported by the Russian Foundation for the Humanities (grant N 02-05-12010).

References

1. Bjorner D, Kotov V (1991) Images of Programming. Dedicated to the Memory of A.P. Ershov, North-Holland, Amsterdam
2. Brusilovsky P (2001) Adaptive hypermedia. User Modelling and User-Adapted Interaction 11: 87-110
3. CS Recognizes Pioneers in Central and Eastern Europe (1998) IEEE Computer 6 : 79-84
4. Ershov AP (1966) ALPHA – an automatic programming system of high efficiency. J ACM 13:17-24
5. Ershov AP (1975) A history of computing in the USSR. Datamation 21: 80-88
6. Ershov AP (1981) Programming, the second literacy. In: Computer and education. Proc. IFIP TC-3 3rd World Conf. on Computer in Education (WCCE 81), North-Holland, Amsterdam, Pt. I, 1-17.
7. Ershov AP, Monakhov VM, et al (1985) Foundations of informatics and computing machinery: experimental text-book for secondary school, Prosveshchenije, Moscow, Pt.1. (In Russian).
8. Ershov AP, Shura-Bura MR (1980) The early development of programming in the USSR. In: A History of Computing in the Twentieth Century, Acad. Press, New York, p. 137-196.
9. European Virtual Computer Museum. Development of Computer Science and Technologies in Ukraine. URL: http://www.icfcst.kiev.ua/museum/
10. Impagliazzo J, Campbell-Kelly M, et al (1999) History in the Computing Curriculum. IEEE Annals of the History of Computing 21: 4-16
11. Kasyanov VN (2000) SIMICS: information system on informatics history. In: Proc. Intern. Conf. on Educational Uses of Information and Communication Technologies. The 16th IFIP World Computer Congress, PHEI, Beijing, p 168
12. Kasyanov VN (2005) SVM – Siberian Virtual Museum of Informatics History. In: Innovation and the Knowledge Economy: Issues, Applications, Case Studies, IOS Press, Amsterdam, Part 2, pp 1014-1021
13. Kasyanov VN (2006) Museums and Internet: New Possibilities. In: Informational techniques in Humanitarian Researches, NSU Press, Novosibirsk, Issue 10, pp 88-96 (In Russian)

14. Kasyanov VN, Nesgovorova GP, Volyanskaya TA (2003) Adaptive hypermedia and its application to development of virtual museum of Siberian informatics history. In: Proc. 5th Intern. Conf. PSI-2003, Novosibirsk, pp 10-12 (In Russian)
15. On-line Museum of Computer History. Project of MGTU. URL: http://museum.iu4.bmstu.ru/project.shtml
16. The CIMI Profile Release 1.0H A Z39.50 Profile for Cultural Heritage Information. URL: http://www.cimi.org/old_site/documents/HarmonizedProfile/HarmonProfile1.htm
17. The Ershov Arhchive. URL: http://www.iis.nsk.su
18. The Russian Virtual Computer Museum. Project of Eduard Projdakov. URL: http://www.computer-museum.ru/
19. The Virtual Museum of Manchester Computing. URL: http://www.computer50.org/kgill/
20. Virtual Museum of Informatics History in Siberia. URL: http://pco.iis.nsk.su/svm/
21. Virtual School Museum of Computer Science. URL: http://schools.keldysh.ru/sch444/MUSEUM/
22. Virtuelles Museums der Informatik. URL: http://www.fbi.fh-darmstadt.de/~vmi/

ICT for Success of Education from an Indian Perspective

Rakesh Mohan Bhatt

Dept. of Computer Science, HNB Garhwal University, Srinagar (Garhwal) 247 174 India; rmbhatt77@yahoo.com

Abstract: India has been trying to uphold the status of education for many years. However, due to poor educational infrastructure, social segregation, and non-conducive economic conditions, maximum learners are deprived of education. India has a large number of students from primary to higher levels. Only around 40 percent can improve to gain their higher studies after completing their primary or middle level education. Due to the convergence, electronic-informational environment has been emerging at a very fast rate. Now, the education system seems to follow its use in delivering and managing the education in a need-based way. There is an up surge of computer and Internet connections in schools. Almost every university will be creating its own network and will be under a single net in the coming future. Certainly, these efforts will make the education in a cost-effective manner. Further, creation of the collaborative teaching and learning environment is essential so that the dropout rate remains low and the requirement of increasing number of learners and teaching load can reach a resolution by ICT means. The present paper discusses the education scenario, the upcoming efforts in the ICT developments and need of the collaborative environment for success of education in India.

Keywords: ICT, Education, India

1 Introduction

Indian has twenty-eight states and seven Union Territories (UTs) that cover a population of 1.065 billion. The total literacy rate has increased to 65.8 percent. India has the second largest elementary education system in the world, having an intake around 1.5 million children of the age group 6-14. There are 324 universities, 16,000 colleges for higher education enrolling about 9.28 million people. Thus, India has a large number of students from primary to higher levels (www.education.nic.in). However, conditions deprive maximum learners of an

---

Please use the following format when citing this chapter:

Bhatt, R.M., 2008, in IFIP International Federation for Information Processing, Volume 269; *History of Computing and Education 3*; John Impagliazzo; (Boston: Springer), pp. 147–155.

education. After completing the primary or middle level education, around 40 percent learners fail to seek a higher education.

The applications of amalgamation of ICTs will have far-reaching implications in shaping the society. Due to this convergence, electronic-informational environments are emerging at a very fast rate. The education system seems to follow its use in delivering and managing the education in a need-based way. Further, excellent efforts are in progress in telecommunication services for creating and accelerating the open and collaborative learning environment. Thus, a new educational scenario is emerging by applying and executing ICT services. Hence, the definitions of formal and non-formal education systems are somewhat being diluted, and existence of an ICT-based education services are emerging. To elevate its status by analyzing some points, viz. education scenario, emerging ICT efforts, challenges and outcomes, respective issues emerged and discussions and conclusions have been made, as we will see in the following sections.

2 Education Scenario

If we look into the history, the growth of enrollment in primary, upper primary, secondary, and senior secondary levels have occurred 6, 14, and 20 times during the years 1950-1951 to 2001-2002. An increase of 24 and 12 times in the number in the higher education institutions providing general and professional education, respectively, were recorded and ten times the number in universities has been observed during this period. The government spends approximately 4% of the GNP on education whereas as per the recommendation of National Policy on Education, the aim is to achieve 6%, which seems very far. Several efforts in the past have been recorded (Bhatt 1998, 2006) but still more efforts are required.

India has around 50% of its population below the age of 25, of which 25% are children. A large number of the children fail to complete their primary level of education. This dropout rate falls in the range of 50-60 percent of the total intake. According to the report of the World Bank, about 60.7 million children of age group 6 to 10 years have joined the schools whereas 30.2 million could not obtain the opportunity. Further, for higher education, only 6% (Deshmukh 1999) falling in the age group of 17-24 years was able to enroll. If we analyze the development in the literacy improvements, we find that India had 18.33 percent literacy rate at the time of Independence in 1947; which has now been increased to 65.8 percent. Nevertheless, India still has one-third strength of the non-literate of the world's illiterate mass. This ratio is very high and estimates the figure around 400 million. If we observe globally, we examine that since 1960, students numbers have increased by 6.5 times until 1995 (Gautam, 1999). Now about 16,000 colleges (1849 for women) have the enrolment of 9.28 million and the faculty strength is around 0.436 million.

The plan to pool the learners' stream right from the beginning, i.e., from the primary school level, the scheme should be very well thought and analyzed to take the benefits of ICT services. The chain of dropouts from primary to higher level can be very well controlled and checked. During the year 1998 (www.education.nic.in), the strength of children in the primary schools was 106 million, and only 39 million students were studying in the middle standard and 23 million at the secondary followed by 6.5 million at the tertiary level. As per the Institute of Applied Manpower Research (IAMR), New Delhi, until 1997 India had approximately 0.6 million primary schools, 0.15 million middle schools and 0.1 million high/higher secondary schools. We also observe that the dropout rate is very high at the primary level.

To alleviate the increasing dropout rate, students should have to be positively motivated. By providing the better options available with the ICT aided services, the country can also develop and maintain this affinity. However, if the commitment to fulfill the objectives set for the education systems comes from the learners as well as from the education providers, then success is achievable. This socially and vocationally relevant new mode of learning should enable education to keep high the literacy rate and simultaneously keep the rate of dropouts. We observe that under the influence of ICT, distance education has been taking a considerable lead. Only 12% (Kishore, 1998) of the learners were being catered to at the higher education level through distance education providers; nonetheless, with the ICT enabled services, the number of learners is increasing. This mode of learning can also be covered under the net-based learning (Sj0helle, 2005) in addition to the conventional system.

3 Emerging ICT Efforts

ICT has imparted strength to all organizations. Thus, innovation through ICT has occurred and taken for the developmental works as a necessary tool (Talera et.al., 1995). Therefore, developmental issues, which are difficult to analyze and understand particularly in India where diversity exists in many forms, ICT can help significantly, taking into account the fact that ICT itself does forward the solutions. Under the pressure of growing population and increasing demand for ICT enabled information in India, it is required to look for the new generation of technologies that deliver information to a host of potential users including researchers, educators, business groups, and policy makers.

Until 1999, India had 75 million televisions in households with an estimated 362 million TV viewers. Further, estimates report that only 7.1% of the population has a telephone, 2.4% has a mobile, 0.72% has the PC, and only 1.75% of the population has an internet connection (Vikas, 2004). Some years back personal computer market has shown the growth of 70% (Chandragupta, 2000) which is ever increasing since then. By March 2000, internet connection holders were only at 1.2 million; this has now reached around 10 million. Some years back, India had 3.6 PCs per 1000 people as compared to 362 in the US. To increase this ratio, IT task force of the Government of India (Sesagiri, 2000) has envisaged raising this ratio to 1 PC per 50 people by the year 2008. India's IT spending is about 0.7 per cent of GDP.

Under the operation knowledge (www.nic.in), the government's IT Action Plan envisages - IT for all by 2008. In this connection, the government launched to have an internet facility in all educational institutions in all states. The government also has programs on the anvil to create SMART schools and virtual institutions. More than 1000 pilot projects are under operation by the government for spreading IT among the masses. It has spent about $14.55 billion in these projects. They estimate the success rate at 40%. The initiatives under these projects are like the Vidya Vahini project for providing connectivity to Government Senior Secondary Schools and the Gyan Vahini project to upgrade the IT infrastructure in the higher learning institutions by 2007. Many other initiatives have also been taken such as the Working Group on IT for masses (www.itformasses.nic.in); upgrading the Education and Research Network (ERNET) which connects various universities and regional engineering colleges (RECs) through a high speed network; enactment of the Information Technology (IT) Act of 2000; the Media Lab Asia project for taking IT to the masses. With these efforts, the internet subscriber base is expected to increase to 35 million by 2007 from the earlier level of seven million. It also envisions generating seven million jobs in the sector by 2008. The Department of IT has also instituted a computer literacy excellence award for schools (www.bhashaindia.com/trivia/trivia.aspx). Other initiatives such as Gyan Nidhi (www.cdacindia.com), Vidhya Nidhi (www.vidhyanidhi.org.in), and the Indian National Digital Library in Engineering Science and Technology consortium (INDEST) have emerged and they are gaining popularity among the masses.

Further, to strengthen the mission to disseminate the education, the government launched EDUSAT, an Indian educational satellite, in the year 2004. This provides audio and video communication facilities. In this effort, 58 institutions have access to SITs by the ISRO and UGC to cover 17 regional centres, 12 academic staff colleges, and about 28 universities. This network will be expanding its services in near future (Sharma, 2005). Very recently, to increase the enrollment in the higher education using ICT, the planning commission for the production of knowledgeware and the creation of new infrastructures had allocated more than 100 billion dollars to this endeavor. Efforts are also taking place from the Consortium for Educational Communication (CEC) for the distribution of Vyas Higher Education Channel (Kem, 2008) to enhance the reach of the educational communication at the most remote locations. To deliver the knowledge, courseware on higher education using ICT modes, UGC-CEC has 17

Educational Multimedia Research Centres (EMRCs) located in the different parts of the country. Currently, it covers around 50 areas of interest with the help of its 15,000 repository of programs (www.cec-uge.org).

Recently, the University Grants Commission has decided to establish "A UGC Network" named as UGCNET to provide a seamless, broadband, scalable nation wide inter university link up and create virtual enhancement of the academic structure. University level UGCNET has also begun to cover all universities under an umbrella. To date about 183 universities are covered under this net.

4 Outcome

According to the World Education Report-1998, India had around 45.88% of the world illiterates of the age group of 15+. However, the literacy graph has shown an upward progress of about 11% from the 1991census to 1998 census. In a significant move, three years back, the government had passed the Act 2002, enacted in Dec 2002 that has made free and compulsory education as a fundamental right of all children in the age group 6-14. This step will eventually increase the demand for higher education too. Thus, the tenth five-year plan from the year 2002 to 2007 has recommended about one million teachers for classes 1 through 8. An enhancement of 6% to 10% enrolment in the universities is also expected by the year 2007.

The project "Education for All" has fostered this requirement. Recently, the Data Quest magazine reported that the share of IT area is about 7%. During last year, the country sold about 4 million PCs. The broadband facility started in India in 2000; however, its wide use is still awaited although the users have now started accessing the internet using wireless technology but in small numbers.

To modernize the facilities, extra financial support is required to meet the ever-increasing pressure of new entrants. The ICT role can reduce the burden in many ways at all levels such as with extra working hours, extra teachers, and extra buildings. Learners on computers can involve themselves in a competitive environment, besides gaining pace individually in the learning process. Through network, they can become a team member, and this can benefit a lot in many ways. Thus, asynchronous as well as synchronous mode of learning is achievable.

In the process of controlling and operating the ICT based education process, the evolved collaborative environment may help tackle the issues as:

- Course design and implementation,
- Admission procedure,
- Teaching facilities
- Teaching requirement,
- Establishing learners or target groups,
- Staff members,

- Requirement for relevant hardware and software etc.,
- Area-specific need based education,
- Re-engineering the education process, and
- Other measures to revamp the education system.

The virtual role of ICT has increasingly been becoming the changing factor of the new scenario of education mode, which is now e-learning. Under this mode, a learner gets to pace themselves on his/her own, irrespective of the activities of other learners and simultaneously they can place themselves on the right direction. Further, changes are occurring so fast in the IT industry that it is very difficult to cope with the pace. Therefore, it also becomes important to anticipate these changes accordingly in such a way as to achieve the aims.

5 Challenges

Technological revolution in information science and ever growing demands have propelled the need to have the proper and secure management of emerging massive information, by deploying appropriate communication devices that the required information may be delivered in time and space.

We can consider three tasks associated with the challenge. Heavy investment will be required to procure these items; this is the first task to meet the challenge in meeting the objectives set for education. Then, the second task is to acquire the required ICT infrastructure and applications. The third, and the most important, task is to create the collaborative environment. This third task is the cumulative stage of the progress on the first tow tasks. For the first case, the government is generating the necessary funds; and, for the second case, educational institutions are running several projects and making MoUs with the industries to procure the ICT infrastructure. The third task will facilitate the synchronous as well as asynchronous mode of teaching and learning processes. A collaborative environment means working together in harmony. This harmony consists of X and Y parameters such that:

X is considered as a collaboration in team teaching, and

Y is considered as a collaboration in team learning.

This pair builds up a sense of responsibility, which we can term "shared-responsibility". This is the very important aspect of the collaborative environment. This shared-responsibility allows individual and group learners to improve their skill in depth. We can tremendously increase the level of inspiration. In ensuring the good performance of X and Y parameters; Y will require the learner to stay in his group and interact accordingly; whereas, X will require to inculcate the means of assistance, to notice, and examine/check each learner, in order to observe the progress and evaluation. This kind of environment can support the web-based remotely controlled lectures, and student's lab computers (Curran, 2002).

6 Discussion

In addition, a large numbers of government, public, and private companies have their own enterprise-wide networks. As far as Internet economy is concerned, it is reported (Ahmad 2001) that $22 billion is floating in the internet economy of India and 184 companies has invested in this economy since 2001. In the IT segment, 41 percent of the companies have invested.

In the outsourcing business, 2% is due to IT. Among top 230 out of 1000, world companies are in the outsourcing business, which might be due to presence of existing work force and infrastructure. Outsourcing business has yielded 40% annual increase and estimated 17 billion by 2008, which was 1.5 billion during 2001-02. In the ITES sector, the National Association of Computer Manufacturers (NASSCOM) has also estimated a growth of about $ 24 billion by 2008 (Singh, 2004).

Therefore, here, ICT based education can fill the gap between the industry and education. However, side-by-side updating and orientation in the education are needed as per the industry practices and techniques. An exploding crunch of skilled or professionals is expected in the industries. For example, in the field of IT, a crunch 500,000 employees by 2010 is pegged by the NASSCOM. Towards this realization, NASSCOM and UGC have recently made a tie-up to accelerate the industry-academia interface (Agrawal, 2005) so they can share current tools, practices, and knowledge. These developments will strengthen the teaching/learning system and the ICT infrastructure.

7 Conclusion

Information Communication Technologies (ICT) has been adjudged the best tool to offer its services in a number of ways particularly for education. In the view of increased population and poor educational infrastructure, the current emerging digital scenario can pave the way for better means of education in India. We have noticed significant observations in the integration of the existing technological infrastructure, which will certainly allow the smooth delivery of the ICT services to education.

The creation of the collaborative teaching and learning environment is essential so that the dropout rate can be kept low and the requirement of increasing number of learners and teaching load can also be resolved by ICT means. Further, developments towards to create the industry and academia interface will strengthen the teaching/learning system and ICT infrastructure. This will also enhance the employable stature of the learner. Therefore, to make out education success, we need ICT applications to widen its scope especially in the rural areas where the majority of the target groups reside. Only then will it fulfill the expectation of a substantially raising in enrolment of the learners by effective deployment of the education channel and the creation of the collaborative learning environment.

Acknowledgments: Author wants to acknowledge the encouragement received from his respected and beloved father late Sri Rameshwar Prasad Bhatt and his late uncle Sri Dwarika Prasad Bhatt. The support received from Computer Society of India is most sincerely acknowledged.

References

1. Ahmad, Tufail: The internet economy of India ed. Osama Manjar, Madanmohan Rao and Tufail Ahmad, 10-16, Inomy Media Pvt. Ltd., New Delhi, (2001).
2. Agrawal, N.M and Rao M. R.: IT education and industry needs – gaps, concerns and solutions, CSI Communication, April, 28, 10, 17 Mumbai (2005).
3. Bhatt, R. M.: Progress for virtual-teaching process in India, in Teleteaching' 98 Distance learning, Training and Education, Ed. Gordon Davis,120-123, Austrian Computer Society, Austria(1998).
4. Bhatt, R. M.: Growth of computing technology for education in India, in The History of Computing in Education, Ed. J.A.N. Lee & John Imagliazzo, 91-102, Kluwer, Canada(2004).
5. Chandragupta, Amritkar (2002) Digital Age, 1, 5, Feb. 5, 2000, Mumbai
6. Curran Kevin: A web-based collaboration teaching environment, IEEE, July-Sept. ,70-76,(2002)
7. Deshmukh, K. G.: University and higher education in the 21st century, University News, 36,28 (1999)
8. Gautam, Hari : Our Education System, Univ. News, (27) 24, 12(1999)
9. Kem, T. R., CEC Television News, vol.6,No.02, pp1-2(2008).
10. Kishore S (1998) Student support & quality indicators in distance education, Indian Journal of Open Learning, 1998, (7), 2, 205.
11. Sesagiri N. in Yojna-a publication of planning commission, Govt. of India, New Delhi, Vol.10, Jan.,pp4-10, (2000)
12. Sharma, G. D. (2005), Reaching out to all with quality higher education : The philosophy approach and methodology towards the use of EDUSAT Network in higher education, CEC Television News, (2), 10,13-14.
13. Singh, Nikita, "IT carers for you", CSI Communication, January, pp. 13-16, Mumbai, (2004).
14. Sj0helle Kibsgaard Dagrun: Learning potential in net communication, in proced. of the IFIP WCCE-2005, Univ. of Stellenbosch, Cape Town, South Africa, 4-7, July,2005 *ISBN 1-920-01711-9, 2005.*(2005)
15. Talero & Gandette: Harnessing information for development: A proposal for World Bank Group Vision and Strategy, IT for development, Vol. 6, pp145-188(1995)

16. Vikas Om:IT for masses: Hope or Hype?, CSI Communication, Dec., (28) 6, pp 8-11 Mumbai, (2004).
17. www.education.nic.in Accessed 16 Oct 2007
18. www.bhashaindia.com/trivia/trivia.aspx Accessed Sept. 2007.
19. www.cdacindia.com Accessed 12 Feb 2007.
20. www.itformasses.nic.in Accessed 25 Aug 2007.
21. www.nic.in Accessed 14 June 2007.
22. www.vidhyanidhi.org.in Accessed 11 May 2006.
23. www.cec-uge.org Accessed 11 Jan 2008.

Sinhala Computing in Early Stage – Sri Lanka Experience

S.T. Nandasara[1] and Yoshiki Mikami[2]

[1] University of Colombo School of Computing, Sri Lanka, nandasara@yahoo.com
[2] Nagaoka University of Technology, Japan, mikami@kjs.nagaokaut.ac.jp

Abstract: Sinhala writing system used in Sri Lanka is a syllabic writing system deriving from *Brahmi* and it consists of vowels, consonants, diacritical marks, and special symbols. Several of these are combined to form complex ligatures. Total number of different glyphs is almost close to 2300. Thus, all computer equipment for Sinhala language needs to provide for this degree of complexity in both display and printing but without adding any extra complexity to the keyboard or the input systems. In this paper, we discuss how Sinhala computing technology has evolved in early personal computers with limited capabilities and resources.

Keywords: Complex script computing, Sinhala language, Standarisation

1 Introduction

Sri Lanka has a population of 20 million of whom the majorities are Sinhalese (74%). Other ethnic groups are made up of Sri Lankan Tamils and Indian Tamils (18%), Moors (7%), Malays and Burghers. There are three living languages in Sri Lanka. They are Sinhala, Tamil, and English, used for general, everyday communication: both interpersonal and mass communication. Written documents, on paper or other materials, appear in one, two, or all of these languages.

This article focuses on key issues and the structure concerning Sinhala writing at the character level. Then we will discuss some of the major issues involved in design of Sinhala computing interface for early character base machines using 8-bit standard for Sinhala scripts.

Please use the following format when citing this chapter:

Nandasara, S.T. and Mikami, Y., 2008, in IFIP International Federation for Information Processing, Volume 269; *History of Computing and Education 3*; John Impagliazzo; (Boston: Springer), pp. 157–165.

2 Sinhala Scripts Structure and Major Issues

Sinhala script is used for writing the Sinhala language in Sri Lanka is said to be derivatives from the ancient scripts *Brahmi*, known to have existed since third to second century B.C.E. Literary Sinhala obtained its standard in the 14th century A.D., and this standard is respected by the whole speech community of Sri Lanka. Full Sinhala script includes the symbols necessary for writing loan words from Sanskrit and Pali, notably the aspirated consonants.

Formal description of the Sinhala character set can be defined as follows:
Semi-consonants = (ං, ඃ}
Vowels = {අ, ආ, ඇ, ඈ, ඉ, ඊ, උ, ඌ, සa, සaa, ඏ, ඐ, එ, ඒ, ඓ, ඔ, ඕ, ඖ}
Consonants = {ක, ඛ, ග, ඝ, ඞ, ඟ, ච, ඡ, ජ, ඣ, ඤ, ඥ, ඦ, ට, ඨ, ඩ, ඪ, ණ, ඬ, ත, ථ, ද, ධ, න, ඳ, ප, ඵ, බ, භ, ම, ඹ, ය, ර, ල, ව, ශ, ෂ, ස, හ, ළ, ෆ}
Vowel signs = {◌්, ◌ා, ◌ැ, ◌ෑ, ◌ි, ◌ී, ◌ු, ◌ූ, ◌a, ◌aa, ◌ෙ, ◌ේ, ◌ෛ, ◌ො, ◌ෝ, ◌ෞ}
Non-vocalic strokes = {්‍ර, ්‍ය}

2.1 Major Issues in Writing Systems

We must consider the following points for use of the Sinhala writing systems. Firstly, every vowel except the first one has a corresponding vowel sign that can be attached to consonants to make composite characters. Secondly, when vowels appear at the beginning of a word, vowels are written as independent letters. Thirdly, there are two commonly used diacritical marks: '*anuswar*' and '*visarga*', like most of the Indic languages. Fourthly, unlike in English, vowel signs are attached to the right, left, above or below to its fix position or variable position. When we attach some modifiers, it changes the original shapes of the consonants. Appearances of modifiers are also differed according to the consonants. Next, there are two special symbols (non-vocalic strokes) corresponding to the sound of 'r' and 'y' called *rakaransaya* and *yansaya*. Lastly, when Sanskrit and Pali words are adopted into Sinhala, they are transcribed in the compound manner in which they are written in Sanskrit and Pali. This composition is effected by the union of one or more consonants, or their parts or symbols, with a vowels-consonant or its parts or symbols, and vice versa.

2.2 Complex Ligature and Character Positioning

In Sinhala language, combinations of consonants, vowel signs, and diacritical marks are constructed in a different way according to the shape of the Sinhala letter. Some would create a rather uneven, irregular, and illogical outer appearance.

Every combination is constructed in the way according to the shape of the Sinhala letter. Forty-one (41) consonants and sixteen (16) vowel signs combined to form glyphs. Thereafter, each united glyphs can further combined with 2 special symbols, rakaransaya and yansaya and then even further it can be combined with 2 diacritical marks (semi-consonants) and after all it will produce more than 2300 "usable" combinations used for Sinhala writing. For example consonant ka (ක) with vowel signs and non-vocalic strokes will produce following combinations;

ක, ක්, ක, කා, කැ, කෑ, කි, කී, කු, කූ, කෘ, කෲ, කෙ, කේ, කෛ, කො, කෝ, කෞ, ක්‍ර, ක්‍රා, ක්‍රැ, ක්‍රෑ, ක්‍රි, ක්‍රී, ක්‍රෙ, ක්‍රේ, ක්‍රෛ, ක්‍රො, ක්‍රෝ, ක්‍රෞ, ක්‍ය, ක්‍යා, ක්‍යැ, ක්‍යෑ, ක්‍යි, ක්‍යී, ක්‍යු, ක්‍යූ, ක්‍යෙ, ක්‍යේ, ක්‍යෛ, ක්‍යො, ක්‍යෝ & ක්‍යෞ.

Consequently, Sinhala characters can be divided in to three main groups. (1) Those having a normal 'x' height, (2) Those which have an ascender, similar to 'l' and (3) Those which have a descender, similar to 'g'. However, this positioning is more complicated when single or multiple vowel signs are attached to the same character (see Figure 1).

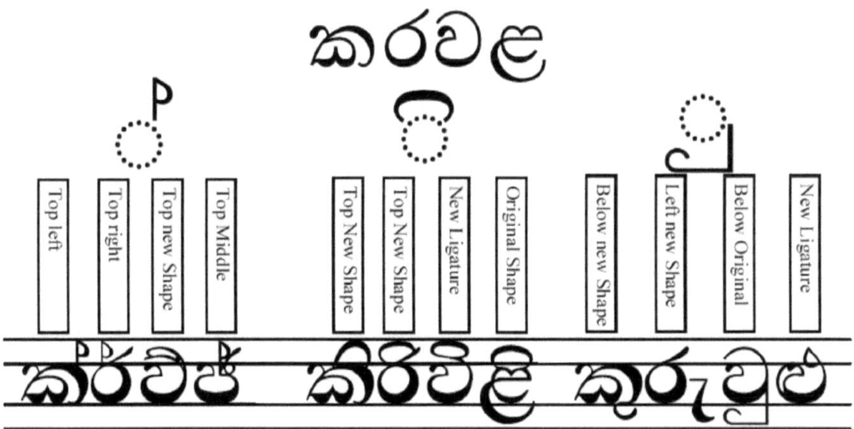

Figure 1 Shapes and New Positioning are given when combining Vowel Signs with Consonants.

3 Major Steps in Sinhala Text Processing

With the introduction of BBC microcomputers to the University of Colombo in 1982, I myself developed a set of Sinhala Bitmap fonts for computers. Using this Sinhala font set, daily TV programme schedule was transmitted for public by the National TV Station and it was the first attempt to use computers with local languages. Introduction of IBM PCs for data processing, need of developing proper application was the major challenge to language like Sinhala where existing technologies were far behind to handle such complex scripts. The very first Sinhala word processor developed by one Chinese company in 1984 was not successful in Sri Lanka. Thereafter, there was another word processor developed by GIST in India. This was also not successful. Some local computer venders were interested in developing software for IBM compatible personal computer end up with a patent disputes over the software developed by one company against other company.

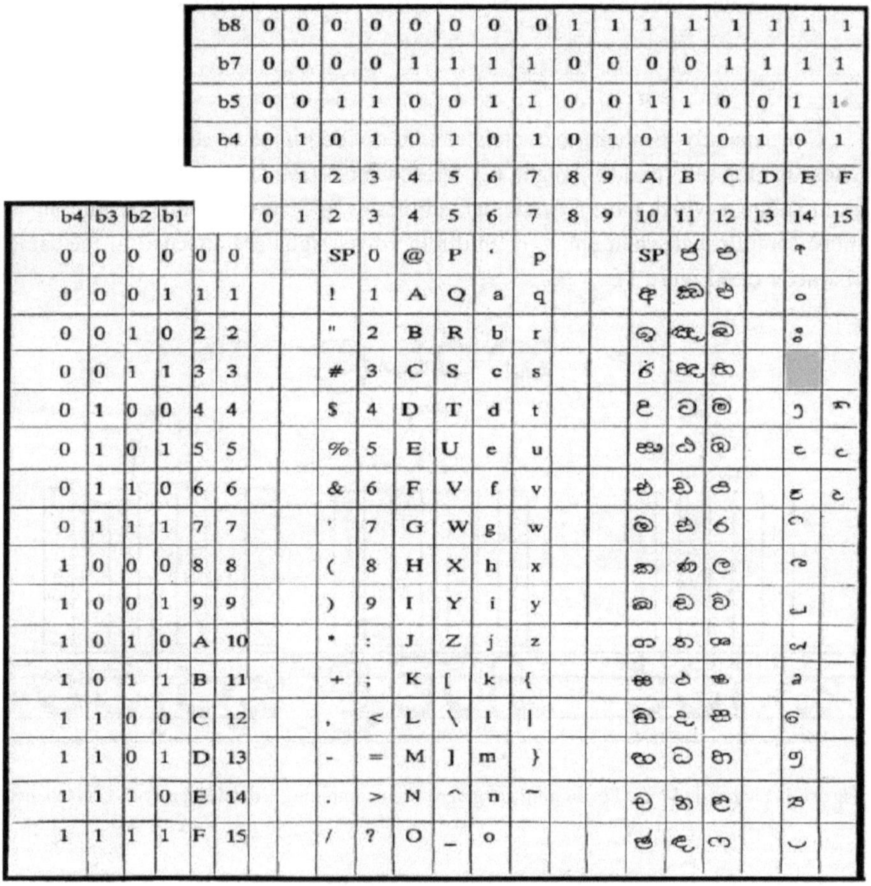

Figure 2 First ever encoding for Sinhala Character Set submitted for the public comment, 1990.

Since mid 1980s, a number of steps were taken by the government to formulate Sinhala language related discrepancies, such as different alphabetical orders used by different dictionaries. Due to the importance of information interchange among computers in national language and the requirement for a standard code was identified by the Information and Technology Council of Sri

Lanka (CINTEC) in 1985. One of the committee's initial endeavours was to establish a standard code for information interchange in Sinhala.

Because of the collaborative work with the Thammasat University, Thailand, and the inputs from the CINTEC Working Committee on the Use of Sinhala and Tamil in Computer Technology, the draft standard was released as a CINTEC publication [1] to the public for comments and observations in March 1990.

After receiving the public comments and recommendations, the first ever standard (Figure 2) was approved by the Council of CINTEC and the Sri Lanka Standard Institute on the advice of its Working Committee for Recommending Standards for the use of Sinhala Script in Computer Technology [2][3][4][5].

3.1 Standard Keyboard for Sinhala

At this stage, it is important to indicate that for the development of the appropriate electronic keyboard layout where again CINTEC took the initiative. Having agreed that a large number of Sinhala typists were using the government approved *Wijesekera*[1] Sinhala Typewriter Keyboard, CINTEC first developed and obtained government approval for the "Extended *Wijesekera* Keyboard for Electronic Typewriters" (*see* Figure 3), the intention being the introduction of electronic typewriters then used as an interface for microcomputer input.

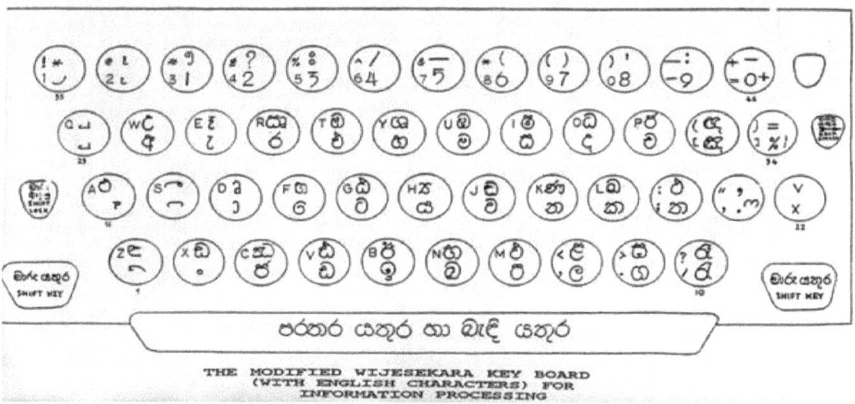

Figure 3 Extended *Wijesekara* Keyboard for Electronic typewriters used interface for microcomputer input (1989).

[1] *Wijesekera* Typewriter Keyboard was approved by the government of Sri Lanka as a National Sinhala Typewrite in 1968.

3.2 Input Method for Sinhala Character Set

Sri Lankan software industry had suffered with legal dispute on patent issues of software implementation as mentioned earlier; few individuals had started their own Sinhala word processors. In the meantime, the Institute of Computer Technology (ICT) of the University of Colombo, initiated collaborative work with Thammasat University to incorporate Sinhala capabilities for personal computer. The SLASCII standard was used to create the first ever Sinhala/English bilingual character based API called SBIOS (Sinhala BIOS) and then Sinhala keyboard layout was used with Sinhala word processor WT Ver. 1.0 (well known as "*Wadan Tharuwa*")[2] developed in early 1990s for IBM-PC computers (See Figure 4). According to *Wadan Tharuwa*, Sinhala words are input and stored letter-by-letter from left to right. This is a three-layer system for the cells that contain symbols in base level, above or below levels. The base character will be stored first, followed by the upper and then lower if the case arises. System will alarm for illegal input key sequence such as there cannot be any diacritic at the lower level after the upper level diacritic is placed.

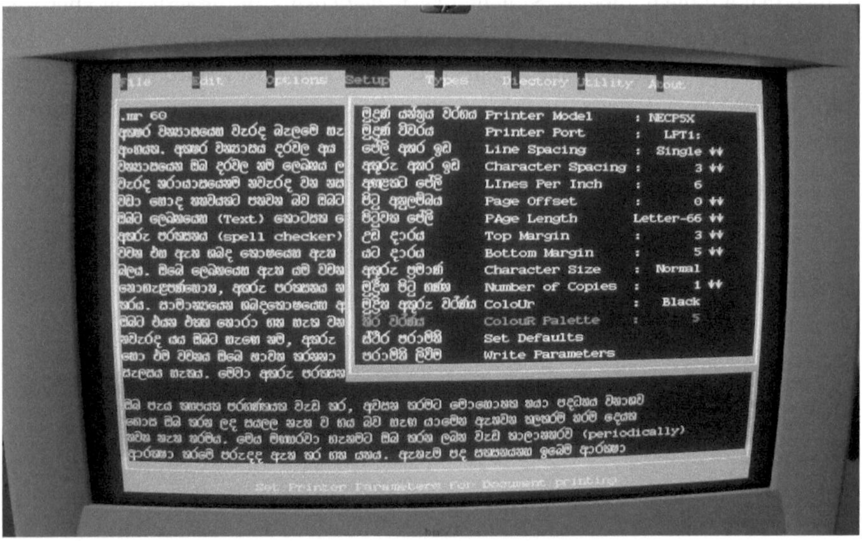

Figure 4 Sample VGA screen shot of Bi-lingual Sinhala/English Word Processor "*Wadan Tharuwa*" in early 1989. (Photo: author's collection)

[2] *Wadan Tharuwa* is a one of the earliest bi-lingual and menu-driven commercial word processor released in Sri Lanka to run on IBM-PC and it was conformed to SLASCII. The name "*Wadan Tharuwa*" meaning "Word Star" was developed by the author, S T Nandasara.

SBIOS API input method provided a sequence checking mechanism to ensure the validity of the input sequence in one of the three levels of strictness; base level: pass through, lower level: basic check, and upper level: strict check.

This mechanism of sequence checking is provided for three reasons.

1. To maintain logical sorting order of the alphabet,
2. To maintain the visual correctness of the character display,
3. To maintain the correctness of the use of diacritical marks.

SBIOS has also specified the cursor movements and editing behaviour for Sinhala WT. We must move the cursor from cells to cells. However, we must skip all characters in other levels than the base level. Text deletion using the "Delete" key must also remove all characters in the current cell, including the above and below levels. Meanwhile, character-by-character, right-to-left, removal is still possible by using the "Backspace" key, where the order of removal is considered by the order they are stored. At a later stage, extra capabilities added to maintain a diacritical marks, mathematical and phonetic symbols for DOS operating system [6][7]. Language was selected by toggling the Shift-Ctrl key combination whenever is required.

3.3 From Bitmap to Open Font

During mid 1990s introduction of Desk Top Publishing (DTP) with PC, there was a demand for quality printing in desktop computers. The first attempt to introduce Sinhala Desktop publishing for IBM PC was available with Xerox Ventura®. One of the early outline fonts for Roman scripts was available with Xerox Ventura® for WYSIWYG (What You See Is What You Get) DTP in 1994. However, there was no whatsoever technical support given by Xerox Ventura® how non-Roman fonts to be installed with this DTP package. Thanks to the reverse engineering efforts and tag concept was used to format text and paragraphs within the package, *Athwela* was developed in 1994 to support tri-lingual (Sinhala, Tamil & English) DTP with Xerox ventura® (see Figure 5).

This move in character rendering technology with Bit Map Font technology for laser printer opened the way to the next stage of text processing, and it coincides with the emergence of new design of Sinhala character code.

Apple Macintosh® came with their early version of word processors with Sinhala language support with laser printer technology.

3.4 Current Development Platform Status

The extraction and inclusion of Sinhala code page in UCS/Unicode has made possible to connect Sinhala community to global cyberspace. However, in order to be really connected, we should do localization on proprietary or open platforms accordingly. Currently Microsoft Windows platform is widely used in Sri Lanka. Microsoft does not provide proper Unicode support input method for Sinhala. It is planning to be released with its next version of the operating system. However, Sinhala language kit (beta version) released by Microsoft in early 2005 for Windows XP/SP2 can be used with the third party keyboard input methods.

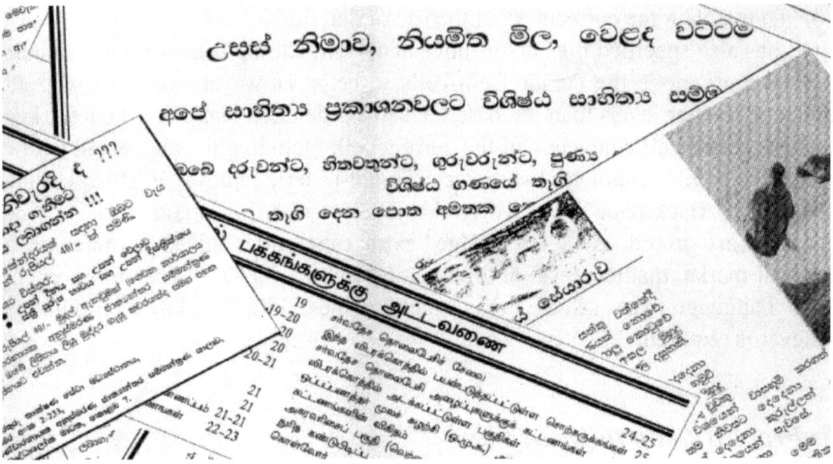

Figure 5 Sample tri-lingual laser documents from *Athwela* DTP Package.

4. Conclusion

Sri Lanka has always been independent in her island history. Thus, the Sinhala language remains unique and cannot be automatically handled by technologies originated from the west. However, writing systems for various southeast and south Asian languages, such as Tamil, Thai, Khmer, and Myanmar have a lot of commonalities, and these language communities, could share a lot of common challenges to more ahead in their own text processing.

References

1. Nandasara, S. T., Disanayaka, J. B., Samaranayake, V. K., Seneviratne, E. K., and Koannantakool, T., 1990. – *Draft* Standard *for the Use of Sinhala in Computer Technology,* Approved by the CINTEC on the advice of its working committee for recommending Standards for the Use of Sinhala and Tamil Script in Computer Technology.
2. Working Paper, 1985. *Order of Alphabet and System of Transliteration,* CANLIT & NARESA.
3. SLS 1134:1996. *Sri Lanka Standard SLS 1134:1996-Sinhala Character Code for Information Interchange,* SLSI publication.
4. Nandasara, S. T., and Samaranayake, V. K., 1991. *A Standard Code for Information Interchange in Sinhalese,* ISO-IEC JTC1/SCL/WG2 N673, October.

5. SLS 1134:2004. *Sri Lanka Standard SLS 1134:2004-Sinhala Character Code for Information Interchange,* SLSI publication.
6. Nandasara, S.T., Sri Lanka Experience of Development of Tamil Input/Output/Display Methods, TAMILNET'97 – International Symposium, Singapore, May, 1997
7. Nandasara, S. T., Samaranayake, V. K., *Current Development of Sinhala / Tamil / English Trilingual Processing in Sri Lanka*, MLIT-2, November 7-8, Tokyo, Japan, pp. 181-192, 1997.

A Brief History of Choosing First Programming Languages

Leila Goosen

University of Pretoria, South Africa; lgoosen@gk.up.ac.za

Abstract: Choosing the *best* computer language for introducing students to programming is often an emotional issue, leading to protracted debates for many years. This paper aims to document how the development of programming languages has influenced the educational processes of choosing an introductory language since the early days of computing, by exploring some of the "programming languages that have been selected over the last couple of decades and the rational for those selections". [1]

Keywords: History, Selection criteria, First programming language

1 Introduction

Choosing the *best* computer language for introducing students to programming is often an emotional issue, leading to protracted debates over the years [2-6], e.g.

1976: "The selection of languages for use as pedagogical aids in the teaching of computer science is still a big issue at most universities." [7]

1979: "What is a good programming language for beginners?" [8]

1982: "With the diversity of high-level programming languages available, selecting the "right" one for a computer science curriculum or course can be a befuddling process." [6]

1986: "Which computer languages should we be teaching our students - and why?" [9]

1989: "There is increasing discussion about the primary programming language used for undergraduate courses in Computer Science." [10]

So, why is it necessary to pay so much attention to which programming language you start with? [11] The choice of an introductory programming language "is probably the most significant of" the "factors that will shape the competency of the next generation of computer users" [8]. Luker regards "the language used for CS1 and CS2 … as a crucial factor in students' subsequent progress in the discipline" [10].

Please use the following format when citing this chapter:

Goosen, L., 2008, in IFIP International Federation for Information Processing, Volume 269; *History of Computing and Education 3*; John Impagliazzo; (Boston: Springer), pp. 167–170.

2 First Choices

As high-level programming languages became established, faculties, for the first time, needed to start making decisions on which language(s) to implement for teaching [6]: According to [1], they needed to decide whether to move to one of the higher level programming languages, or to continue teaching assembly language programming in introductory courses. Around the mid 1970s, [12] was convinced that the most currently accepted solution" in "to use an existing high-level language".

Another part of the "quarrel" focused around whether a "pedagogical" or a "real" language should be used [12], i.e. languages specifically written for teaching programming, as opposed to languages used in industry. "Is it necessary to teach the languages which are most widely used outside the classroom in order to keep the curriculum relevant to the real world?" [7] According to [13], choosing languages "based on their current *popularity* or the likelihood of their future popularity … has a number of practical benefits." If students, for example, "are constantly reading advertisements for COBOL programmers" [7], they could be more "motivated to study a language that they have heard of" [13]. Similarly, students' interest stems from the fact that they know that a certain language is in demand from "employers, who request that people master the language they will use" [12] in their workplace.

Last, but not the least, [13] also mentions that "a good selection of books and language implementations will be available for a popular language." This brings up text availability as one of the pedagogical factors in support of the process of teaching programming [7]: Especially in introductory courses, students as novice programmers can greatly benefit from the security provided by a readable text. However, if only a small number of texts are available to support a specific language, this may result in the inability to find a suitable text to support a course in that language.

In an effort to facilitate the decision making process [7], in 1976, produced one of the first examples where they applied a set of criteria "to a list of potential languages". In that paper, they also discuss issues with regard to resource constraints, and the influence that cost efficiency could have.

As the "(o)ldest general language in use and the first to become widely used" [14], FORTRAN was most often selected to open "the doors of computing to large numbers of scientists", "mathematicians and engineers who made up computer science faculties at the time" [1]. Compared to other languages of that era, COBOL has a "unique English-like style" [14]. As it was widely used in business data processing, especially departments offering computing courses as part of Business Information Systems programs selected this option. BASIC is "(t)he simplest and one of the most widely used languages" [14]. Because it usually was the only programming language available on personal computers [8], it often became the first language of students at various educational levels.

Giangrande points out that at that stage "there was no named methodology associated with assembly languages, FORTRAN, or COBOL" [1]. Smith criticizes the use of specifically FORTRAN in an introductory course for the effect it had on future programming [7]. As weaknesses in programming languages yet again became a problem, a new methodology, called *structured programming*, emerged. The support of control structures, like while loops, if-then-else statements, etc. for good programming techniques, is something that was lacking in the older languages, e.g. FORTRAN and COBOL [7]. This ensured that these were superseded by a variety of newer programming languages that "incorporated constructs that supported structured programming." [1]

3 The Rise and Fall of Pascal

Until recently (mid 1990s), Pascal used to be the most widely adopted programming language [11] "for introductory computer science courses" [1]. According to [12], one of the principal advantages of Pascal is that it is a simple, small and concise language" specifically designed for teaching structured programming. These "qualities make it usable in a great variety of problems (and not only in numerical calculations), with fair efficiency, and without frustrating restrictions." In 1975, the creator of Pascal himself [15] described the some of the merits of the language "with respect to ease of programming, … efficient implementability" by means of the compiler and interpreter used for the so-called p-code, and easy, practical portability "to a large number of computer systems" [1]. The fact that Pascal and most of the development environments "came with a lot of support and documentation" [11] also made it popular among students.

"During the 1980s, several important languages were created and several languages of the 1970s became popular." [13]. Early in the 1980s [6] mentions some of the comparison criteria for languages such as FORTRAN, COBOL and Pascal. Languages should support "good software engineering practices", as well as showing the existence of control structures to support a preferred programming methodology, adequate diagnostic aids and other programming tools and literature and program libraries for the language.

"(T)he availability of adequate local and vendor support for the implementation of the language" [6] and direct costs with regard to items such as "license fees, and software maintenance contracts" should also be included in calculations.

Although Pascal, BASIC, FORTRAN and COBOL were all abstractions of assembly language [4], that provided big improvements over assembly language, their primary abstraction still required one to think in terms of the structure of the computer, rather than the structure of the problem one was trying to solve. The effort required to perform this mapping, and the fact that it was extrinsic to the programming language, produced programs that were difficult to write and expensive to maintain.

According to [13] "(t)he most striking trend in the field of programming languages" in the 1980s had "been the rise of paradigms, of which the object-oriented paradigm is the best-known." As "support for the creation of objects as instances of a class," [1] function overloading, inheritance and polymorphism became more common, Pascal's popularity gradually began declining - an increasing number of institutions were choosing to introduce undergraduates to programming by teaching object oriented languages, such as C/C++ and Java.

References

1. Giangrande, E.: CS1 programming language options. Journal of Computing Sciences in Colleges. Vol. 22, pp. 153-160 (2007).
2. Ali, A.I., Kohun, F.: Suggested Topics for an IS Introductory Course in Java. In: Proceedings of the Informing Science and Information Technology Education Joint Conference (2005), pp. 33-49, Available via http://pro-ceedings.informingscience.org/InSITE2005/I19f28Ali.pdf. Accessed 25 Apr 2007.
3. Duke, R., Salzman, E., Burmeister, J., Poon, J., Murray, L.: Teaching programming to beginners - choosing the language is just the first step. In: Proceedings of the Australasian Conference on Computing Education. pp.79-86. ACM Press, New York (2000).
4. Goosen, L.: Criteria and guidelines for the selection and implementation of a first programming language in high schools PhD thesis, North-West University (Potchefstroom Campus) (2004); http:// www.puk.ac.za/biblioteek/proefskrifte/2004/goosen_l.pdf
5. Mannila, L., de Raadt, M.: An objective comparison of languages for teaching introductory programming. In: Proceedings of the 6th Baltic Sea conference on Computing education research. pp.32-37. ACM Press, New York (2006).
6. Tharp, A.L.: Selecting the "right" programming language. In: Proceedings of the thirteenth SIGCSE Technical Symposium on Computer Science Education SIGCSE '82. pp. 151-155. ACM Press, New York (1982).
7. Smith, C., Rickman, J.: Selecting languages for pedagogical tools in the computer science curriculum. In: Proceedings of the sixth SIGCSE Technical Symposium on Computer Science Education SIGCSE '76. pp.38-47. ACM Press, New York (1976).
8. Wexelblat, R.L.: First programming language: Consequences (Panel Discussion). In: Proceedings of the 1979 annual conference ACM '79. p.259. ACM Press, New York (1979).
9. Baron, N.S.: The future of computer languages: implications for education. In: Proceedings of the seventeenth SIGCSE Technical Symposium on Computer Science Education SIGCSE '86. pp. 44-49. ACM Press, New York (1986).
10. Luker, P.A.: Never mind the language, what about the paradigm? In: Proceedings of the twentieth SIGCSE Technical Symposium on Computer Science Education SIGCSE '89. pp.252-256. ACM Press, New York (1989).
11. Gupta, D.: What is a good first programming language? Crossroads. Vol. 10, p. 7 (2004).
12. Lecarme, O.: Structured programming, programming teaching and the language Pascal. ACM SIGCSE Bulletin. Vol. 6, pp. 9-15 (1974).
13. King, K.N.: The evolution of the programming languages course. In: Proceedings of the twenty-third SIGCSE technical symposium on Computer science education SIGCSE '92. pp. 213-219. ACM Press, New York (1992).
14. Bergin, T.J.: A history of the history of programming languages. Communications of the ACM. Vol. 50, pp. 69-74 (2007).
15. Wirth, N.: An assessment of the programming language PASCAL. In: Proceedings of the international conference on Reliable software. pp. 23-30. ACM Press, New York (1975).

Programming in Japanese for Literacy Education

Ken Okada, Manabu Sugiura, Yoshiaki Matsuzawa, Megumi Araki, and Hajime Ohiwa

Keio University - Graduate School of Media and Governance
5322 Endo, Fujisawa-shi, Kanagawa-ken, 252-8520 Japan
squeaker@crew.sfc.keio.ac.jp

Abstract: We have developed a programming language Kotodama (means "what you speak becomes reality") in which a source program can be read as authentic Japanese language and be executed as a programming language at the same time. We put Kotodama into a teaching environment Squeak developed by Alan Kay and have developed several programming courses on it. We have found that explanation of a programming language becomes unnecessary and that we can concentrate on algorithm development by examining a program text that can be read as Japanese. We believe that this programming course can work as natural language writing course as well for precise description.

Keywords: Programming in Japanese, Word order, Postfix notation, Algorithm education

1 Introduction

When personal computers appeared, a programming language BASIC first appeared and users would learn programming by using it. However, various software applications had been commercially available and it soon became unnecessary for users to learn programming.

We believe that leaning how to use application software does not form a literate person for information society. Instead, we believe teaching the essential understanding of the computer by programming is to form literacy for the people in information society.

At first, the work of programming occurred in assembly language. It used mnemonics that corresponded to the machine instructions. Then, high-level

---

Please use the following format when citing this chapter:

Okada, K., Sugiura, M., Matsuzawa, Y., Araki, M. and Ohiwa, H., 2008, in IFIP International Federation for Information Processing, Volume 269; *History of Computing and Education 3*; John Impagliazzo; (Boston: Springer), pp. 171–176.

programming languages such as FORTRAN appeared. Programming languages after FORTRAN were designed as abbreviated languages of English.

Research on machine translation (MT) has long occurred but few reported its application for programming languages. As is well known, MT is useful when the scope of translation is limited to the narrow area. Programming would be one of the most suitable areas of MT application.

Squeak by Alan Kay is an excellent environment for teaching programming, and people reported many good results for introductory programming education. However, when applied for the Japanese, it does not work as it does for Western people. This is because a program appears in the form of the English language, as is explained in the next section. We extended Squeak eToy so one can write a program in the Japanese language; we named it "Kotodama on Squeak" to solve the problem.

2 Word Order

In Squeak, a program is composed of by arranging scripting tiles so that the composed tile script becomes a program based on English. Figure 1 is a tile script for commanding the star forward by five dots. In this expression, the subject comes first, the verb comes next, and the object comes at the end.

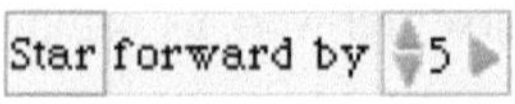

Figure 1 An example of Squeak command in English

In Japanese, the subject comes first, the object comes next, and the verb comes last. The word order "object verb" is same as that of the postfix notation and very effective for stack operation. The word order of "Kotodama on Squeak" is different from English word orderIn Japanese, Squeak (Squeak Nihongo) in which an English word is replaced by the corresponding Japanese word, the verb comes next to a subject.

"Kotodama on Squeak" enables one to write a program in Japanese. Figure 2 is a tile in "Kotodama on Squeak". The verb is located at the end, following Japanese word order.

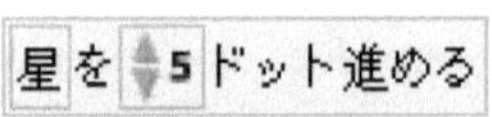

Figure 2 Kotodama on Squeak command in Japanese

It is very difficult to understand a tile script of the replaced words in the Japanese Squeak. To illustrate this, Figure 3 shows the translated English script of the tile script of Figure 2 without changing the word order. ("[p]" shows the particle). Native English people would feel strange to see the verb that comes at the end. It is what happens to Japanese users while they use the Japanese Squeak.

Figure 3 Translated English command of Figure 2 with the same word order

Let us imagine that we use the tile script shown in Figure 3. An instructor must explain that its meaning is "Star forward by 5". This is what happens when we use Japanese Squeak.

When we use "Kotodama on Squeak", the instructor would say that one must just read the tile script and think what is wrong with it, if a learner realizes that something is wrong because his/her program does not work as expected.

3 Tiles Whose Meaning can be Understood by its Reading

In Squeak eToy, tiles exist that are not easy to understand for the novices. The test tile shown in Figure 4 is one of them.

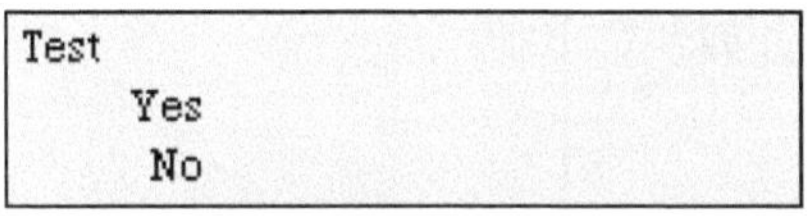

Figure 4 Test tile in Squeak

It is difficult for the beginning programmers to understand the meaning from this. Only those who know the concept of condition branching would understand the meaning of "Test", "Yes", and "No".

In "Kotodama on Squeak", the corresponding tile script is understood only by reading the tile. Figure 5 shows such a test tile.

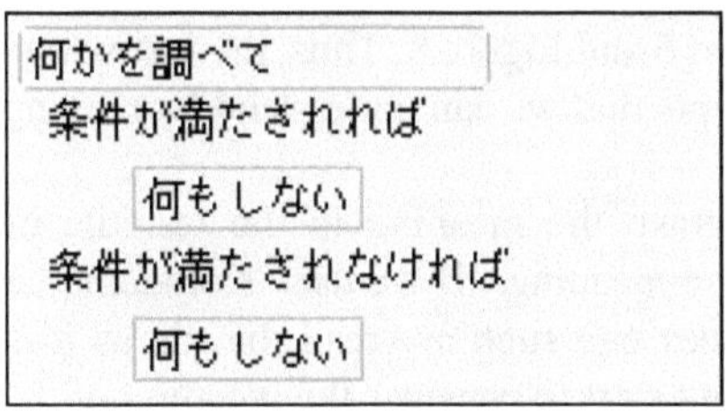

Figure 5 Test command in Kotodama on Squeak

Figure 6 shows the tile in which the Japanese text of Figure 5 translates into English.

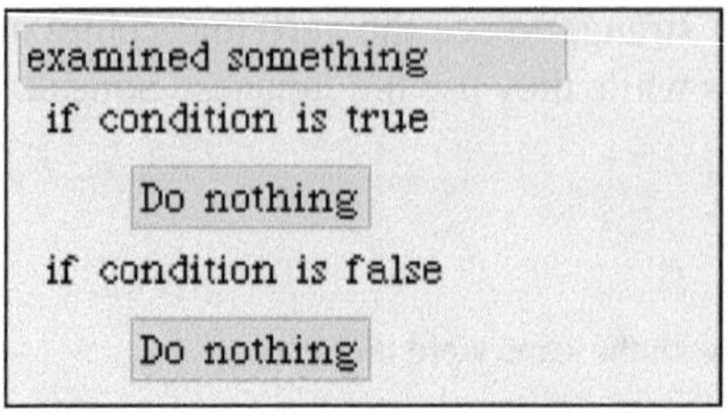

Figure 6 English translation of Figure 5

In "Kotodama on Squeak", a tile shows such script as the one which even a program beginner understands the meaning by reading. When one reads, "examined something", they immediately understand its meaning. In addition, when we read the expressions under it, we will also understand their meanings.

Good readability of the tile in "Kotodama on Squeak" occurs when we place some tile on the conditional part of the test tile. Figure 7 is such an example in which the color judgment tile appears on the conditional part. Figure 8 shows its English translation.

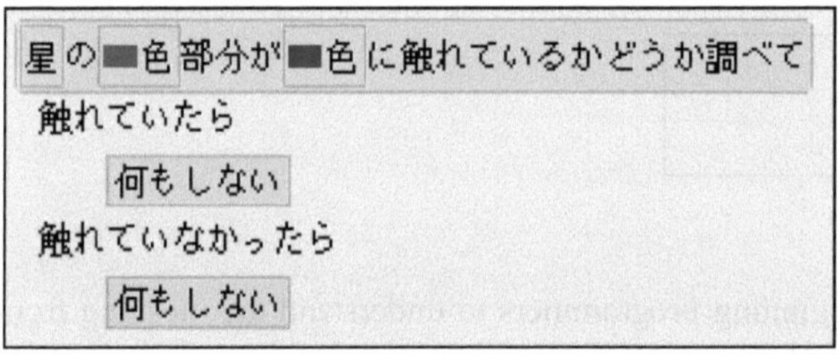

Figure 7 What is to be done is described in Japanese in Kotodama on Squeak

In the test tile of "Kotodama on Squeak", when we make some condition, the expression of the corresponding second and fourth lines change according to the content of the condition as is shown in Figure 6 and Figure 8. Thus, the instruction of Squeak becomes easy because it uses scripts that we can understand by reading them, as we did in the last section.

Because it is difficult for novices to grasp the meaning in the test tile of Squeak eToy, its instructor has to explain the meaning. If we use "Kotodama on Squeak", the instructor's explanation becomes one such as "read the tile as it is and think what it means". Eventually, learners start to consider the meaning of the tile by reading it for themselves while variously changing it for reaching the desired result. "Kotodama on Squeak" promotes the learners' self-study attitudes.

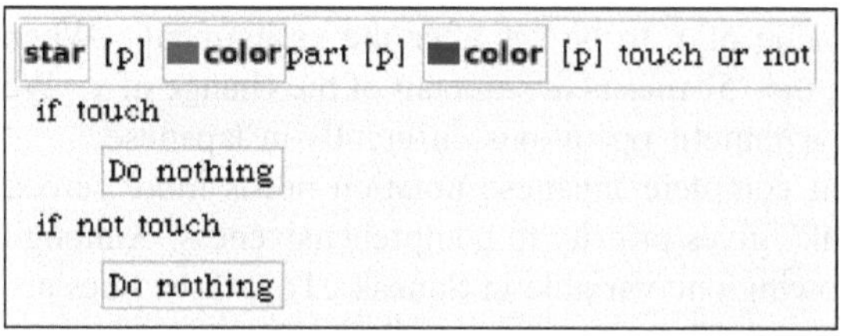

Figure 8 English translation of Figure 7

4 Interface to Understand the Operation Method

In Squeak eToy, an interface requires explanation to understand its effects. Figure 9 shows such an interface when we combine the variable tile and the assignment statement tile.

Figure 9 Prepared tiles for assignment

It is very difficult for a beginner to remove the tile as is expected from the interface. We can take out the assignment statement tile by clicking the arrow image. Without instruction, it is difficult to form this operation. It is necessary to click the arrow part of the assignment statement tile to obtain the increase type tile as shown in Figure 10. This operation is also difficult for novices.

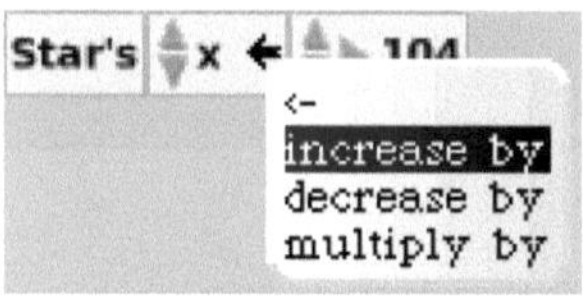

Figure 10 Increment statements for the variable "Star's" in Squeak

We can modify the interface for manipulating the variable in "Kotodama on Squeak". We need one such modification because the current value of a variable is always displayed. It is difficult for the programming beginners to understand the concept of the variables. Therefore, by always displaying the current value, we force the learners to be conscious of the variable and its current value.

Another modification is to separate the assignment statement tile and the increase type tile. We do this because the meaning of the object in the sentence is different in the former and latter statements. For example, when writing “Star’s x set to 5”, the “5” means the value of x to be set after the assignment. When writing “Star’s x increase by 5”, the “5” means the amount of the change of x. We denote notations for setting and arithmetic operations differently in Japanese.

There is a disadvantage that complete Japanese notation needs more screen space, but “Kotodama on Squeak” gives priority to comprehensiveness. Although we use one line of space for showing one variable in Squeak eToy, three lines are necessary in “Kotodama on Squeak”. Therefore, we install the geometry category by using three screens.

The interface design philosophy of “Kotodama on Squeak” is that one can understand the meaning of a program just by reading it. Therefore, together with the features of preceding sections, the learner’s self-study attitude is advanced.

5 Conclusion

“Kotodama on Squeak” is a programming environment intended for introducing programming for Japanese novices. We provide several courses for K-6 to K10 and university students. Learners can understand the effects of a program by just reading the source program as a Japanese text. We have found that education for algorithmic developments can be taught in shorter hours than the one taught by using conventional programming languages, because grammatical explanations are unnecessary. The user-friendly nature of Squeak also contributes to successful educational results. We find that using natural language is very effective for teaching programming. It could be useful for precise description of a natural language as a part of traditional literacy education.

Erratum to: History of Computing and Education 3 (HCE3)

John Impagliazzo (ed.)

This book was originally published with a copyright holder in the name of the publisher in error, whereas IFIP International Federation for Information Processing holds the copyright.

The updated original online version for this book can be found at
DOI 10.1007/978-0-387-09657-5

J. Impagliazzo (ed.), *History of Computing and Education 3 (HCE3)*, DOI 10.1007/978-0-387-09657-5_13,

MIX
Papier aus verantwortungsvollen Quellen
Paper from responsible sources
FSC® C105338

If you have any concerns about our products,
you can contact us on
ProductSafety@springernature.com

In case Publisher is established outside the EU,
the EU authorized representative is:
Springer Nature Customer Service Center GmbH
Europaplatz 3, 69115 Heidelberg, Germany

Printed by Libri Plureos GmbH
in Hamburg, Germany